Sisters and Strangers

Women in the Shanghai Cotton Mills, 1919-1949

Sisters and Strangers

WOMEN IN THE SHANGHAI COTTON MILLS, 1919–1949

Emily Honig

Stanford University Press
Stanford, California

Stanford University Press
Stanford, California

© 1986 by the Board of Trustees of the
Leland Stanford Junior University

Printed in the United States of America
Original printing 1986

Last figure below indicates year of this printing:
01   00   99   98   97   96   95   94   93   92

Chinese calligraphy by Weiguo Yu

CIP data appear at the end of the book

For my parents,
Victor and Lorraine Honig

Acknowledgments

Those of us who began our graduate study of Chinese history at Stanford University in the mid-1970's consider ourselves extremely fortunate. We had two extraordinarily generous advisors, Harold Kahn and Lyman Van Slyke, and we had each other. This book is one product of the intellectual companionship we developed. These companions—Katheryn Bernhardt, Helen Chauncey, Gail Hershatter, and Randall Stross, as well as Harold Kahn and Lyman Van Slyke—have contributed to this project at every stage and in every possible way: helping formulate the topic, strategizing about how to conduct research in the People's Republic of China, solving computer problems, thoroughly criticizing every page of the manuscript, and providing constant, unfailing encouragement.

I could not have conducted my research in Shanghai without the assistance of many groups and individuals. Fudan University hosted me in Shanghai and did everything for me that a *danwei* can do for its members. I am particularly grateful to my advisors in the History Department at Fudan, Yu Zidao and Huang Meizhen, for accepting me as their student, alerting me to sources, and providing valuable guidance for my research. I also wish to thank Shen Yixing at the Institute for Historical Research and scholars at the Institute for Economic Research of the Shanghai Academy of Social Sciences for assisting me in arranging and conducting interviews and for sharing with me their own views of the history of the Shanghai working class. Students in the 1977 class in the History Department at Fudan University, particularly Li Biyu and Zhao Xiaojian, helped me read documents, translate tapes of interviews from local dialects into Mandarin, and reminded me constantly to have a sense of humor in contending with the bureaucracy. My experience conducting research in Shanghai was made especially rich by friendships with two women, both now octogenarians—Cora Deng (Deng Yuzhi) and Talitha Gerlach. They entertained me with waffle parties and shared with me their memories of living with and teaching pre-Liberation women workers. No statement of gratitude can adequately express my debt to the women workers who patiently answered my questions about their life histories; without their assistance this book could not have been written.

When I returned to the United States and embarked on the process of writing and then revising my dissertation, I was assisted by many people. In addition to those already mentioned, I wish to thank members of the Stanford Women's History Writing Group who read, commented on, and raised questions about several chapters of this book: Antonia Castañeda, Estelle Freedman, Gary Sue Goodman, Gayle Gullet, Lois Helmboldt, Gail Hershatter, Valerie Matsumoto, Joanne Meyerowitz, Vicki Ruiz, and Francis Taylor. Weiguo Yu offered his expertise in Subei dialect to check the translations of the taped interviews, and his knowledge of Subei life to clarify many of the local customs described by women workers. I am also very grateful to Margery Wolf, Susan Mann, Marilyn Young, and Lisa Rofel for comments on the manuscript and for ongoing discussions that have constantly forced me to refine—and sometimes change—the ideas developed in this book. I had the good fortune to spend a year revising my dissertation under the direction of Frederic Wakeman, Jr. His suggestions and enthusiasm were invaluable. I also benefited from Joseph Esherick's and Kay Ann Johnson's systematic comments on the entire manuscript, as well as from comments by Andrew Walder, Lynda Shaffer, Philip Huang, Janet Salaff, Laurie Coyle, and Christine Kelley on specific chapters. I am indebted to Nancy Butcher for her meticulous editing of the final manuscript.

Financial support for my dissertation research was provided by the Committee on Scholarly Communication with the People's Republic of China and by the Social Science Research Council. A postdoctoral grant from the American Council of Learned Societies made it possible for me to spend the year 1982–83 revising my dissertation, and the Center for Chinese Studies at the University of California, Berkeley, provided me with office space in which to work during that time. My research was facilitated by the generosity and assistance of archivists at the International Labor Organization, the World Young Women's Christian Association in Geneva, and the Young Women's Christian Association National Board Archives in New York. Sage Publications has granted permission to reproduce as Chapter 5 a slightly different version of my article "The Contract Labor System and Women Workers: Pre-Liberation Cotton Mills of Shanghai," *Modern China*, 9 (October 1983), no. 4: 421–54. © 1983 Sage Publications, Inc.

Three individuals deserve more than thanks: my parents, Victor and Lorraine Honig, who taught me to seek to understand people whose lives are very different from my own, and Gail Hershatter, who has been a friend, collaborator, and critic in my attempts to do so.

E.H.

Contents

Tables and Maps

Sisters and Strangers

Women in the Shanghai
Cotton Mills, 1919-1949

Introduction

Modern industrial capitalism in twentieth-century China, as in England and the United States a century earlier, was built on the intersection of textile manufacture and female and child labor. In Shanghai, China's largest industrial center prior to 1949, cotton was king and the majority of mill workers were women. Including those employed in the silk and tobacco factories, women accounted for almost two-thirds of the total industrial work force in Shanghai. By themselves, female cotton mill workers represented more than one-third of the famed Shanghai proletariat.

As in the British mill towns of Lancashire and Manchester, the emergence of modern machinery and large-scale industry in Shanghai have been equated with the emergence of a "new working class."[1] And as in England, the emergence of this new working class coincided with years of constant popular agitation: the May Fourth demonstrations of 1919, the birth of the Chinese Communist Party in 1921 and its growth thereafter, the strikes and riots of the May Thirtieth Movement of 1925, and the Nationalist Revolution of 1927. In China it has seemed natural to assume that the cotton industry was, as E. P. Thompson wrote of nineteenth-century industrial England, "the agent not only of industrial but also of social revolution, producing not only more goods but also 'the Labour Movement' itself."[2]

This assumption is what drew me initially to undertake a study of women who were cotton mill workers in Shanghai. The only major study of the Chinese labor movement by a Western scholar, Jean Chesneaux's *The Chinese Labor Move-*

ment, 1919-1927, describes the politicization of the Shanghai proletariat and the process through which workers became class-conscious revolutionaries.³ Although the primary concern of his study is the political issues of the labor movement, he also chronicles the transformation wrought in social relationships by the industrial revolution in China: the transition from peasant to proletarian, from the dissolution of traditional village-oriented social ties to the emergence of new social relationships based on allegiances between urban workers, from membership in traditional mutual aid societies and native place associations to affiliation with modern labor unions and the Chinese Communist Party. From Chesneaux's pioneering study I inferred that since women cotton mill workers represented more than one-third of the Shanghai industrial proletariat, they too must have experienced these transformations and become militant participants in this revolutionary movement of the 1920's.

I began my study by focusing on issues that precede the role of women in the labor movement and in the Chinese revolution: the nature of work, social relations within the work place, the formation of the working class, and the transformations women underwent as they became members of an urban industrial proletariat. These issues have been ignored or treated only tangentially in the historical literature. In fact, there have been no studies by Western scholars of urban women workers in modern Chinese history.

Studies of pre-Liberation Chinese women have generally centered on those who became famous as politicians or as intellectuals, or on the mobilization of women by the Chinese Communist Party.⁴ In contrast, the subjects of this study are women whose names have never appeared in the historical record. Many, in fact, had names that articulated and reinforced their insignificance. Chen Zhaodi, one of the women whose experiences will be related in the chapters that follow, was one of hundreds of women workers whose name, which meant "summoning little brother," expressed her parents' disappointment at having given birth to a daughter.

There were several reasons for focusing on the cotton industry. The first, most obvious, one was size: the overwhelming majority of female factory workers, and of all factory workers, in Shanghai were employed in cotton mills. Second, the cotton industry was the most modern of the so-called modern enterprises in Shanghai. Many of Shanghai's women industrial workers never entered factories at all, but actually worked at home under a putting-out system. Others, who did leave home to work in factories every day, labored in small workshops or sheds, where they performed unmechanized tasks such as wrapping cigarettes. Large numbers of women workers operated machines in factories in seasonal industries, such as silk reeling, which could employ them only for part of the year. In contrast, women in the cotton mills—almost all of whom were hired as machine operatives—worked in factories that employed several thousand workers, where machines were kept running twenty-four hours a day, twelve months of the year. Thus, if there was in Shanghai any group of women workers who might be called members of a modern industrial proletariat, it was the women cotton mill workers. They were the furthest removed from the rural economy, with its patterns of seasonal labor and household production.

Focus on the cotton industry also compels us to look beyond localism. Before Liberation more than half the cotton mills in Shanghai were owned by British and Japanese capitalists. The cotton industry thus offers an opportunity to examine how imperialism affected the formation and politicization of the work force.

With the idea of examining the relationship between the exploitation endured by women in the Shanghai mills and their participation in the Chinese revolution, I set out in 1979 to begin my research in Shanghai. There I met a group of Chinese scholars who, since the 1950's, had been studying the history of the Shanghai labor movement. They too saw the cotton mills as the epitome of the modern, large-scale enterprises that Marxist theory had predicted would lead to the development of a revolutionary class consciousness among workers. And they too believed that the mills exemplified the ways foreign ownership contributed to the exploitation of women workers, and hence to their propensity to strike and to join the Chinese Communist Party. This group of scholars, the Shanghai Labor

History Committee, had therefore coordinated extensive efforts to interview women who had been cotton mill workers before Liberation and to collect news articles concerning work conditions and strike activity. Individual cotton mills undertook the project of compiling factory histories. These studies focused exclusively on two themes: the varieties of exploitation endured by women workers before Liberation and their heroic participation in the labor movement. The underlying premise of all these collections was the existence of a direct equation between workers' poverty and oppression and their militancy: the more oppressed they were, the greater the likelihood that they would unite in acts of collective resistance.

Archival materials and interviews with pre-Liberation mill workers and managers led me to question this premise. This research alerted me to an entirely different group of issues concerning the work and political experience of pre-Liberation female cotton mill workers: the persistence of divisions among women based on native place, the divisive effects of imperialism, and the role of Shanghai's criminal underworld organization, the Green Gang, in mediating relations between workers and capitalists. Pre-Liberation surveys of working-class life, reports by social reformers and political organizers, local newspaper articles, and factory records all confirmed that these issues were indeed historically significant. The evidence made it clear that this was not a story of rural peasants who severed their ties to the countryside and became urban workers, nor was it simply one of victims of industrial poverty who became class-conscious revolutionary heroines.

The women who worked in the Shanghai mills had a variety of geographic and social origins. In Shanghai, natives of a particular region congregated in certain departments of the mills and lived in the same neighborhoods. There is evidence that even as late as the 1960's a workshop in the cotton mills was often staffed by people from one particular rural district. Most weavers, for example, were from Wuxi, most spinners from Shanghai, and most rovers from Subei. In Shanghai even today people from particular villages often remain clustered in distinct neighborhoods, where they continue to speak the dialect and preserve many of the customs of their hometowns. The persistence of these patterns of localism as long as thirty years after Liberation made it clear that urban life and factory work did not necessarily bring together people with different social and geographic origins.

Localism—expressed in dress styles, eating habits, marriage customs, and dialects—was the basis of the most important divisions and antagonisms among workers. Most women workers had been born either in villages of Subei (the part of Jiangsu north of the Yangzi River, also called Jiangbei) or in those of Jiangnan (the part of the province south of the river). Local slang, even today, confirms regional biases and stereotypes. One of the most common and offensive curses is to call someone a pig from north of the river. There seem to be countless variations on the basic curse "You Jiangbei swine!"—for example, "You're as filthy as a Jiangbei person!" or even "You're as lewd as a Jiangbei person!" News reports confirm that people from Shanghai still refuse to consider introductions to potential marriage partners from Subei. Students worry that they might be sent to teach in Subei neighborhoods of Shanghai, where the pupils are allegedly "not as motivated to study as Shanghainese." The perdurance of these regional prejudices underlines the fact that the pre-Liberation female work force was in no sense a homogeneous one. Women were more likely to perceive their fellow worker from a different region as their foe than they were to see the capitalist as the enemy.

These divisions among women workers, which are not entirely different from those found among textile workers in other historical contexts, were exacerbated in the Shanghai mills by imperialism. My research suggested that there was something overly simplistic about previous assessments of imperialism's effect on the formation of the working class and working-class consciousness. Such assessments had stressed the cruelty inflicted on Chinese workers by foreign mill owners, and the consequent solidarity and nationalism instilled in the workers. I found instead women from Subei who insisted that they had preferred to work in the Japanese mills, where they did not have to contend with the condescending attitude expressed toward them by the Chinese mill managers. This in turn increased the contempt of Jiangnan workers for those from Subei, whom they accused of being unpatriotic. Even for many women from Jiangnan, better pay and more comfortable working conditions made the Japanese-owned mills preferable to those owned by Chinese capitalists. Imperialism, it seemed, had not fostered the solidarity of workers in opposition to the capitalists, but instead had created even greater divisions and antagonisms among them.

I went to Shanghai looking for a history of workers and capitalists. Both workers and capitalists, however, in their memories of pre-Liberation life, recalled a third, equally important, group—the Green Gang.* Aside from discussions of the role of the Green Gang in controlling the labor movement in the late 1920's, little mention has been made of the Green Gang in previous studies of Shanghai's modern history. Yet pre-Liberation local newspapers, factory records, and surveys of Shanghai's social conditions all corroborated the importance of the Green Gang in the Shanghai mills.

All the mill managers I interviewed recalled a past during which they lived in terror of the Green Gang. When they opened cotton mills they were forced to pay gang leaders a "protection fee," and often had to offer them membership in the company's board of directors. Many had been kidnapped and held for ransom by gang members; it was commonplace for mill managers and owners to hire bodyguards to protect them from this menace.

Women workers also lived in terror of the Green Gang. If they themselves had not been attacked by gang members, some of their relatives and friends had been. To avoid harassment, they paid part of their monthly earnings as a protection fee to a neighborhood gang leader. Some women were beholden to gang members for their jobs in the mills. As a result, many of the organizations women spontaneously formed derived from their fundamental need for protection from the gang.

*In addition to the Green Gang there were a Red Gang and myriad smaller gang organizations in Shanghai. Most documentary sources, as well as the pre-Liberation factory workers and managers whom I interviewed, use the term "Green Gang" to refer both to the Green Gang itself and to most other gang organizations. Except where specified, I have adopted this broad usage of "Green Gang."

A vivid example of the power of the Green Gang is the contract labor system. Under this system a recruiter went to rural villages and purchased teenage girls from their parents, kept them in his or her house in Shanghai, and hired them out to the cotton mills. The contractor kept the money earned by the girls in the mills. Previous writers have attributed the existence of the contract labor system to the foreign ownership of many of the cotton mills: unfamiliar with the Chinese language and lacking contacts of their own, foreign mill owners allegedly had no choice but to rely on these labor recruiters, whose brutal treatment of their girls was the subject of many contemporary exposés. Although few of the women I interviewed had actually been hired through this contract labor system, they invariably recounted the plight of contract workers as emblematic of the cruel conditions resulting from the foreign presence.

The mill managers interviewed offered a different interpretation of the contract labor system. They understood the system not as a product of the foreign presence, but rather as an expression of the power of the Green Gang. Factory records and industrial surveys, I found, supported their view. The contract labor system clearly was not confined to foreign-owned mills; there was ample evidence that capitalists opposed the system; and finally, the development of the system coincided almost exactly with the rise of the Green Gang in Shanghai.

In many ways the presence and power of the gang made the process of industrialization and the experience of women workers in Shanghai different from what they had been in the United States and Europe. The industrial world of Shanghai was not divided simply into workers on one side and mill owners on the other: the gangs affected both. From the vantage point of women mill workers, the gang members who threatened them with rape and kidnapping must have seemed daily antagonists at least as detestable as the mill owners. Under these circumstances, working-class consciousness might have meant something other than the workers' consciousness of their interests as workers in opposition to those of the capitalists who employed them.

Even though my study emphasized the forces militating

against the development of solidarity and working-class consciousness among women workers, it ultimately seemed imperative to reconcile these forces with the record of the militant labor movement of the 1920's. In spite of the record of strike activity in the mills from the time of the May Fourth Movement through the Guomindang coup of 1927, I found almost no evidence that women mill workers of the 1920's were the class-conscious revolutionaries that previous studies had implied. Few women joined the radical labor unions formed during this period; even fewer joined the Chinese Communist Party; and I found no examples of women workers who became leaders of the labor movement during the twenties.

On the other hand, many of the women selected by factory officials for me to interview had been activists in the labor movement during the years between the end of World War II and Liberation. As they told their stories I realized that this was a period of the labor movement about which almost nothing had been written by Western scholars.[5] More concerned with the role of peasants in the making of the Chinese revolution, historians have left the impression that (as Lynda Shaffer put it) after 1927 "China's workers simply rolled over and died."[6] Yet when I supplemented the interviews with documentary research, it became clear not only that there was a militant labor movement in Shanghai during the postwar era, but that women mill workers were at the forefront of that movement, both as leaders and as participants.

This militancy did not mean that women of the 1940's had once and for all severed their ties to the countryside, that regional divisions and antagonisms had diminished, and that they now identified themselves as members of an urban working class. I found that even as women became active members of a revolutionary movement, they still remained members of traditional mutual aid societies and retained their loyalties to gang leaders and to supervisors in the mills. Moreover, the history of the Chinese Communist Party's efforts to organize women mill workers proved to be not simply one of distributing anticapitalist and anti-imperialist propaganda and organizing strikes but also one of burning incense and pledging sisterhood with women workers.

CHAPTER ONE

The Warp and Weft of Shanghai History

The story of women in cotton mills is not unique to Shanghai but is in fact one with universal overtones. The histories of industrial revolution in nineteenth-century Western Europe and the United States, as well as in twentieth-century Japan, also begin with women textile workers. Many aspects of women's experience in the Shanghai mills echo those of their predecessors abroad.

But the experience of Shanghai's women workers is not simply defined by the mills themselves, whose concrete structures, smokestacks, and machinery were essentially the same in all these places. If there are unique aspects to this story, they are to be found in its setting. By the 1930's Shanghai was the largest city in China and the sixth-largest city in the world. Although it was China's major port, financial capital, and biggest industrial center, it was also a city of peasants: many residents still farmed land within the broad municipal limits.

Shanghai was also a semicolonial city. After it had been opened to foreign trade in the mid-1800's, it attracted a large foreign population as British, French, Americans, and Japanese vied to win control of the city and its wealth. Each group of nationals carved out a world of its own in Shanghai. Businessmen were joined by missionaries, who came to proselytize, to educate, and occasionally to get involved in politics. Shanghai's status as a foreign-ruled treaty port also made it a haven for Chinese radical intellectuals fleeing the oppressive jurisdiction of the Chinese government. It was in Shanghai that revolutionaries sought refuge from Qing police in 1911 and that the Chinese Communist Party was founded in 1921.

Finally, Shanghai was a world of teahouses, bars, cabarets,

and brothels: in the 1930's Shanghai boasted more prostitutes per capita than any other city in the world. Many of these entertainment establishments, which earned the city the epithets Sin City, Paradise of Adventurers, and Paris of the East, were run by gang members. The gangs' presence and power made Shanghai a city where kidnapping, murder, and other crimes were commonplace.

All these worlds influenced the experience of women mill workers, even if their daily lives rarely took them beyond the road connecting their homes to the mills. Almost all, at some time, worked in mills owned by foreigners; many were beholden to gang members for their jobs. Some studied in schools run by missionaries, others in schools run by Communist organizers. Unless they participated in major political demonstrations, such as those of the May Thirtieth Movement (1925), they might never see the glamour of the stores and neon lights of downtown Shanghai. But many women had brothers or husbands who carried the wealthy of Shanghai in rickshaws or worked as bellboys in dance halls. Some had sisters who had been kidnapped and sold to brothels. Others had worked as servants in large Western-style mansions owned by foreigners in Shanghai. All these coexisting worlds created the context in which the cotton industry developed and the female work force emerged.

"A Wilderness of Temples and Chopsticks"

The transformation of Shanghai into a modern city began in the mid-1800's, when the Treaty of Nanjing, signed in 1842 at the end of the first Opium War, established it as a treaty port and opened it to foreign trade. The conferring of treaty port status did not immediately result in industrialization. Ironically, the city that by the end of World War I had become the "Lancashire of China" was initially viewed by the British as a market for the textiles produced in Lancashire. "It is the great gate to the Chinese empire," the British botanist Robert Fortune exclaimed when he visited Shanghai in 1843.

No other town with which I am acquainted possesses such advantages. . . . In going up the river towards the town, a forest of masts meets the eye, and shows at once that it is a place of vast native trade. . . . The convenience of inland transit is unrivalled in any part of the world. The country, being as it were the valley of the Yang-tse-kiang [Yangzi River], is one vast plain, intersected by many beautiful rivers, and these again joined and crossed by canals, many of them nearly natural, and others stupendous works of art. . . . The port of Shanghae swarms with boats of all sizes, employed in this inland traffic. . . . Since the port has been opened these boats bring down large quantities of tea and silk to supply the wants of our merchants who have established themselves here, and return loaded with the manufactures of Europe and America, which they have taken in exchange. Our plain cotton goods are most in demand amongst the Chinese, because they can dye them in their own peculiar style, and fit them for the tastes of the people. . . . There can be no doubt that all of the green teas, and perhaps the greatest portion of the black, can be brought to Shanghae at less expense than they can be taken to Canton, or any of the other southern towns. . . . The large silk districts of Northern China are close at hand. . . . Taking, therefore, all these facts into consideration . . . there can be no doubt that in a few years it will not only rival Canton, but become a place of far greater importance.[1]

As Fortune had predicted, Shanghai developed rapidly as a center for foreign trade. Tea exports from Shanghai increased from a million pounds in 1844 to eighty million pounds in 1855. The quantity of silk exported from Shanghai multiplied almost fifteen times during the first decade of foreign trade: in 1844 Shanghai exported 6,433 bales of silk; by 1855 it was exporting 92,000 bales.[2] Shanghai was important not only as a center of trade in goods such as tea and silk, which were produced in the surrounding countryside of Jiangsu and Zhejiang provinces, but also as a trading center for goods produced far inland. The Yangzi River facilitated transport of vegetable oils, animal hides, eggs, and raw cotton from places such as Sichuan and Hankou.[3] It was to perform the tasks required to process these goods for export, such as sorting cotton, silk, eggs, and bird feathers, that women were first drawn into the Shanghai work force.[4]

The growth of foreign trade was accompanied by a transformation in the physical landscape of the city. At the time foreign traders arrived in the early 1840's, Shanghai was a small town surrounded by a wall no more than three and a half miles in circumference. The area inside the wall was "densely studded with houses"; with shops retailing cotton and silk goods, bamboo ornaments, porcelain, and other curiosities; and with stands selling fish, meat, fruit, and vegetables. "Dining rooms, tea-houses, and bakers' shops are met with at every step," Fortune wrote, "from the poor man who carries his kitchen upon his back, and beats upon a piece of bamboo to apprise the neighborhood of his presence . . . to the most extensive tavern or tea-garden crowded with hundreds of customers."[5] A contemporary guidebook described the area as "a wilderness of temples and chopsticks."

In contrast to the crowds and bustle within the city wall, the area outside the wall was an agricultural plain dotted with occasional temples and villages. The land was trisected by the Huangpu River, linking Shanghai to the Yangzi delta, and Suzhou Creek, connecting Shanghai to Suzhou. It was in the area parallel to the Huangpu River, stretching between the wall of the Chinese city and Suzhou Creek, that the first foreign settlements were established when Shanghai was opened as a treaty port. By 1848 the British Settlement extended south to the creek called Yangjing; the French Concession was established across Yangjing Creek in 1849 and occupied the land between the creek and the boundary of the Chinese city (see Map 1). Americans, who did not have a legally recognized settlement at that time, occupied the Hongkou district along the Huangpu north of Suzhou Creek. The settlements were for foreigners only; Chinese could remain inside the old walled city but were to be excluded from the territories purchased by foreigners.

This arrangement did not last more than a decade. During the Taiping Rebellion, which began in 1862 and continued for fourteen years, villages and cities throughout the Yangzi valley were laid waste, and thousands of refugees fled to the safety of the foreign settlements in Shanghai. By the mid-1860's the ideal of a foreigners' enclave had been reduced to a short-lived memory: there were a half million Chinese living in the so-called foreign settlements, compared with a mere one thousand foreigners.

Despite the numerical strength of the Chinese population,

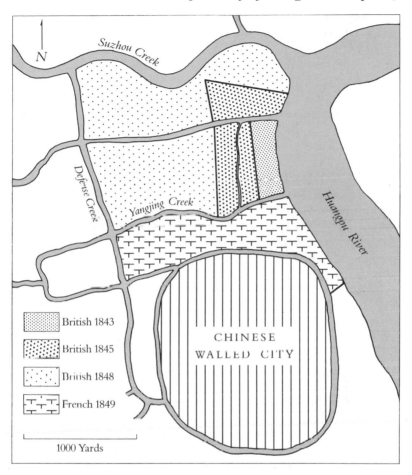

Map 1. Early foreign settlements at Shanghai. Adapted from Rhoads Murphey, *Shanghai: Key to Modern China* (Cambridge, Mass., 1953); reproduced by permission of Harvard University Press.

all government power was maintained by foreigners. In 1863 the area occupied by Americans merged with the British settlement to form the International Settlement, which was governed by an elected body, the Shanghai Municipal Council. (The French Concession remained independent and had its own government council.) Although Chinese residents of the International Settlement were required to pay municipal taxes, they were not allowed to vote; the franchise was a privilege reserved for the foreign land-renters of the settlement. A mixed court, presided over by a Chinese judge and a British officer, was established to handle legal cases involving Chinese residents.[6]

One of the first necessities of the foreigners, to maintain law and order within the settlements, was a police department. Some Sikhs (whom the Shanghainese called Red-headed Number Threes) were recruited for the job, but most police were Chinese. Many had originally been boatmen along the Grand Canal but had lost their jobs in the late nineteenth century, when Manchu rulers decided to transport tribute grain to Peking via sea rather than by boat on the Grand Canal. When these unemployed boatmen came to Shanghai they brought with them the tradition of the Green Gang, a secret society to which most boatmen involved in grain shipment along the Grand Canal had belonged since the early years of the Qing dynasty. Through these boatmen who joined the police department, the Green Gang developed a base of power in the treaty port of Shanghai.[7] From this base it grew into a powerful underworld organization, eventually becoming an organization that members of all echelons of Shanghai society, from politicians and businessmen to workers and entertainers, had to join in order to survive.

Most of the foreigners who inhabited the International Settlement had come to take advantage of the profits to be made by trading in silk, tea, and opium. British and American firms that had initially become prominent as trading houses in Canton, such as Jardine, Matheson and Company (whose trade name in China, Yi He, or Ewo in English transliteration, meant Precious and Peaceful), Russell and Company, and Robert Dent and Company, quickly set up branch offices along the Shanghai Bund—the avenue along the Huangpu River, once a "well-trodden tow path bordering a marsh."[8] The financial organizations that serviced the growing foreign trade also began to migrate toward Shanghai.

In addition to foreign banks, Chinese native bankers also set up shop in the International Settlement. The Shanxi Bankers' Guild established its office in Hongkou in 1892. (The guild building became a tourist attraction because it housed a theater "with a curiously shaped dome in which it is possible to see oneself upside down!")[9] By the late 1800's the community of Ningbo merchants who had moved north to Shanghai was sufficiently large to sponsor the construction of a Ningbo Guild Hall. Along with their counterparts from Shaoxing, the Ningbo merchants were the core of the Shanghai Native Bankers' Guild.[10] Finally, Chinese who had interpreted for foreigners in Canton migrated to Shanghai and became compradores for the large foreign firms.

Trade dominated the Shanghai economy throughout the nineteenth century, forming a base of wealth on which industry slowly began to develop. Shanghai's proximity to the silk-producing center of Jiangnan, as well as its status as a treaty port, made it an ideal place to develop silk-reeling factories, or filatures, to meet the demands of the export trade. Technically it was still illegal for foreigners to operate factories in China, but the Chinese government overlooked these small, low-capital ventures in the foreign concessions.[11] The first mechanized silk filature was built in 1862. Russell and Jardine, Matheson soon built their own filatures, as did several French and Italian entrepreneurs. By 1894 there were approximately 5,000 workers in Shanghai's silk filatures: about half worked in the four foreign-owned firms, and half in the five that were Chinese-owned.[12] During the first half of the twentieth century, Shanghai's silk industry became the second-largest employer of women workers, rivaled only by the cotton industry.

The cotton industry had its inauspicious beginnings during the last decade of the nineteenth century. Li Hongzhang established the first mill, the Shanghai Machine Weaving Bureau, in 1888. When it began operating in 1890 it employed some four thousand workers. They did not work there long, however; in 1893 the mill was destroyed by a fire.[13] In 1891 Li started the New Cotton Spinning and Weaving Bureau, which employed about sixty technicians and three hundred workers, in Yangshupu.[14] Before the end of the Sino-Japanese War, three other cotton mills were built in Shanghai.[15]

By 1894 the development of silk filatures and cotton mills, as well as shipbuilding, machine-repair, and chemical plants, made Shanghai the largest industrial center in China, with more than 36,000 factory workers. This figure represented about 46 percent of the total number of industrial workers in China.[16] Nevertheless, prior to 1895 industry was still subordinate to trade, which remained the cornerstone of the Shanghai economy.

Industrialization

It was not until the end of the Sino-Japanese War and the signing in 1895 of the Treaty of Shimonoseki, which granted foreigners the right to build factories in the treaty ports, that Shanghai began to develop as a major industrial center. Discussions of Shanghai's merits as a trading center and market for Lancashire's products were replaced by proclamations about the potential value of Chinese labor. The members of the Blackburn mission, sent from Great Britain to Shanghai in 1896, insisted on the value of developing the cotton industry in Shanghai. "Comparing this Oriental labour and our own," the report of the mission stated, "there is on the one hand, cheap, plentiful, submissive, capable labour, plus the best machinery we can give it; on the other hand, dear, dictating and exacting labour, plus the same machinery. Can anyone call these equal conditions? Are they not in favour of the Shanghai capitalist, who can see that his money will be more profitably employed by utilising this labour than by selling English piece goods?"[17]

Apparently these exhortations were heeded; the British were the first to take advantage of the newly won privilege for foreigners in China. The largest British mills in Shanghai, the Yi He and the Lao Gong Mou mills, were established by Jardine, Matheson in 1895 and 1896, respectively. The Germans followed suit by building the Rui Ji Mill, and an American company opened the Heng Yuan Mill in 1897.[18]

The Japanese, who eventually dominated Shanghai's cotton industry, made a more modest beginning in the early 1900's by purchasing two bankrupt Chinese-owned mills.[19] Not until 1911 did a Japanese company, the Naigai Wata Company (Nei Wai), construct the first Japanese-built mill on the southern shore of Suzhou Creek in west Shanghai. Naigai Wata, which already operated two cotton mills in Osaka, rapidly became the largest textile conglomerate in Shanghai, eventually operating eleven mills.[20]

After the outbreak of World War I in 1914 there was a dramatic reduction in the import of cotton piece goods into China from abroad, and the cotton industry flourished in Shanghai. During these years the three Chinese families that dominated the textile world of Shanghai throughout the first half of the twentieth century—the Nie, Rong, and Guo families—made their first bids as cotton mill owners. The mills of the Rongs and Guos were the only Chinese holdings that could compete in size with Japanese and British mills.

Originally from Hunan, Nie Zhikui began his career as a subordinate of Zeng Guofan in the battle to suppress the Taipings; later he married Zeng's daughter. Nie was one of the major investors in the New Cotton Spinning and Weaving Bureau in the early 1890's. When this mill, reorganized as Fu Tai, was put up for sale in 1909, Nie bought it and renamed it the Heng Feng Mill.[21] When he died in 1911, his son C. C. Nie (Nie Yuntai) took over. The younger Nie was active in organizing the Chinese Cotton Mill Owners' Association in 1918; he became its first vice-president. After World War I he constructed a new mill in Wusong, invested in the China Machine Works, and (with K. P. Chen and H. H. Kung) formed an organization to foster Sino-American trade.[22] C. C. Nie devoted a great deal of effort to educating his workers and earned a reputation as a "benevolent capitalist." He became a favorite of the YWCA, which had begun work in Shanghai in 1908. One of the first YWCA secretaries was ecstatic when, in order to fulfill his desire to help the poor people who lived in the Yangshupu district, Nie

gave his own beautiful garden, in front of his large European house for use as a Play Ground under the direction of the "Young Women's Christian Association." About two hundred children have participated thus far. Mr. Nieh arranged to have a Chinese entertainment for these children and their parents. A Pine tree in his garden was utilized as a Christmas tree and nearly four hundred bags, containing each a Book on Character building, were given to the children who came. . . . I wish you could have seen the children as they sat on the ground listening to Mrs. Nieh tell the Christmas story. . . . Both Madame and Mrs. Nieh attend a Bible class which Miss Jacob teaches in their home; and we hope they will be baptised before long. Mr. Nieh is to be baptised next Saturday.[23]

The Rong family also made its appearance in the Shanghai textile world during World War I. The Rong brothers, Rong Zongjing and Rong Desheng, came from Wuxi. Sent by his father to Shanghai when he was seven to study in an iron-anchor-making firm, Zongjing, the elder, left Shanghai because of illness but returned in the early 1890's with his brother to become an apprentice in a native bank. Several years later they joined their father in opening a native bank of their own. They made enough money in this enterprise to begin building flour mills in the early 1900's; the Rong family's Fu Xin flour mills dominated Shanghai's flour industry just as their Shen Xin cotton mills would come to dominate the Chinese-owned cotton industry. The Rongs constructed their first cotton mill, Shen Xin Number One, in west Shanghai in 1916. Over the years they established six more cotton mills in Shanghai, as well as one each in Wuxi, Hankou, and Changzhou.[24]

The third "cotton family" was the Guo family. Originally from Xiangshan county in Guangdong, the family had moved to Australia in the mid-1800's. In 1907 the two Guo brothers moved to Hong Kong and opened the first of many Wing On (Yong An in Mandarin) department stores, which made them famous. Eventually they established department stores in Shanghai, San Francisco, and Australia while investing in real estate and insurance in China. In 1921 they built the first of four cotton mills, three in Shanghai and one in its suburb Wusong.[25]

The enterprises built by these and other native capitalists, as well as by foreign investors, produced conspicuous displays of wealth that by the end of World War I dramatically transformed the physical appearance and social structure of Shanghai. The imposing office buildings along the Bund—including those of Robert Dent, the Hong Kong and Shanghai Banking Corporation, the Yokohama Specie Bank, the *North China Daily News*, the Maritime Customs, and Jardine, Matheson—

created the distinctive Shanghai skyline. Stretching west from the Bund to the British Race Course, Nanjing Road (see Map 2), formerly called Great Horse Road, became a bustling shopping street. The city's two department stores, Sincere and Wing On, were "concrete structures with four or five stories, filled with dazzling displays of Chinese and foreign goods and with Chinese hotels and restaurants in the top floors."[26] The stores' towers were illuminated by neon lights at night and symbolized Shanghai's status as China's most modern city.

Beyond the racecourse, Nanjing Road became Bubbling Well Road, "a synonym for the patrician quarter of Shanghai."[27] Due south of Bubbling Well Road, Avenue Joffre, the main thoroughfare of the French Concession, had become an equally elegant residential area for the rich. Wealthy Chinese businessmen had built villas every bit as lavish and extravagantly furnished as those of the foreigners. The residence of one nouveau riche industrialist was described as "a castle-like stone mansion equipped with a swimming pool, tennis courts, one Daimler, two Isotta-Fraschinis . . . and sundry smaller cars."[28] In these estates, as well as in slightly less extravagant residences, tens of thousands of Chinese women, including many migrants from rural areas, found jobs as servants and as wet nurses.[29]

The residents of Bubbling Well Road and Avenue Joffre sought entertainment in the Great World and in the New World—pleasure palaces established during World War I. "On the first floor were gambling tables, singsong girls, magicians, pick-pockets, slot machines, fireworks, bird cages, fans, stick incense, acrobats and ginger," the Hollywood film director Josef von Sternberg wrote after his visit to the Great World.

One flight up were the restaurants, a dozen different groups of actors, crickets in cages, pimps, midwives, barbers and earwax extractors. The third floor had jugglers, herb medicines, ice cream parlours, photographers, a new bevy of girls their high-collared gowns slit to reveal their hips, and under the heading of novelty, several rows of exposed toilets, their impresarios instructing the amused patrons not to squat but to assume a position more in keeping with the imported plumbing. The fourth floor was crowded with shoot-

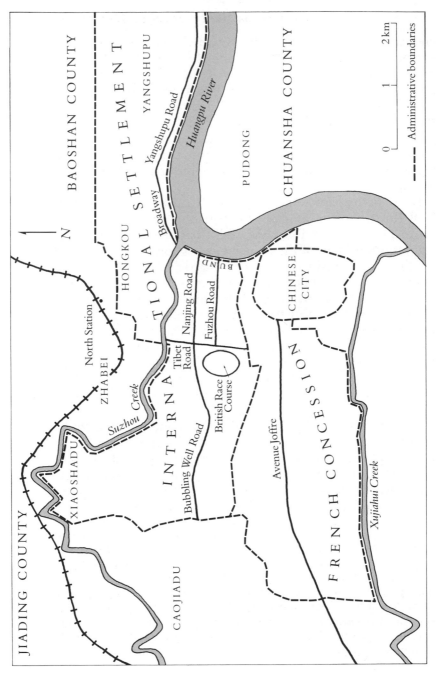

Map 2. Shanghai, 1919

ing galleries, fan-tan tables, revolving wheels, massage benches, acupuncture and moxa cabinets, hot-towel counters, dried fish and intestines, and dance platforms. . . . The fifth floor featured girls whose dresses were slit to the armpits, a stuffed whale, story tellers, balloons, peep shows, masks, a mirror maze, two love-letter booths with scribes who guaranteed results, "rubber goods" and a temple filled with ferocious gods and joss sticks. On the top floor and roof of that house of multiple joys a jumble of tightrope walkers slithered back and forth, and there were seesaws, Chinese checkers, mahjongg, strings of firecrackers going off, lottery tickets and marriage brokers.[30]

Shanghai's famed entertainment industry, comprising these pleasure palaces as well as ballrooms such as the Venus and the Ambassador, offered employment to several thousand women in Shanghai. The amusement centers hired female receptionists to attract customers; the ballrooms hired dance hostesses to provide companionship for the predominantly male clientele. The most famous dancing girls, such as the MGM Ballroom's Five Tigresses and the Paramount's Lilac Lady, took in more than a thousand dollars in a single night.[31]

As alluring as the amusement centers and ballrooms were the teahouses of Fuzhou Road, just a few blocks south of Nanjing Road. The thriving business of the pleasure palaces and teahouses was enhanced by the sexual services of the young Chinese women they offered. In the teahouses, wrote one fascinated observer,

by nine or ten o'clock everything is in full swing. In and out among the square tables, filling the brilliantly lighted rooms, trail slowly little processions of young girls. . . . Clad in silk or satin, adorned with jewelry, their faces unnatural with paint and powder, they follow the lead of the woman in charge of each group. She stops often to draw attention ingratiatingly to her charges and expatiates on their good points. When one is chosen she leaves her to her fate and passes on to dispose of others. . . . Multitudes of victims, having been sold into this slavery when too young to resist, . . . are kept up hour after hour in the close atmosphere of the tea-room awaiting the pleasure of their prospective seducers. Out on the street, by ricksha and on foot, women continue to hurry to the tea houses with their living merchandise, and still they keep arriving till the night is far advanced and business at a stand-still.[32]

Aside from these young girls and the household servants, coolies, and rickshaw pullers whose work took them to the International Settlement, most of the urban poor lived in the factory districts. By the end of the war these districts had developed in areas separated from the downtown business and commercial neighborhoods by the Huangpu River or by Suzhou Creek. Across the Huangpu, almost directly opposite the Bund, was Pudong. Although the Japan-China Spinning and Weaving Company operated several mills there, Pudong was not a major cotton mill district. It was dominated instead by the factory buildings of the British and American Tobacco Company and the docks and warehouses of Mitsui, Standard Oil, the China Merchant Steam Navigation Company, and Jardine, Matheson.

Back across the Huangpu, but east of the mouth of Suzhou Creek, Yangshupu had by 1919 become a mill district. It is hardly surprising that Yangshupu was the first industrial district of Shanghai: the abundance of cheap, undeveloped land and the proximity to water transport made it an ideal site for factories. "Yangtsepoo [Yangshupu] Road, meaning Poplar-Tree-Shore Road, is a continuation of Broadway, and as it is chiefly a street of mills, stands rather low in the social scale," Mary Gamewell noted when she visited Shanghai in 1916. "It runs parallel with the river and should have been a residential avenue, the most beautiful in Shanghai, but somehow the mills got there first and then there was no help for it. . . . The fresh breezes and fine outlook are lost on the tired mill hands shut up behind brick walls from dawn to dusk."[33]

West of Yangshupu and north of Suzhou Creek were two other districts of small-scale factories: Hongkou and Zhabei. Most of Shanghai's silk filatures, as well as several small cigarette, match, and knit goods factories, had been built in these two districts.[34] The most important difference between the two districts was that whereas Hongkou lay mostly within the boundaries of the International Settlement, Zhabei was entirely Chinese-owned and -governed. The Settlement boundary made a similar division between Xiaoshadu and Caojiadu, the two other major cotton mill districts, located even farther west along Suzhou Creek.

By 1919 these six industrial districts supported a population of 181,485 factory workers.* Almost half these worked in Shanghai's 26 cotton mills (11 Chinese-owned, 11 Japanese-owned, and 4 British-owned). Another 40,000 worked in the machine industry, 20,000 in cigarette factories, and 5,000-6,000 in silk filatures.[35] (See Table 1 for a breakdown of male, female, and child workers in various industries for 1929 and 1946.)

Although these districts lay just across the Huangpu River or Suzhou Creek from downtown Shanghai, nothing in their physical appearance belied a proximity to China's most international and cosmopolitan center. There were no large department stores, fancy silk shops, or European-style mansions and villas; nor were there cabarets, nightclubs, and ballrooms.

Most residents of the factory districts lived in two-story Chinese-style houses constructed of mud floors, bamboo walls, and tiled roofs. Lofts made it possible for three or four families to occupy a single dwelling. At night, chickens and ducks often shared the premises. There was neither electricity nor plumbing; residents fetched water from creeks that ran through the neighborhood—creeks used for washing clothes, vegetables, and toilet buckets.

Within the working-class districts existed yet another of Shanghai's distinctive worlds—the shantytowns, tucked away in the curves of Suzhou Creek and along the Huangpu River in Yangshupu, far from the commercial sectors of the city. In these shack settlements, begun by migrants who came to Shanghai early in the twentieth century to beg or work as coolies, refugees from northern Jiangsu, Shandong, and Anhui made their homes in huts made of scrap matting, straw, and broken boards. Inside, straw spread over bricks served as beds, and old tin cans served as stoves. The term *penghu ren*, literally "shack dwellers," became a synonym for "low-class" in Shanghainese.

The expansion of the shantytowns closely paralleled the industrial growth of Shanghai. When Naigai Wata began building mills in the western part of Shanghai in 1911, the shack settlement of Medicine Water Lane sprang up on the south

---

*Shanghai shehui kexueyuan, lishi yanjiusuo, *Wusi yundong zai Shanghai shiliao xuanji* (Shanghai, 1980), p. 11. This figure represented only about 12 percent of the total population of Shanghai, estimated to be 1,538,000 in 1919.

TABLE 1   *Distribution of Male, Female, and Child Workers in Shanghai's Industries, 1929 and 1946*

| Industry | No. of factories | Workers | | | | | | Total |
| | | Male adults | | Female adults | | Children | | |
		No.	Pct.	No.	Pct.	No.	Pct.	
				1929				
Cotton spinning	61	23,064	21%	84,270	76%	3,548	3%	110,882
Silk reeling	107	1,712	3	37,211	73	12,453	24	51,376
Cotton weaving	405	6,547	22	22,394	77	303	1	29,244
Tobacco	90	7,335	30	15,703	65	1,259	5	24,297
Printing	419	9,455	71	630	5	3,252	24	13,337
Knitting	177	2,686	27	7,236	71	203	2	10,125
Machinery	518	6,455	66	0	0	3,300	34	9,755
Shipbuilding	13	5,994	96	0	0	254	4	6,248
Silk weaving	68	2,563	68	1,229	32	0	0	3,792
Eggs	7	1,399	39	2,186	61	0	0	3,585
Glassmaking	30	1,588	52	0	0	1,455	48	3,043
Bleaching & dyeing	48	2,914	100	0	0	0	0	2,914
Match-making	7	911	34	1,232	46	553	20	2,696
Enameling	16	1,857	81	353	15	90	4	2,300
Flour	13	2,112	100	0	0	0	0	2,112
Oil	11	1,951	100	0	0	0	0	1,951
Woodworking	23	1,886	100	0	0	0	0	1,886
Tanning	150	1,552	83.9	2	0.1	296	16.0	1,850
Metallurgy	120	1,133	69	0	0	516	31	1,649
Papermaking	7	872	56	681	44	0	0	1,553
Soapmaking	36	800	72	305	28	0	0	1,105
TOTAL	2,326	84,786	30%	173,432	61%	27,482	9%	285,700
				1946				
Cotton spinning	38	10,365	22%	35,306	77%	418	1%	46,089
Cotton weaving	42	4,284	40.71	6,236	59.27	2	0.02	10,522
Rubber	8	1,579	44	1,875	53	95	3	3,549

Industry								
Cigarettes	10	453	14	2,842	83	120	3	3,425
Wool textiles	9	1,095	32	2,271	66	58	2	3,424
Silk textiles	6	578	30.7	1,294	69.0	6	0.3	1,878
Machinery	14	1,506	85	17	1	242	14	1,765
Knitting	12	365	22	1,243	75	45	3	1,653
Hemp	2	529	35	974	65	0	0	1,503
Flour	5	999	99.8	0	0	2	0.2	1,001
Glassmaking	9	557	69	16	2	235	29	808
Towels & blankets	5	261	37	424	61	13	2	698
Match-making	4	249	40	348	56	22	4	619
Enameling	4	569	95	13	2	19	3	601
Papermaking	5	409	68	189	32	0	0	598
Shipbuilding	2	544	93	0	0	38	7	582
Medicine-making	4	128	23	426	77	0	0	554
Underwear	3	174	33	338	54	15	3	527
Printing	4	359	84	36	8	34	8	429
Oil	3	360	100	0	0	0	0	360
Needlemaking	5	170	55	122	39	17	6	309
Hatmaking	3	175	59	107	36	16	5	298
Thermos	3	207	76	44	17	20	7	271
Electric equipment	4	155	70	41	19	25	11	221
Soapmaking	4	181	83	32	15	6	2	219
Food canning	2	126	63	69	34	6	3	201
Soft pipe making	3	48	28	107	64	13	8	168
Metallurgy	3	78	52	16	13	32	25	126
Seasonings	2	101	32	20	16	2	2	123
Acid/alkali	2	95	100	0	0	0	0	95
Can manufacturing	2	38	44	48	55	1	1	87
Belt-making	1	26	32	54	68	0	0	80
Plastic manufacture	1	48	100	0	0	0	0	48
Tanning	1	33	100	0	0	0	0	38
TOTAL	225	26,859	32%	54,508	66%	1,502	2%	82,869

SOURCES: For 1929, Shanghai Bureau of Social Affairs, *Wages and Hours of Labor, Greater Shanghai, 1929* (Shanghai, 1929). For 1946, Shanghai shehuiju, *Shanghai gongchang laogong tongji* (Shanghai, 1946).

bank of Suzhou Creek, and Piaoziwan on the north bank. Despite frequent fires that sometimes destroyed entire hut settlements in a single night, these shantytowns were repeatedly rebuilt.[36]

Industrialization and Politics

By 1919 Shanghai had become the major industrial, commercial, and financial center of China. As the May Fourth Movement demonstrated, however, it had not yet challenged Peking as a locus of major intellectual and political movements. This situation began to change during the ensuing decade, and women cotton mill workers, already the largest single component of Shanghai's working class, were with increasing frequency the objects of and participants in economic, intellectual, and political movements. *New Youth*, edited by left-wing May Fourth intellectuals, heralded the change in May 1920 by publishing an issue devoted to labor conditions in Shanghai. Editor Chen Duxiu himself wrote a lengthy section of this special labor issue investigating the recruitment of women from Hunan to work in a Shanghai cotton mill.

After the founding of the Chinese Communist Party in Shanghai in 1921, an increasing number of radical intellectuals migrated to Shanghai. Their ranks included people who became active as labor leaders, such as Deng Zhongxia and Xiang Jingyu, as well as writers, such as Lu Xun and Ba Jin. Although few of them ever worked in factories themselves, they produced some of the most eloquent descriptions of factory life and the labor movement, including the waves of strikes that swept Shanghai after 1921, that were written during this period.[37] The strikes, particularly a dramatic strike of women silk workers in Zhabei in 1922, drew the attention of foreign missionaries to labor conditions. The missionaries' concern led to the formation of the Shanghai Child Labor Commission in 1922. Appointed by the Municipal Council, its members included Song Meiling, Agatha Harrison (the industrial secretary of the YWCA), and representatives of major industrial firms such as Naigai Wata and Jardine, Matheson. In 1924 the commission published the results of its extensive survey of working conditions, as well as a report stating its recommendation that the employment of children under ten years of age be prohibited. Unfortunately, by the time the Municipal Council submitted this recommendation as a bylaw to be voted on by the electorate of the International Settlement, the riots following the May Thirtieth Incident of 1925 had swept the city, and the bylaw was never adopted.[38]

The May Thirtieth Movement of 1925 began on May 15, when a cotton mill worker named Gu Zhenghong was shot and killed by Japanese guards at the Nei Wai Number Five Mill in Xiaoshadu. This incident triggered massive student demonstrations protesting foreign control in Shanghai. The tension escalated on May 30, when students were arrested and riots broke out as crowds demanding their release clashed with the police. Ten people were killed and fifty injured when Sikh policemen under British command opened fire on the crowd. The next day, May 31, the Chinese General Chamber of Commerce declared a strike of workers, students, and merchants. The strikers' demands ranged from establishing Chinese control over the police in Shanghai and representation on the Municipal Council to improving labor conditions in Shanghai's factories.[39]

Strike activity, particularly in Shanghai's cotton mills, continued with increasing intensity under the direction of the Shanghai General Union. Paving the way for the Northern Expedition, which set out from Guangzhou in 1926 to wrest control of China from the warlords, the Shanghai General Union mobilized another general strike in 1927 and was successful in establishing a provisional municipal government in Chinese-controlled Zhabei. Chiang Kai-shek, leading his National Revolutionary Army, was able to enter Shanghai at the end of March without firing a single shot. On April 12 Chiang's soldiers, assisted by armed members of the Green Gang, launched a coup that devastated the labor movement and inaugurated the period known as the White Terror.[40]

Japanese in Shanghai

These events took place against a background of increasing dominance by the Japanese over Shanghai's economic life during the 1920's. Japanese ascendancy was most dramatically evident in the cotton industry, which had expanded rapidly in the decade since World War I.

In 1919 the number of cotton mills (and spindles) owned by the Japanese in Shanghai was about the same as the number owned by the Chinese. This balance shifted quickly, for a number of reasons (see Table 2). First, the tariff revision of 1918, by imposing higher duties on imports of the finer-quality yarns and cloths that the Japanese had been exporting to China, made it more advantageous than before for the Japanese to locate their manufacturing operations in Shanghai. Second, laws regulating night shift employment in Japan made China, which was free of such restrictions, attractive to employers.[41] Between 1919 and 1925 the number of Japanese-owned mills in Shanghai increased from 11 to 32. Most of the new mills belonged to large conglomerates. The number of Chinese-owned mills increased from 11 to 22 during the same period, but most of the Chinese mills belonged to small companies: each company owned only one mill, or occasionally two. In 1925 the 32 Japanese mills belonged to only 11 different companies, the 22 Chinese mills to 18 companies.[42]

The increasing Japanese role in the cotton industry was mirrored outside the textile world. In the early 1920's Japanese companies purchased three wharf frontages, two in Pudong and one in Yangshupu, and the number of Japanese-owned banks increased steadily.[43] By 1930 the Japanese had replaced the British as the largest community of foreigners in the International Settlement. Their ranks swelled from a mere eight hundred in 1890 to ten thousand in 1920 and to thirty thousand in 1930—triple the British population at that time. The Japanese population formed a community called Little Tokyo in the part of Hongkou just north of Suzhou Creek.

There, north of Soochow Creek . . . Japanese shopkeepers and small traders lived in Chinese houses that had been transformed into regular Japanese homes. They lived there, squatting on the mat-covered floor, bathing in boiling hot water, leaving their shoes out in the hall. They taught their Chinese "boys" how to prepare tempura and sukiyaki, and sent them down to the Hongkew market to get their fresh supplies of Japanese fish and Japanese crabs and soy bean paste and raw ginger and Japanese vegetables—fresh from Kyushu. In their dainty shops, they sold Japanese cotton, toys, phonograph records, bicycles and a great many Chinese things, too.[44]

These consumer items were the target of the anti-Japanese boycott of 1931, organized in response to the Japanese seizure of Manchuria. As the boycott developed in Shanghai, Chinese firms refused to handle Japanese goods, Chinese banks refused to honor Japanese bills of lading, and some 70,000 tons of Japanese cargo backed up at the harbor. Whenever a Japanese ship docked, picket teams gathered on the nearby wharf. One result of the boycott was that a large number of Japanese mills in Shanghai were forced to cease operations temporarily, leaving many Chinese workers unemployed.[45]

Tension between Chinese and Japanese came to a head with the Shanghai Incident of 1932. Following skirmishes between Chinese and Japanese civilians on the outskirts of Shanghai, the Japanese consul general demanded that the anti-Japanese boycott be suppressed and the anti-Japanese propaganda campaign silenced. By the time Wu Dezhen, the mayor of Shanghai, communicated his acceptance of the Japanese demands, the Japanese navy had already taken the matter into its own hands. The admiral of the Japanese naval forces demanded that the Chinese Nineteenth Route Army withdraw from Zhabei. On January 28, 1932, when Chinese forces stood fast, the Japanese attacked on the pretext of defending Japanese residents in nearby Hongkou and the so-called undeclared war began. The biggest battles of the ensuing weeks were fought in Zhabei, the district surrounding the North Railway Station, a primary target for Japanese bombs.

Large sections of densely populated Chapei were laid waste. Fighting raged in the streets [and] spread into Hongkew, which was part of the International Settlement. Tenement houses burned down or collapsed under incessant shell fire. Industrial plants were blasted to pieces—among them the modern plant of the Commercial Press which had supplied three out of every four schoolbooks used in China during the last thirty years. Churches, schools, hospitals, cotton mills, and a Chinese university, were destroyed.[46]

Some 200,000 workers lost their jobs, and many their homes as well, as a result of the Japanese bombardment of Shanghai. The fighting lasted until a truce was signed on May 5.

TABLE 2   *Size and Work Force of Cotton Industry, Selected Years, 1921-1947*

Year	No. of mills	No. of spindles	No. of looms	No. of workers
1921				
Chinese	23	499,346	3,940	—
British	5	259,286	2,153	—
Japanese	24	352,180	1,986	—
Total	52	1,110,812	8,079	33,174
1922				
Chinese	24	624,142	4,240	40,739
British	5	257,866	2,800	13,000
Japanese	22	586,828	2,968	13,370
Total	51	1,468,836	10,008	67,109
1924				
Chinese	24	665,798	4,410	47,437
British	5	250,516	2,863	19,000
Japanese	28	629,368	3,929	43,428
Total	57	1,545,682	11,202	109,865
1925				
Chinese	22	677,238	5,090	44,934
British	4	205,320	2,348	16,500
Japanese	32	939,428	5,836	59,262
Total	58	1,821,986	13,274	120,696
1927				
Chinese	24	711,756	5,116	49,908
British	4	205,320	2,348	16,500
Japanese	30	947,540	7,710	58,113
Total	58	1,864,616	15,174	124,521
1928				
Chinese	24	776,388	7,384	50,555
British	3	153,320	1,800	13,000
Japanese	32	1,010,000	8,356	53,123
Total	59	1,939,708	17,540	116,678
1929				
Chinese	28	818,088	6,338	56,376
British	3	153,320	1,900	13,000
Japanese	30	1,054,344	8,820	58,029
Total	61	2,025,752	17,058	127,405
1930				
Chinese	28	953,646	7,007	63,243
British	3	177,228	2,480	13,189
Japanese	30	1,148,184	8,846	54,606
Total	61	2,279,058	18,333	131,038

TABLE 2 *(continued)*

Year	No. of mills	No. of spindles	No. of looms	No. of workers
1931				
Chinese	28	1,068,920	7,864	65,146
British	3	170,610	2,691	13,000
Japanese	30	1,253,100	13,685	51,103
Total	61	2,492,630	24,240	129,249
1932				
Chinese	28	1,082,148	7,238	65,638
British	3	183,196	2,891	13,000
Japanese	30	1,284,872	12,353	42,435
Total	61	2,550,216	22,482	121,073
1933				
Chinese	31	1,126,204	7,854	55,826
British	3	184,908	2,890	13,000
Japanese	30	1,287,608	13,278	44,940
Total	64	2,598,720	24,022	113,766
1934				
Chinese	31	1,131,444	8,337	52,407
British	4	184,908	2,891	13,000
Japanese	30	1,324,872	13,637	47,502
Total	65	2,641,224	24,865	112,909
1935				
Chinese	31	1,118,218	8,540	45,159
British	4	227,148	4,021	10,000
Japanese	30	1,314,388	15,208	44,863
Total	65	2,659,754	27,769	100,022
1936				
Chinese	31	1,114,408	8,754	54,818
British	4	221,336	4,021	12,221
Japanese	30	1,331,412	17,283	49,842
Total	65	2,667,156	30,058	116,881
1942				
Total	22	—	—	8,177
1943				
Total	22	—	—	3,934
1947				
Chinese	80	2,212,648	23,822	96,692
British	3	45,260	24	829
Total	83	2,257,908	23,846	97,521

SOURCE: Shanghaishi mianfangzhi gongye tongye gonghui, *Zhongguo mianfang tongji shiliao* (Shanghai, 1950).

By 1932 the Shanghai economy was suffering from the worldwide depression, and the textile industry was particularly hard hit. This time, however, it was the Chinese capitalists who were forced to close the gates of their mills. Ironically, this was in part a result of the anti-Japanese boycott, which (in the words of Kang Chao) had "triggered a price war in which the surviving powers of the two groups of mills were subject to test."[47] To sell their yarn during the boycott, many Japanese firms had drastically reduced their prices, and Chinese mill owners had no choice but to do the same.[48] Severe floods along the Yangzi River in 1931 increased the mill owners' problems by making raw cotton hard to get and therefore expensive. As a final blow, the Japanese occupation of Manchuria eliminated one of the most important markets for goods produced by the Chinese-owned mills. By mid-1933, 12 of the 31 Chinese-owned mills in Shanghai had completely shut down. Most others had reduced their hours.[49] The other major employer of women workers, the silk industry, was equally hard hit. In 1930 there had been 107 Chinese-owned filatures operating in Shanghai; by 1935 the number had dropped to a mere 30.[50] The outlook for women workers in Shanghai during the depression years was thus particularly bleak.

The plight of Shanghai's women workers during the early and mid-1930's attracted the attention of social reformers, including the YWCA Labor Bureau (established in 1921), now headed by Cora Deng. Under her direction, the number of night schools run by the YWCA for women workers in Shanghai multiplied, and the content of the classes became increasingly radical. The Labor Bureau recruited a number of Chinese women who had studied sociology and social work in the United States to serve on its staff. In addition to writing prolifically about the conditions of women workers, they encouraged their students to write articles describing their own working lives. Many of these articles were published in the YWCA's Chinese journal. At the same time, under the direction of American sociologist Herbert Lamson, students such as Yang Meizhen in the Sociology Department of Shanghai College (founded in Yangshupu in 1906 by the Baptist Church) conducted surveys of women workers in the factory district surrounding their school. The conditions of women workers during the depression also captured the attention of members of the League of Left-Wing Writers, founded in Shanghai in 1930 following the White Terror. During these years Mao Dun wrote his novel *Midnight,* describing the predicaments of workers and capitalists in the silk filatures, and Xia Yan produced his piece of "journalistic fiction" *Contract Labor,* exposing the conditions of female contract workers in the Shanghai cotton mills. The written record generated by these people makes the 1930's uniquely rich in accounts of the lives of women workers.

War with Japan

Shanghai's economy had barely begun to recover from the depression when the War of Resistance Against Japan broke out in 1937.* Immediately following the Marco Polo Bridge Incident on July 7, thousands who lived in the Chinese districts of Shanghai, rightly predicting that the war would spread south, began to flee to the safety of the International Settlement.

They were crossing the bridges that led into safety, more of them every day. Rents went up in the Settlement and in Frenchtown. Seven dollar rooms could be had for twenty-five. . . . The refugees squatted on the foreshore of the Bund in the blistering heat and did not move. They camped there, with the milch cows that some of them had driven along. Many of the men and women were herded into refugee camps that were improvised, by the municipal authorities, in Chinese amusement parks.[51]

Many factory owners whose mills were in the Chinese sections of Shanghai joined the move to the foreign settlements.[52]

Not until August 13, when Japanese troops moved into Wusong and Jiangwan, did fighting break out in Shanghai. Most of the factories in Shanghai were forced to suspend operations because of shelling, bombing, and street fighting.

*For the Chinese, World War II began with the Japanese attack in 1937. They refer to the war from 1937 to 1945 as the War of Resistance Against Japan, hereafter referred to as simply the War of Resistance.

Ironically, the most severe damage was inflicted on August 14 when Chinese planes aiming at the Japanese warship *Izumo*, docked in the Huangpu River just offshore from the Bund, missed their target. Instead they dropped two bombs at the junction of Great Horse Road and the Bund: one crashed through the roof of the Palace Hotel, the other landed in front of Victor Sassoon's Cathay House. Only a half hour later another Chinese bomber accidentally hit the Great World amusement center, and several weeks later yet another Chinese plane dropped a bomb farther up Great Horse Road, causing severe damage to both the Wing On and Sincere department stores.[53] Fighting between Chinese and Japanese continued until November, when Chinese troops retreated from Shanghai. From the end of 1937 until the outbreak of the Pacific War in 1941, the International Settlement was a "lonely island."[54]

In spite of the widespread destruction, the early years of the war were the first period of prosperity the cotton industry had known in a decade. Some mills that had not moved from the areas outside the Settlement boundaries were taken over by the Japanese.[55] Mills in the International Settlement, however, quickly resumed operations. In addition, seven new cotton mills registering under British or American company names were constructed in 1938.[56] High prices commanded by yarn and cloth made mills lucrative enterprises; the profits of the British-owned Yi He Mill, for example, trebled from 1937 to 1938. The profits earned by the Yong An Number Three Mill, the only Yong An mill inside the Settlement, more than compensated for the losses incurred by the company's three idle mills.[57] Other Shanghai industries experienced the same prosperity, and life in the city remained deceptively normal for a people at war. A YWCA secretary visiting Shanghai in early 1938 wrote home:

I have been back in Shanghai now for almost six weeks. . . . The first days of my return were a disappointment. I expected a war-torn Shanghai with a pale-faced population struggling in poverty and want and suffering from disorder and daily threats of violence. Instead I found everything quite normal. The streets [of the International Settlement] were crowded because of the augmented population, but people went about their business as usual. The restaurants were doing a prosperous business, and the theaters were even fuller than before the war. Many of the dancing halls have added a new feature—roller skating![58]

Not until December 1941, when the Japanese finally invaded the International Settlement, did this state of artificial normality come to an end. The first local incident of the Pacific War took place in the middle of the Huangpu River, where both Japanese and American ships were moored. Well before dawn on December 8 the Japanese gunboat *Izumo* pulled alongside two American ships and forced them to surrender.

When daylight came it was evident that the Japanese had planned their taking-over of the Settlement in some detail. Aircraft flew over the town dropping thousands of leaflets in various languages, exhorting the population to keep calm and trust the benevolence of the Imperial Japanese forces. By 10 A.M. sentries were already mounted at the British, American and Dutch consulates, the Municipal Building, the banks, cable offices and public utilities. The American Club was at once taken over by the Naval Landing Party. There was now a barrier at the Garden Bridge over the Soochow Creek, sealing off the Japanese quarter from the rest of the Settlement.[59]

Barbed-wire barricades were set up throughout the city, and Japanese sentries posted at all bridges. The Chinese were required to bow and express greetings as they passed the sentries; otherwise they would be stabbed with bayonets. British and American residents were required to register with the Japanese army, to wear red armbands, and to obtain permission from the Japanese before changing residence. Some were rounded up and interned in a house on Haiphong Road. "Shanghai, once the world's noisiest city, has become strangely silent," one foreign observer wrote at the time.[60]

Japanese administrators took over all British and American businesses, as well as the Chinese-owned mills that had registered after 1937 under British or American trade names. In some mills, production of yarn and cloth continued; in others, machinery was scrapped and used to manufacture ammunition for the Japanese army; in a few, operations were shifted to the production of army uniforms. By 1942 the number of spindles operating in the formerly Chinese-owned mills had been reduced by one-third, and the number of functioning looms cut in half.[61] The number of cotton mill workers in Shanghai had dropped to just over 8,000; by 1943 it was at an all-time low of less than 4,000[62] (see Table 2).

Toward Liberation

When the Japanese surrendered and the war ended in 1945, the International Settlement and the French Concession belonged to the Chinese government for the first time since their inception more than a century before. The government permitted foreign businesses, banks, and factories (except those owned by the Japanese) to resume operations. Although the Japanese had removed the machinery from some cotton mills, most had not suffered extensive damage during the war and should have been able to resume operations almost immediately. Yet most of the Shanghai mills remained closed through the fall of 1945; according to one estimate, only about 10 percent of the available spindles were operating in November.[63] It was almost a year after the war's end before the cotton industry began to revive.

This slow recovery, Suzanne Pepper argues in her study of the Chinese civil war, was due less to damage and disruption caused by the war than to corruption among the military and government officials who took over after Japan surrendered. The first military units to enter Shanghai after the surrender confiscated large quantities of raw materials, and while they were at it, dismantled and sold factory equipment for their own profit.[64]

In October 1945 the Committee for the Supervision of Enemy and Puppet Properties and the Bureau for the Disposal of Enemy and Puppet Properties were established to organize the process of taking over the factories, warehouses, and other properties that had originally belonged directly or indirectly to the Japanese. During their first month of work these two committees uncovered more than five hundred cases of attempts by Chinese military officials to conceal enemy property in the Shanghai area.[65] The members of these committees were not innocent of the crimes they accused their military predecessors of having committed. Corruption was so rampant that Chiang Kai-shek himself wrote a letter to the mayor of Shanghai, reporting reliable rumors that

the military, political and party officials in Nanking, Shanghai, Peiping and Tientsin have been leading extravagant lives, indulging in prostitution and gambling, and have forcibly occupied the people's larger buildings as offices under the assumed names of various party, military or political organizations. The worst conditions are said to be found in Shanghai and Peiping. I wonder if these officials are aware of what they are doing. Have you heard or seen anything in this connection?[66]

These problems were inherited, and indeed aggravated, by the China Textile Reconstruction Corporation (CTRC), established by the Executive Yuan in December 1945 to assume ownership of all cotton mills throughout the country that had formerly belonged to Japanese capitalists. Cases of corruption, bribes, and irregularities on the part of CTRC officials were common.[67] And the legacy of equipment problems compounded these difficulties: when the corporation took over the eighteen ex-Japanese mills in Shanghai in early 1946, there were complaints that "the machinery was mostly in great disorder and the buildings were in a dilapidated state." For several months these mills operated only day shifts.[68]

In the mill workshops the people who assumed managerial positions were not necessarily skilled technicians. "In the past, when our factory was under the management of the Japanese, if any spindle was out of order, they would immediately get it repaired," a woman who worked in one of the CTRC mills in Shanghai told a news reporter.

Now everything is managed carelessly. If the machine is a little out of gear, no one would attend to it—just keep on operating it as usual. As a result, machines wore out quickly. I am afraid that after a couple of years, all the spindles will become unworkable. Whenever we have any difficulty with our machine and go to ask those technicians, the answer we get would either be "Oh, this I don't know," or "Ah, that I don't know." They would give you no clear answer at all. Yet it is said that they are all university graduates. Whenever they have any difficulty, they will have to consult their text books. In handling the machinery they are no better than the workers.[69]

The mills controlled by the CTRC prided themselves on offering services for workers ranging from shower facilities and basketball courts to schools for their children and maternity leave. But the bureaucratic procedures attached to these benefits rendered them almost meaningless to the workers.

The problems of the cotton mills were only one symptom of a larger economic crisis. The most conspicuous manifestation of this crisis was an unprecedented inflation, which made it necessary "to carry a suit-case full of bank notes in order to do a morning's shopping."[70] Workers frequently went out on strike, demanding that their wages be adjusted to the cost of living and that their employers give them fixed amounts of rice and cloth. Between 1946 and 1949 the labor movement was for the first time since the 1927 coup and White Terror as active as it had been in the mid-1920's. In the first six months of 1946, for example, there were some 250 strikes in Shanghai.[71] These strikes, largely a product of the severe economic disruption of the postwar years, were for the most part orchestrated by the Chinese Communist Party. The CCP had been operating underground for more than a decade, but after the Japanese surrendered it began to actively develop branches in enterprises throughout Shanghai. Strikes involved not only factory workers but also workers at the Shanghai Customs Bureau, the American Power Company, the French Tramway Company, and the department stores.

During this time Shanghai was also the scene of frequent student demonstrations demanding an end to the civil war that had broken out between the CCP and the Guomindang (GMD) in 1946. These demonstrations reached a climax at the end of January 1948. Within one week there were three major strikes: a student strike at Tong Ji University, brought to a bloody end by the GMD; a strike of workers at the Shen Xin Number Nine Mill, in which several workers were killed and five hundred injured by GMD army units dispatched to halt the strike; and a strike of some ten thousand dance hostesses.[72]

While these movements swept Shanghai, the GMD was rapidly losing territory to the Communists in northern China. By early 1949 the CCP had crossed the Huai River and was moving south toward Nanjing and Shanghai. As the armies hurried south, Communist cadres in Shanghai were mobilizing workers to form "factory protection teams." The actual arrival of the People's Liberation Army in Shanghai in May was almost anticlimactic. "When the KMT [GMD] gave up Shanghai they did fight, but more for show than for effectiveness, and most of them got away with their skins whole," one foreign resident wrote.

Our building is high, and from my office window I could see them, and later watched the battle raging on the other side of the river some days before it closed in on our side. At night we used to go up on the roof and see the red patches on the horizon, each night a little nearer until the final blaze of petrol dumps, explosion of arsenals, and the crash of guns not so very far away. It all happened very quickly, save in our section of the city where we had the whizzing bullets along four sides of our building for three days, while friends in all other parts of the city phoned us at intervals and invited us to come and celebrate with them. It was a strange feeling to know the silence after the last burst of shooting, to see the yellow uniforms of the Liberation Army creeping up the opposite side of the street and then be able to go out to survey the new face of Shanghai.[73]

There were parades and processions in the streets in the days that followed. Yet in the cotton mills the liberation of Shanghai scarcely interrupted production, and work continued almost entirely as usual. Not until the political campaigns of the 1950's were radical changes made in the ownership, management, and organization of production in the mills.

During the decade after Liberation Shanghai's economic and social landscape, as well as its physical landscape, was transformed once again. Industries, trade companies, and banks originally owned by foreign and Chinese capitalists were gradually taken over by the Chinese government. Their offices lining the Bund became the headquarters for the new Shanghai municipal government, the Federation of Labor, and the Women's Federation. The Shanghai Club—famous since the early twentieth century for housing the longest bar in the world, and thus a favorite gathering place of foreign businessmen—was turned into a seamen's club. In the rest of the city the formerly thriving world of teahouses and cabarets dwindled in the wake of a massive campaign to eliminate opium smoking and prostitution.

Thus, after 1949 the mill buildings and machinery were much the same as they had been before, but the social environment was utterly different.

CHAPTER TWO

Inside the Mills

The cotton mills of Shanghai were by no means identical, and even individual mills changed over time. However, for the purposes of understanding the world in which working women spent more than half their waking hours, let us look at the structure and operations of one fairly typical mill, the Shen Xin Number One Mill, in 1925.[1]

Tour of a Mill

The main office of the company that owned the mill was located not in Caojiadu, where the mill was constructed in 1915, but on Jiangxi Road in downtown Shanghai near the Bund. In this office the owners (the Rong brothers of Wuxi) and the general and assistant managers made all decisions about purchasing raw cotton and machinery, and selling finished yarn and cloth. As in most Chinese-owned mills the majority of the managerial staff were friends or relatives of the owners. Every day they entertained the cotton brokers who came to show them samples of raw cotton, and bargained with them about the price. These managers paid only occasional visits to the mill itself.[2]

The task of translating management plans into production was the responsibility of engineers, who coordinated all the steps involved in turning raw cotton into yarn, and yarn into cloth. Having studied textile engineering at the Nantong Textile Institute or in Japan or England, they scarcely disguised their contempt for their superiors' ignorance. "They didn't even know which kind of cotton was good and which was bad," complained one engineer who had worked at a Shen Xin mill.[3]

To observe the mill operations, one had to leave the offices in downtown Shanghai and follow Suzhou Creek as it wound west, all the way to Caojiadu. At the point where the creek suddenly curved north, cotton mills and other factories could be seen flanking the river. Nothing distinguished the appearance of the Number One Mill from that of nearby factories. It consisted of several brick structures covering an area of more than eight acres. In addition to the main production workshops the complex included two business offices, six cotton and yarn warehouses, a machine repair shop, an engine room, and six dormitories. Most of the people who lived in the dormitories were not workers but members of the mill staff, supervisory personnel whose status fell between that of the engineers and that of the workers. Most were middle school graduates who had gone through a two-year apprenticeship program. While in that program they studied all aspects of textile production and management, and were required to live in the dormitories. At the end of the program they became overseers in individual workshops, and eventually they might be promoted to supervise all the workshops of the spinning or weaving section.[4]

The process by which cotton was turned first into yarn and then into cloth began outside the back gate of the factory, along the bank of Suzhou Creek. Here boats delivered raw cotton grown in Jiangsu, Shaanxi, and Hebei to the mill. Before being shipped the cotton was ginned (that is, the seeds were removed from the cotton fibers) and compressed into tightly packed bales for transportation.

Bare-chested coolies wearing knee-length cotton shorts and straw sandals unloaded these bales, which weighed close to five hundred pounds each, and carried them to the receiving room of the mill for storage. When the cotton was to be used, it was transported to the blowing room. Here, in one of the noisiest and dustiest departments of the mill, the first steps of preparing the cotton for spinning were carried out. The dirty, matted cotton was torn apart, fluffed, and cleaned. One group of male workers, called bale breakers, used hand trucks to take the bales from the entrance of the blowing room to a large scale. They weighed each bale, placed it in a row according to the grade of the raw cotton, used a mattock to break open the iron bands around each bale, and tore the wrapping away. Now another group of men took over. They pulled layers of cotton from the tops of the bales and fed the cotton into the first machine, which removed seeds, stalks, leaves, and sand and blended the different grades of cotton. What emerged from the other end of the machine were white fluffy clumps of cotton. These clumps were stuffed into a feeder, which spread them out to form sheets of still-fluffy cotton and rolled the sheet to form a cotton "lap." Coolies used carts to move the cotton laps from the blowing room to the carding room, inside the two-story spinning building. In the carding room male lap carriers lifted the heavy laps onto their shoulders and positioned them at the front of the carding machine. As the sheets of cotton passed through this machine, they were pressed between a series of small metal flats and a large cylindrical drum covered with thousands of fine wire teeth. The teeth combed the cotton, forcing the fibers into a regular, parallel pattern while removing any dust and short fibers that remained in the cotton. After several hours the metal teeth on the carding machine would become covered with lint. To keep the machine running effectively, highly skilled workers called strippers, working in teams of two, would lift open the metal cover of the machines and run a stripping brush across the metal teeth. Cotton emerged from the carding machine as long, ropelike strands of yarn called slivers, which were fed into a three-foot-tall, round can. About every forty-five minutes, a can filled up and male workers replaced it with an empty one.

The cans of cotton slivers were taken to the drawing frame, which marked the first point in the process involving women workers. Most women in this room were in their mid-twenties and, like almost all women in the mill, were illiterate. They placed six cans of slivers on one side of the drawing frame and fed the end of each strand into the machine. Occasionally a sliver broke. Then the machine automatically stopped, and the operator repaired the broken sliver and reset the machine. As the six slivers passed through the machine, they were combined into one strand. On the other side of the machine a series of rollers drew out one continuous sliver of uniform thickness. Women on this side of the machine removed cans full of coiled slivers and provided empty cans as necessary.

This drawn sliver was still neither thin enough nor strong enough for spinning; in fact, it was two hundred times too thick. Before it could go to the spinning workshop, it had to be attenuated and twisted on three machines in the roving room: the slubber, the intermediate frame, and the roving frame.

In the warm, noisy, and dusty roving room, cans of drawn slivers were lined up along one side of the slubbing machine. The tasks involved in operating this machine, as well as most machines in the spinning room, required manual dexterity rather than physical strength. Because mill managers believed that women's fingers were more dexterous than men's, they hired increasingly large numbers of young women.

On one side of the slubber women moved cans of slivers into place. A woman doing this had to first thread the sliver onto the slubber, and then pull a lever that started the machine. Occasionally a sliver broke, and she then quickly rejoined the broken ends by rubbing them together between her palms. When one can of drawn slivers was used up, she switched off the machine, pushed the empty can out of the way, grabbed a full can, and moved it into place. She then joined the end of the sliver in the new can to the end of the sliver from the old can, which was already in the machine. After splitting the two ends in half, she rubbed them together between her palms until they were joined. Then she switched the machine back on.

On the opposite side of the slubber, the sliver came across a set of rollers, which drew it out to make it thinner and then stretched it down toward the front of the machine. Along the way the sliver was twisted by the rapidly rotating flyer and then, for the first time, was wound onto a bobbin. A woman tending the front of the slubbing frame removed bobbins as they filled up, placed them on top of the machine, and replaced them with empty bobbins. Every so often she collected the full bobbins and put them into a crate, which a male worker then hauled to the intermediate rover. The women who operated the intermediate and the final roving frames performed essentially these same tasks. On the intermediate frame two strands of slubbing were drawn together and twisted to make an even thinner sliver. The roving frame, which rotated even faster than the intermediate frame, performed the process a third time. By the time the sliver was wound onto the bobbins of the roving frame, it had begun to look like thread.

Several employees in the roving room were not ordinary workers. First, a general supervisor, called the Number One, was responsible for allocating work for the entire department. But because the roving room was very large, there were several "small Number Ones" who supervised workers in each section of the workshop. Red bands across their blue work aprons identified them as small Number Ones. None of the Number Ones operated machines: they walked back and forth past the rows of machines, cajoling delinquent workers. In addition to the Number Ones there was a secretary, a woman who kept track of how much work each employee did. Her pay was not much more than that of ordinary machine operators, but her work was much lighter, sometimes allowing her to sit on a stool and knit or mend clothes.

In addition to the female machine operatives, there were several male mechanics who tended broken machines. Most of these mechanics were in their mid-twenties or early thirties and had had some education before beginning work at the mill. Much to the consternation of mill management, most of the mechanics, as well as many of the foremen and the guards, were members of the Green Gang.

Beyond the seemingly endless rows of intermediate frames and roving frames was the spinning room. The Shen Xin Number One Mill, which was of average size, had almost 40,000 spindles mounted on several hundred rows of spinning frames. The spinning room held the largest concentration of workers, roughly one-third of the total of 5,000. Most of the workers assigned to this workshop were teenage girls, but there were also a number of "child workers." "The whole plant was literally overrun with small girls between twelve and fourteen years," an American observer wrote after touring the mill. "With youngsters as small as seven years of age running all over the mill, some evidently trying to learn mill processes, it is impossible to tell which were being employed and which were just being provided with amusement."[5]

Workers in the spinning room performed three procedures. Men unloaded carts of bobbins from the roving room and placed them on top of the spinning frames. Women operators, tending about 175 spindles each, attached a bobbin and pulled the end of the thread through the spindle. As the thread ran through the rapidly revolving spindle, it was once again drawn thinner and twisted, and finally wound onto another, smaller, bobbin. Whenever threads broke, women piecers quickly tied the snapped ends back together. Doffers, many of whom were boys only ten to twelve years of age, replaced full bobbins with empty ones.[6] In twenty-four hours each spindle could spin about one and a half pounds of very coarse (twelve- to sixteen-count) yarn.[7]

Most of the yarn was sent to the weaving department, but a small portion was prepared for packaging and sale. This portion was taken to the reeling room. As in the spinning department, the women's main tasks were operating machines that twisted two strands of yarn together, joining broken threads, and replacing full bobbins with empty ones. From bobbins the yarn was reeled into hanks, which were taken to the packaging department, weighed, bundled, and sent to the warehouse.

Most of the yarn produced in the spinning department bypassed the reeling room and went instead to the weaving workshop, located in a building about a half mile away. The yards between the buildings were "littered with crates of new machinery . . . exposed to the elements, which in Shanghai, winter and summer, are mean."[8]

Before it was ready for use on the loom, the yarn had to go through several preparatory processes. First it was divided into two types: the warp (the threads running the length of the fabric) and the weft (the threads drawn across the loom, over and under the warp threads). The yarn that came from the spinning room could be used as it was for weft threads. These threads were simply attached to a round rack at the side of a loom. The yarn that would be used as warp, however, had to be wound, warped, sized, and drawn in before it could be woven on the loom. First, because the thread on each bobbin was much too short to be used as warp thread, yarn from many bobbins was joined to form a continuous thread up to 27,000 feet long. In the winding room these threads were wound onto a cone that was much bigger than the original bobbins. The women in this department replaced bobbins of yarn, pieced broken threads, and put full cones into a crate. They also had to watch for and eliminate kinks and weak spots in the thread, which could cause breakage during weaving.

Male workers moved the crates of thread cones to the adjacent warping room. On one side of this big, airy room were rows of racks on which nine or ten cones were stacked. In the middle of the room there was no machinery, just a dense web of taut threads from these cones, stretching all the way across the room. At the far end of the room was a frame holding a warping beam, a large cylinder onto which the threads were wound. A woman warper first fed the threads through guides on the front side of the frame, wound the ends onto the beam, and then used a pedal to make the cylinder rotate. From time to time, she stopped the machine to fix a broken thread. When the beam was full, a male worker helped her lift the heavy beam onto a hand truck, which carried the entire beam to the hot and humid sizing room next door.

Sizing, a yellowish, pasty starch, was applied to the warp threads to make them strong enough to withstand the friction and tension they would be subjected to on the loom. The men who worked in this department were among the most highly skilled and highly paid workers in the mill. First, depending on how many threads were required for the warp, several beams were set on racks at the head of the sizing machine. For example, if the final warp was to have 2,000 threads, then four beams of 500 threads each would be meshed together as they went through the sizer.

Once the beams were set up, a worker turned a handle that controlled the flow of hot sizing solution into the tank of the machine. Steam valves along the bottom of the tank kept the liquid boiling while the thread wound off the beams and passed through the solution. As the thread emerged from the solution, two rollers pressed out excess liquid. The machine attendant then had to feel the hot thread and decide whether the thread had absorbed enough sizing. The thread then passed between two steam-heated revolving drums for drying. Finally it was wound onto a weaver's beam set on a stand at the other end of the sizing machine.

There was one more operation before weaving: drawing-in, which set the pattern for the cloth. In a startlingly quiet and brightly lit room were seven or eight frames. A weaver's beam was placed on one side of each frame; a woman worker sat on the other side. She used a long thin metal hook to pull the end of each thread, one by one, through the holes in a series of metal tabs in the frame between her and the beam. This was extremely painstaking work, requiring intense concentration. After she had completed this process for a beam, which might hold one or two thousand threads, the entire frame was carried to the weaving room and attached to a loom.

"The weaving shed is a most interesting sight, . . . the rattle of the machinery being almost indescribably loud to a visitor, yet to the busy operative it is hardly realized. The shuttle in each loom often passes across the sley two hundred times a minute."⁹ The weaving room contained some 1,200 looms. Young "battery girls" scurried from loom to loom, replacing empty weft bobbins with full ones. Each weaver, considered skilled only after two years of work, watched several looms at once. She could sit on a narrow wooden bench while working, and weaving was thus suitable for older women with bound feet. Whenever a weft thread broke, the weaver stopped the machine, rethreaded the shuttle, which carried the weft back and forth across the loom, and reset the loom. As the cloth was woven it rolled onto another beam. Tuners, all trained male workers, adjusted and repaired the equipment. Whenever a weaving beam was used up, a tuner set up a new one on the loom.

The rolls of woven cloth were taken to the inspection room, where women examined the cloth for defects. Men in the bundling department packed the rolls and transported them to the warehouse. The cloth produced at the Shen Xin Number One Mill was sold on the market as Man and Bell cloth.

Sexual Division of Labor in the Mills

One striking aspect of the Shen Xin Mill was the segregation of male and female workers: in some departments most workers were male, whereas in others most were female. Even in workshops with both male and female workers, labor was strictly divided according to the particular tasks to be done. In the roving department, for instance, men moved the cans of yarn and women tended the machines. However, the principles by which jobs were allocated to men or women were not absolute, and they varied widely among the mills in Shanghai. In general the division of labor reflected estimations of the strength, dexterity, and skill required for each job, weighed against the availability and price of three kinds of laborers: men, women, and children. Each sector was paid different wages, even when its members performed tasks identical to those of another group.

We know very little about the composition of the work force in the mills during the late nineteenth and early twentieth centuries. Many managers and workers recall that the mill work force was originally composed primarily of men and children. Most workers in the spinning department of Shen Xin One when it opened in 1915 were ten-year-old boys, and a minority were young girls.[10] A Japanese survey published in 1908 commented on the difficulty of finding women workers at that time, noting that because many women had bound feet they were not suitable for mill work that required workers to stand for great lengths of time.[11] Another problem, a mill manager recalled, was traditional attitudes: "At that time if a woman went to work in a factory, people thought it was bad luck. Women who worked in factories were looked down upon."[12]

The first survey that shows a sexual division of labor by department was published in the special labor issue of *New Youth* (May 1920). Although the authors do not tell us how many men, women, and children worked in each department, their study does provide a general picture. We find that in some mills there were operations that were clearly the domain of male workers: blowing, carding, packing, sizing, and drawing in. Throughout the mill men did all machine repairs, oiling, sweeping, and carrying of cotton, yarn, and cloth. Other departments, such as the spinning, roving, and weaving departments, used both male and female workers. No departments had exclusively female workers.[13] A large number of workers (although the survey does not specify a percentage) were children.

Over the next thirty years this pattern changed; there was an increasing tendency to employ women. Jobs that in the 1920's were considered too demanding for women were considered appropriate for women of the 1940's. Changes in the division of labor were almost always the result of specific political circumstances, such as the labor movement, or of economic constraints, such as those imposed by the depression.

The first major changes in the division of labor took place during the 1920's in the wake of a series of strike waves beginning in 1922 and lasting until the coup of 1927. Not coincidentally, mill managers began at that time to stress the advantages of female laborers. "With male workers disputes often arose. There would be arguments and strikes," recalled one engineer who had helped direct the shift toward hiring more women in the 1920's. "Women workers were more stable."[14] During this period women became the majority in two of the biggest departments: spinning and roving. Managers had little doubt that women could easily work in the spinning department, where most of the jobs required dexterity for tying knots. It was more difficult to integrate women into the roving department, and the process of substituting women for men took place in stages. Before the 1920's women were hired to work on the roving frame, but male workers continued to operate the slubber and the intermediate rover. Beginning about 1922, however, mill managers began to hire women to work these first two frames in the roving department. Because this work was considered dirty and arduous, many mills found that local women were not willing to do it; instead they had to recruit women from the countryside for these jobs (see Chapter Three).

The men who had originally held these jobs did not willingly give them up. One man who had been working at the Nei Wai Number Five Mill at this time remembered that the Japanese managers came and talked to the male workers. " 'Our factory is going bankrupt, and cannot keep running. We will give you some money, and you can go look for other ways of making a living,' they said to us. Just like that they eliminated us one by one, and then recruited women to do our jobs."[15] In February 1925, notices were posted in the Nei Wai and Tong Xing mills that large numbers of male workers in the roving departments were being laid off. Workers organized in opposition, and by the end of February workers at Japanese-owned mills throughout Shanghai had gone out on strike.

This strike and the strikes of the May Thirtieth Movement only three months later perhaps made managers realize that they could not eliminate male workers from the mills as easily as they had anticipated. "With the May Thirtieth Movement," two former mill managers recalled, "you could not be so obvious about using women to replace male workers. You had to wait until there were empty slots. Then, you could use women to fill in and gradually replace the men. It took several years."[16] By the end of the 1920's most of the machine operators, from drawing through roving, spinning, and reeling, were women (see Table 3).

Many of the "women" employed during this period were in fact girls no older than twelve or thirteen, and some were even younger. They were assumed to be both easier to manage and less expensive than adult men. "Originally most of the assistants in the mills were child workers," one manager recollected.

Wages for child workers were very low, but their efficiency was also very low, so it was not really worth it. Worker efficiency was one of our biggest problems, so after about 1924 we did not use child workers anymore. For example, in the spinning room we originally used mostly young girls as doffers. We had thought that they would work fast. But later we discovered this was wrong. We found that if we

TABLE 3 *Sexual Division of Labor in Selected Shanghai Mills, 1929*

Department	Male adults		Female adults		Children		Total
	No.	Pct.	No.	Pct.	No.	Pct.	
SPINNING							
Blowing	824	97%	26	3%	0	0%	850
Carding							
Stripping	216	100	0	0	0	0	216
Carding	417	88	56	12	0	0	473
Other	163	100	0	0	0	0	163
Roving							
Foremen/forewomen	65	23	220	77	0	0	285
Drawing	11	1	2,046	99	0	0	2,057
Roving	66	1	5,138	97	89	2	5,293
Other	373	79	6	1	92	20	471
Spinning							
Foremen/forewomen	48	15	273	85	0	0	321
Piecers	7	0.1	9,330	98.9	101	1	9,438
Doffers	180	32	0	0	388	68	568
Other	491	78	35	5	105	17	631
Reeling							
Forewomen	0	0	289	100	0	0	289
Reelers	0	0	9,199	100	0	0	9,199
Other	334	71	136	29	0	0	470
Baling							
Weighing	62	100	0	0	0	0	62
Bundling	416	99	4	1	0	0	420
Other	65	64	37	36	0	0	102

	Count	%	Count	%	Count	%	Total
Waste cotton picking	77	10	610	80	76	10	763
Mechanical							
Repairers	1,780	100	0	0	0	0	1,780
Mechanics	263	91	0	0	25	9	288
Smiths	789	100	0	0	0	0	789
Coolies	911	63	169	12	285	20	1,365
WEAVING							
Warping							
Foremen/forewomen	7	47%	8	53%	0	0%	15
Warping	70	18	328	82	0	0	398
Warp winding	48	8	268	43	314	49	630
Sizing	65	100	0	0	0	0	65
Weft winding	0	0	1,200	100	0	0	1,200
Drawing in	0	0	190	100	0	0	190
Other	188	57	108	33	31	10	327
Weaving							
Foremen/forewomen	47	26	131	74	0	0	178
Weaving	910	16	4,827	84	0	0	5,737
Other	57	100	0	0	0	0	57
Finishing and mechanical							
Finishing	412	80	54	10	49	10	515
Mechanics, smiths	497	100	0	0	0	0	497
Coolies	257	95	14	5	0	0	271
TOTAL	10,116	22%	34,702	75%	1,555	3%	46,373

SOURCE: Shanghai Bureau of Social Affairs, *Wages and Hours of Labor, Greater Shanghai, 1929* (Shanghai, 1929), pp. 98–102, 106–9.

used older girls they worked faster, so we did not have to employ as many. Then we started trying to use girls who were about twenty years old. The same was true of piecing.[17]

Despite the mill owners' intentions there were significant numbers of child workers until 1949. Their role in the work force, however, does appear to have declined after 1937.

Further changes in the division of labor took place during the depression of the 1930's. Cotton mill owners, forced to scale down their operations and often to close their factories for a period of time, sought to do everything possible to reduce production expenses. Hiring women to do some of the jobs formerly done by men was one solution.

Most of the jobs women had been hired to perform before the 1930's required patience, good eyesight, and manual dexterity, all presumed to be the particular virtues of women. The jobs given to women in the mid-1930's fell into a different category. For the first time women were called on to perform tasks that required some physical strength and thus had formerly been described as men's work. In most mills this meant that women began to work in the bundling room and that they took over the stripping operations in the carding room. One manager remembered that "around 1930 those of us who were managers began to do research about how to increase the number of women workers and reduce the number of male workers. It was probably around 1933 that the job of packing the small bundles was changed to women. Stripping also started using women. Blowing, since it was too hard, still used men. As things developed, the role of women in the cotton mills was getting more and more important."[18] In some cases, even the jobs that were considered the most physically taxing were done by women during the economic crisis of the 1930's. "Most of the men day-shift workers have been discharged," wrote a young woman who worked at the British-owned Yi He Mill in Yangshupu. "Formerly these men worked at carrying heavy loads. Now the women workers have to do this. In factory rooms you will see young twelve- and thirteen-year-old girls carrying the loads of cotton and yarn which used to be carried by adult men."[19] Even in the most extreme cases,

TABLE 4   *Extent of Female Work Force at Shen Xin Nine During the Depression*

Year	Number of male workers	Number of female workers	Total	Percent female
1932	1,263	4,039	5,302	76.2%
1933	1,187	3,629	4,816	75.4
1934	877	3,944	4,821	81.8
1935	782	3,652	4,434	82.4
1936	851	3,928	4,779	82.2

SOURCE: Shanghai shehui kexueyuan jingji yanjiusuo, *Rongjia qiye shiliao*, vol. 1 (Shanghai, 1980), p. 557.

however, the technical jobs, such as machine repair, remained the domain of male workers.

These changes did not always result in an increase in the total number of women workers in the mills. But even when the absolute number of women in a particular mill decreased, their relative number increased. At the large Shen Xin Number Nine Mill, the percentage of female workers rose from 76.2 percent to 82.2 percent between 1932 and 1936, whereas the total number of workers fell (see Table 4).

During this time the jobs performed by women suffered drastic wage reductions, but the wages paid to male workers actually rose slightly during the economic crisis. Looking again at Shen Xin, we find that female spinners who had earned 0.432 *yuan* a day in 1931 earned only 0.327 *yuan* in 1935; wages paid in the stripping department, recently taken over by women, dropped from 0.530 *yuan* in 1931 to 0.447 *yuan* in 1935.* In contrast, the wages paid to male packing workers rose from 0.557 *yuan* in 1931 to 0.689 *yuan* in 1935, and the earnings of electricians rose from 0.587 *yuan* to 0.708 *yuan*. This phenomenon occurred also at the Yong An mills. Workers in the departments that were primarily male, such as the blowing, baling, and maintenance departments, all received wage increases; workers in the primarily female departments, such as the roving and spinning departments, experienced substantial decreases.[20]

Although saving money was the primary reason for hiring more women, they were perceived to have one additional as-

*A *yuan* (Chinese dollar) was worth $0.30 in 1931.

set: they were dispensable. During a period of economic in-
stability and frequent plant closures, management believed
that it was preferable to lay off women. "We liked to use more
women during this time," one manager recalled. "If production was uneven and we had to reduce the number of workers,
it was easier to lay off women. We rarely laid off male workers.
This was because in general women were not responsible for
supporting their family."[21] This logic was echoed by an editor
of *Textile Weekly*, who maintained that there was "not really a
direct relation between our mills reducing work and unemployment, since most of our workers are young women who
have worked for less than two years."[22]

The final transformation of the work force took place after
World War II. By 1948 women made up almost 80 percent of
the work force in most of the mills taken over by the China
Textile Reconstruction Corporation. In some mills there were
as many women as men in the blowing and carding departments; virtually all the workers in the roving, spinning, drawing, and baling departments were female. In the weaving department, sizing was the only job still done primarily by men.
The distinctions between skilled and unskilled work, and between male and female work corresponded almost exactly. Almost all men remaining in the mills performed tasks requiring
a high degree of skill: they were technicians, machine repair-
ers, and electricians. Women did the unskilled jobs: they were
machine operators.[23]

The foremost division in the cotton mill work force, then,
was that between male and female workers. But the women
that made up the work force at any given time were by no
means a united or homogeneous group. Age and marital status
created distinctions—twelve-year-old girls worked alongside
married women in their twenties who already had children.
Furthermore, groups of women in a mill usually ate different
foods, wore different styles of clothing, and spoke mutually
incomprehensible dialects, according to their places of origin.
An examination of the origins and the implications of these
divisions among the female work force is the subject of the
next chapter.

Origins of the Workers

"With the mill woman, as with all others of her sisters, there are class distinctions," a YWCA secretary reported from Shanghai in 1907.[1] To contemporary observers throughout the first half of the twentieth century it was obvious that there was no typical female cotton mill worker. There were very poor women who lived in straw huts, ate little besides vegetable scraps discarded in the street, and wore ragged cotton clothes. There were also fashionable women who wore long, high-heeled shoes, and spent part of their earnings to have their hair curled and to buy cosmetics and jewelry. In other words, some women were financially better off than others.

Usually these economic differences reflected differences in geographic origins. Although the majority of women who worked in the cotton mills came either from Shanghai proper or from villages in neighboring Jiangsu and Zhejiang, their particular native place was crucial in shaping their experiences in Shanghai, both inside and outside the mills.

Geographic Origins

In surveys of the origins of women mill workers from the 1920's to the 1940's, the native places that appear most often fall within the geographic area bounded by the Huai River on the north, the Grand Canal on the west, and the southern bank of Hangzhou Bay on the south. Mills typically employed women from three areas: Shanghai proper and its suburbs, Jiangnan villages and towns near cities such as Wuxi and

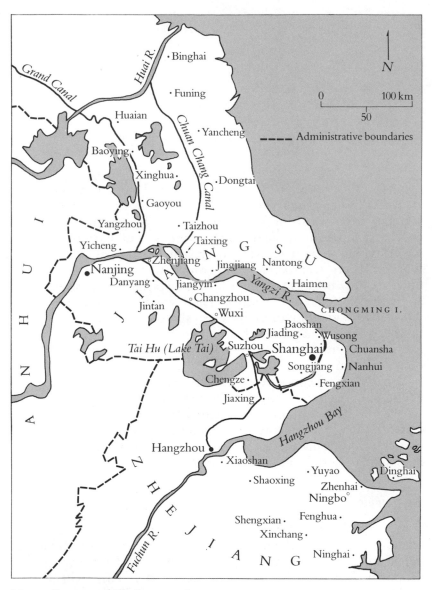

Map 3. Jiangsu and Zhejiang provinces

Changzhou, and Subei villages, from Nantong in the south to Funing in the north[2] (see Map 3). Because place of origin was one of the main ways by which women workers in Shanghai identified themselves as similar to or different from each other, it is important to look briefly at each of the three major areas from which they came. Differences in the rural experiences of women help explain their different experiences in the mills, as well as their relationships with each other.

SHANGHAI

The women workers referred to as locals did not live in the downtown financial district, in the plush Western residential district, or even in the Chinese city. They lived rather in the suburbs where the first cotton mills were built. During the first two decades of the twentieth century, the areas that were to become the mill districts of Yangshupu, Xiaoshadu, and Zhabei were as undeveloped as the bustling financial district had been only a half century earlier: they were "cultivated fields, dotted here and yonder with a village, and always and everywhere graves, rising in pyramidal grass-grown mounds."[3]

Before the mills were built the residents of Yangshupu, for example, were peasants who grew primarily rice, winter wheat, and cotton. When Herbert Lamson studied the industrialization of this district, he found only a few "rugged and strong" women doing farm work. Most women's major occupation, in addition to housework such as cooking, sewing clothes, and making shoes, was handicrafts: spinning yarn and weaving cloth. "The work done was slow and the product small," Lamson reported.[4]

By the early 1930's most women in these villages had given up handicrafts and entered the recently constructed mills. When Lamson surveyed four villages in Yangshupu in 1930, he found that all 26 girls between the ages of fifteen and nineteen worked in mills, as did 21 of the 23 women who were twenty to twenty-four years old.[5] One reason was the gradual decline in the market for handicraft goods these women had formerly produced. As factory-made goods replaced home-made articles, women were left unemployed. The Republican-

period gazetteer for Chuansha county, bordering Yangshupu,
reported about 1927 that

women's subsidiary industry was making lace and weaving towels.
It is like the situation with weaving cloth: thirty years ago it was
extremely widespread, but now there is scarcely any. Ten years ago
lace-making and weaving towels were widespread. At that time 13-
or 14-year-old girls could earn three or four *jiao* [one-tenth of a *yuan*]
a day making lace. Now they can only get about one *jiao* a day for
making lace. Thus, except for the busy farm season, during the fall
and winter women have no work. . . . So the women are entering
the western spinning mills, and becoming women workers.[6]

Mill work was unquestionably the most lucrative of the
options available to the women of these villages. By the early
1930's women could earn almost twice as much in the mills
as they could through traditional handicraft production. Lamson compared the average annual earnings for each occupation available to women as follows: factory workers could
earn $180.95 a year; farm workers, $160.51; seamstresses,
$103.20; handicraft workers, $96.00; and sorceresses and heal-
ers, $60.00.[7]

Because they lived in the mill districts, most of these women
did not have to move when they began working in the factories. Even if the mill was five miles from their home village,
they would walk or ride a wheelbarrow to work and then return home after work.

In addition to the women of suburban Shanghai's peasant
families, there was another group of "native" workers: the
women of families who had migrated to Shanghai in the late
1800's. Fleeing famine in Shandong, Anhui, and northern
Jiangsu and hoping that the men could find work as coolies in
the rapidly expanding commercial sector of Shanghai, many
of these families had made their homes in straw huts in squatter
settlements or on the boats that had transported them to
Shanghai. "The characteristic feature of the Chinese Bund is
its boat population," Gamewell noted during her 1916 visit to
Shanghai.

For more than half a mile little boats called sampans, protected by a
low arched covering of bamboo mats, line the shore and extend well

out into the [Huangpu] river. Each tiny sampan swarms with life as if it were an ant-hill. The occupants are permanent householders and their habitations are anchored. Many of them were originally famine refugees from the north. Most of the men earn a living as wharf coolies. The wives add a little to the income by gathering rags to make into shoe soles and by patching and darning old garments for coolies without families who pay a few cash in return. Planks set on stakes serve as footpaths to connect the boats with the shore, and little toddlers run about on the narrowest of them at will, yet rarely tumble into the water or soft mud below. Births, marriages and funerals lend variety to the life of the boat people. Two or three empty coffins usually stand about on the wharf ready for an emergency, and are meanwhile useful as benches, especially for the women when they sew.[8]

These boat settlements were not limited to the broad Huangpu River. Similar clusters of boats were moored along Suzhou Creek as it wound across Shanghai, and along Hongkou Creek, which stretched north, forming the border between Hongkou and Yangshupu. In short, wherever there were waterways, there were boat settlers.

As the cotton industry began to demand increasing numbers of female workers, some refugee women sought jobs in the mills. Both of the women living in a "boat-hut" that Lamson visited in 1929 worked in cotton mills.[9] And in 1937, when Cora Deng interviewed several hundred women factory workers, she found that a sizable number of cotton mill workers were boat dwellers.[10]

By the 1920's, another group of Shanghai natives was available for work in the mills: the daughters of the first generation of Shanghai's working class. The *China Yearbook* of 1924 announced the birth of an urbanized proletariat: "Some gambled away their savings and cannot return to the native villages. Some refuse to leave the cities, with their freedom, their night life and opportunities for culture and pleasure, for the dull life of the farm. These and their children form the permanently urbanized laborers, and their number will undoubtedly increase as China becomes more industrialized."[11]

Yet even if one counts the peasant women from the environs of Shanghai, the women of migrant families that lived on boats or in straw shacks, and the daughters of urban workers, the women from Shanghai were always a minority of the female mill work force.[12] This was partly because the native work force alone could not meet the labor needs of the rapidly increasing mill operations. Equally important, however, was the attitude of the mill managers, who by the mid-1920's publicly praised the advantages of rural recruits. "Most native women have families," an article in the journal of the Chinese Cotton Mill Owners' Association noted. "Therefore they regard work as a 'supplementary job,' and they do not do it wholeheartedly. Because of marriages and funerals they often request days off. This lowers work efficiency, and for this reason outsiders are better workers than locals."[13] It was from villages in Jiangnan and Subei that most of the women mill workers came.

JIANGNAN

The women who migrated from villages surrounding such Jiangnan cities as Wuxi or Changzhou came from one of China's richest agricultural areas. The fertile soil, a relatively warm, wet climate, and good irrigation systems made double-crop rice production possible; areas close to the southern banks of the Yangzi River grew cotton. Since the Ming dynasty this area had been famous as one of the foremost silk-producing districts in China.[14]

Republican-period surveys of Jiangnan villages suggest that women did not play a major role in agricultural production, but instead engaged in a variety of handicraft industries. In the area around Lake Tai they raised silkworms and spun and wove silk. In other areas they spun and wove cotton, braided reeds, made grass paper, or raised hens and gathered eggs.[15] As mentioned earlier, the decline of rural handicrafts attendant to industrialization caused the emigration of large numbers of women from the villages. For women such as Fan Xiaofeng, the relation between the decline of handicrafts and emigration was immediate and direct. She recalled leaving her home in 1932:

I came from Wujin Xian, in Jiangsu, near Wuxi. In that area we raised silkworms. Every year, in the season around the Spring Festival, we would raise silkworms. That way we could supplement our peasant income. We did this in my house. Everyone would take part. Later, when silk imports started, it destroyed our market, and we could not get any money for selling our silkworms. Without that money we didn't have enough to get by. So my parents tried to think of ways to send us children to work.[16]

Fan went to Shanghai to work in a cotton mill, and in the late 1940's became a well-known union activist.

The forces causing the displacement of women like Fan from the rural economy are clearly illustrated by the case of Kaixiangong, a silk-producing village studied by Chinese anthropologist Fei Xiaotong in the 1930's. Kaixiangong, near the town of Chengze, is six miles southeast of Lake Tai and eight miles west of the Grand Canal and the Suzhou-Jiaxing rail line. Some 90 percent of the land in Kaixiangong was cultivated in rice. On the remaining land the villagers grew wheat, rape, various green vegetables, and mulberry trees, which provided food for the silkworms.[17]

The women's long skirts indicated to Fei that this was an area where women did not work in the fields. The men did the farm work; the women were responsible for household maintenance chores and silk reeling.[18] By asking families about their household budgets, Fei found that the income derived from women's silk-reeling work could hardly be called supplementary or secondary: in fact it often provided more than half the family's total income. Without this income from women's work, peasant families in the area would have been unable to make ends meet.

Fei estimated that a family would need about two hundred dollars a year for their basic expenses. An average peasant family would produce 51 bushels of rice a year. After consuming 42 bushels the family would have a surplus of 9 bushels to sell, bringing them $22.[19] How much of the remaining $178 could be garnered through silk production? During the 1920's, when the silk industry was prosperous, Fei calculated that an average household could earn $250 a year from production of raw silk.[20] Thus, according to Fei's calculations, the income from women's work would have been more than enough to meet family expenses. "Under these conditions," Fei wrote, "the standard of living was much higher than the minimum

expected standard given above. The villagers had then sufficient money to finance . . . various recreative and ceremonial
activities."[21]

Beginning in the late 1920's the silk industry around Kaixiangong declined dramatically. First, industrialization reduced the market for homespun and -woven silk. Then the
Japanese saturated the U.S. silk market in 1934, virtually destroying the Chinese silk export trade.[22] These events had a
profound effect on the village's economy. By 1935 the price of
native silk had dropped from one dollar per *liang* (1.8 ounces)
to approximately thirty-three cents per *liang*. Thus, even if a
family produced the same amount of silk as in the past, they
would only earn a profit of $45. As Fei showed, the result was
that many women who were formerly the principal "bread-
winners" in their families were left unemployed.

The present decline of the silk industry has dislocated the traditional
adjustment of economic activities. The size of farms has remained
the same while the silk industry has been taken over by modern factories. The small farm cannot absorb the female labour that has been
set free by the industrial change. The maladjustment is seen in the
leisure enjoyed by the women in the village and the higher mobility
of female population from the village to the town.[23]

At the time he conducted his investigation in 1936, Fei found
that 80 percent of the 106 girls between the ages of sixteen and
twenty-five had taken jobs in factories outside Kaixiangong.[24]

The decline of the silk industry seems to explain why there
was such an exodus of women from the village, and furthermore, why they often left their husbands or fathers on the land.
The women's work had been rendered superfluous; because
agriculture was still viable, there was no reason for men to
leave. But where did the women go when they left the village?
Some were recruited by, or found jobs in, factories close to
their home village. Modern silk filatures being constructed in
Wuxi and in the nearby town of Chengze could provide employment for some of the women. But with more efficient
mechanized production the factories did not require as many
laborers as handicraft production had. Fei found that the work

that had previously provided income for 350 village women required the labor of only 70 women in the factory at Chengze, leaving almost 300 women from Kaixiangong jobless.

Some migrated to Wuxi, which by the late 1920's had become an industrial center with nearly fifty steam-powered silk filatures, as well as five flour mills, nine cotton mills, eighteen oil-extracting plants, and a soap factory. As in Shanghai, the silk filatures and cotton mills relied primarily on female labor. At least some of the women who migrated to Shanghai to work in the mills had begun their careers in Wuxi mills. The prospect of higher wages motivated some to move downriver, as is suggested by "The Two Sisters of Wusih," a story that appeared in the *North-China Herald* in 1928.

There were two sisters employed in a mill at Wusih. The elder was 24 and was earning $15 per month. The younger was 17 and earned a lesser sum. A Wusih woman named Chang, now resident in Shanghai, paid a visit to her home in that city and got to know the two girls. She told them that Shanghai was a place where the factory chimney stacks were like a forest. If they would come to this happy land they could without difficulty earn $40 each per month.[25]

In addition to higher wages, women migrated from Wuxi to Shanghai for its more plentiful and stable jobs.[26]

Whereas the decline of rural handicrafts and the limited opportunities provided by local factories might have been reasons for women to migrate from Wuxi to Shanghai, social and economic links between the two cities were equally important. First, Wuxi was the home of the Rong family, owners of Shanghai's largest Chinese-held cotton mill complex, as well as its largest flour mill. When the Rong brothers, Rong Desheng and Rong Zongjing, opened their first cotton mills in Shanghai, they relied on family networks to recruit a core of administrative staff and technicians. For example, when the Shen Xin Number One Mill was established in 1914, the Rong brothers hired a general manager from Wuxi, who in turn recruited a group of skilled male workers from the villages in the vicinity of Wuxi and Changzhou. Some female Number Ones also were from Wuxi.[27] The Number Ones played a major role in deciding who would be hired, and it was inevitable that they would provide opportunities to their own friends and relatives.

Even in the mills not owned by the Rong family, many of the managers and engineers came from Wuxi or Changzhou.[28] These people, who went to Shanghai to work as technicians or managers, provided an important connection with village workers. Furthermore, since the construction of the Nanjing-Shanghai rail line in 1908, there was a constant flow of people between cities like Wuxi, Changzhou, and Shanghai. Both workers and staff were likely to return to their home villages for the Spring Festival and other holidays, and ceremonial occasions such as marriages or funerals.

SUBEI

Translated literally, Subei refers to the area of Jiangsu north of the Yangzi River, including everything from Haimen and Nantong, on the river's edge, to Xuzhou and Lianyungang, at the distant northern edge of the province. In general usage, however, this geographic term refers to a somewhat less extensive area, that is, the plain stretching from the Huai River down to Yangzhou and Taizhou in the south, bordered on the west by the Grand Canal and on the east by the sea. Even a superficial acquaintance with the varied topography and economy of this area leaves one wondering how it came to be subsumed under one name. As the name of its major city, Yancheng (Salt City), suggests, the area in the north consists of land reclaimed from the sea, suitable for little but producing salt and raising pigs. Since wheat, not rice, is the basis of their diet, these people are considered northerners by natives of Shanghai. The land farther inland, west of the Chuan Chang Canal, is not so salty and hence can support cotton. Still farther west, stretching south toward Yangzhou and Taizhou, the land is broken by a series of lakes and marshes, and is thus wet enough to grow rice. Yangzhou, at the southwest corner of Subei, is its only sizable city. As the transshipment point on the Grand Canal for Yangzi trade, from the seventh century to the eleventh it had been one of China's major trading cities. Later it gradually declined in importance, although it remained the home of the great salt merchants of Jiangsu[29] (see Map 3).

Because of this geographic diversity, it is futile to make generalizations about the role of women in the rural economy of Subei. Certainly the women of families that depended for a living on salt production did work very different from that done by women of families who grew rice or cotton. But several commonalities in the experiences of women from different parts of Subei distinguished them from women who came from Jiangnan villages or from Shanghai proper. First, although the accent of a woman from Yangzhou was different from that of a woman from Yancheng, both spoke a variant of Subei dialect. This was a language entirely different from the Wu dialect spoken by the population of Jiangnan.

Second, almost all women from Jiangnan villages engaged in some kind of handicraft work. But handicraft industries were much less widespread in Subei, except for the area around Taixing, where there was some cotton spinning and weaving. Subei women, it seemed, played a far more active role in agricultural work. In Taizhou and Yangzhou, one woman recalled, there was a saying, "Planting fields, sowing the seed, women must be in the lead; eating fish, eating meat, women must take the back seat."[30] One of the few persons to write about Subei women in the 1930's, herself a Subei native, noted that "when it is time to irrigate the fields and spread fertilizer, women practically fly back and forth carrying shoulder poles loaded with seventy or eighty pounds of night soil."[31] Women were also responsible for feeding pigs, cutting wheat, planting rice seedlings, drying and hoeing grass, harvesting cotton, and rowing boats. In short, women seemed to do almost all the work that men did, plus housework.[32]

Finally, the patterns of migration from Subei were very different from those from Jiangnan, where (as stated above) there was a substantial outward migration of women who left without their families when they could no longer find employment in the local handicraft sector. To be sure, some women left their families behind when they migrated from Subei. Labor contractors from Shanghai frequently recruited teenage girls from the area around Yangzhou and Taizhou. And some women,

having heard of the abundant opportunities for employment
in cotton mills, went to Shanghai on their own. In one newspaper account two teenage girls from Taizhou, both of whom
were "adopted daughters" in the homes of their future husbands' families, persuaded their guardians to let them go to
Shanghai together. "They had seen so many friends and neighbors, one by one, go to Shanghai to get work in the cotton
mills, and they wanted to go too," the newspaper reported.[33]

Most women, however, did not leave the Subei countryside
alone, to seek a fortune in the mills or to temporarily supplement family incomes. They left permanently, with their families. This may have been partly due to the distance between
Subei and Shanghai: from Yancheng, for example, it took four
days' travel by boat to reach Shanghai. But the most important
reason was that when people left Subei it was often because
floods, droughts, or other natural disasters had destroyed their
crops. Serious floods devastated large parts of northern Jiangsu in 1911, 1921, and 1931. During the last, floodwaters from
the overflowing Grand Canal and Huai River left 61.4 million
mu (9.8 million acres; a *mu* is 0.16 acre) of cultivated land under
as much as twenty feet of water. More than three million families throughout Subei were starving and homeless. Under
these circumstances, the men's need to relocate was as great as
the women's; usually whole families migrated to Shanghai.[34]

Although rural poverty is the ever-present background of
migration from Subei, poverty alone does not fully explain
patterns of migration. Why, for example, did women tend to
come from some villages and not from others that were at least
as poor? Randall Stross's research found almost no emigration
from Liuhe, one of the poorest of the poor Subei districts.[35]
Similarly, their poverty does not explain their choice of desti-
nation, for not all migrated to Shanghai. In the first decades of
the twentieth century, there were many seasonal migrants,
moving from one rural area to another. One report in 1921
estimated that every winter 4,000–5,000 poor peasants from
Subei went to the area around Zhenjiang in search of farm
work; when it was time for the spring planting, they returned
to their homes north of the river.[36] Some 50,000 Xinghua families went south of the river every winter during the mid-
1930's, and peasants from Baoying and Yancheng headed for

Liuhe to work on seasonal harvest teams.[37] Others settled in small industrial centers such as Wuxi, where (as in Shanghai) they were the major source of unskilled labor.[38]

For those who migrated to Shanghai from Subei, as for those from Jiangnan, social connections seem to have been a key factor underlying migration to the city. Social connections between Subei villages and Shanghai, however, were very different from those tying Jiangnan villages to Shanghai. Whereas Wuxi had exported capitalists who played a major role in developing Shanghai's industry, and Ningbo had exported bankers to Shanghai, Subei's major human export traditionally was poor peasants.

It is not clear when migrants from Subei became a considerable part of Shanghai's population. We know that large numbers of people had fled famine in Subei in the mid-1800's and were granted licenses to come to Shanghai as beggars. In October 1865 the *North-China Herald* reported: "They have come from the northern part of this province, where the country has been devastated by locusts, and are traveling with a passport, given to them by the chief magistrate of the place from which they have come—specifying the reasons for their traveling, and testifying to their good character, declaring that they are good, but *distressed* people."[39] In Shanghai these refugees, as well as those who came in subsequent years, filled the ranks of beggars, coolies, and shantytown dwellers. It is probably no coincidence that the majority of Shanghai's rickshaw pullers (there were nearly 100,000 men working as rickshaw pullers by the mid-1930's) and the women mill workers from Subei came from the same villages: Dongtai, Yancheng, Funing, Gaoyou, and Taixian.[40] Those peasants who came when the mills were expanding and seeking women workers most likely had friends, relatives, or acquaintances from their home villages who had been part of a previous generation of migrants to Shanghai.

Pride and Prejudice in Shanghai

Shanghai, Jiangnan, and Subei were thus the areas from which most women mill workers came. Even after they came to Shanghai, they often continued to dress, eat, and speak in the manner of their hometown and thus could immediately be identified as Wuxi folk, Yancheng folk, and so on. "All had their own customs," Chen Zhaodi explained.

People from Subei liked to wear red, brightly colored clothes. People from Wuxi, Changzhou, and Tongzhou had their own looms, so they wore clothing they had woven themselves. They had little square scarves they would wrap on their heads. They also had long aprons. People from Nantong liked to wear long aprons too. People from Yangzhou liked to dress up their hair. They would wear a bun. People from Changzhou and Wuxi liked to wear hairpins.

People from Ningbo liked to eat seafood. They didn't even remove the scales and steam it. We Shanghai people didn't like it that way. Shanghai people liked their food saltier. People from Anhui liked theirs hotter and people from Shandong liked meat dishes, with lots of garlic.[41]

The particular district from which a woman came not only manifested itself in her physical appearance and customs, but also shaped her career, both inside and outside the cotton mills.

Each sector of the Shanghai labor market was dominated by people from one rural area. As mentioned earlier, rickshaw pullers came from certain Subei villages. Most maids were from Shaoxing and Changzhou, coppersmiths were from Ningbo, and bathhouse atttendants were from Yangzhou. Subei people dominated the cotton-spinning industry, Ningboese staffed the tobacco factories, local Shanghainese worked in the knitting mills, workers from Changzhou and Wuxi almost exclusively made up the work force of cotton-weaving factories, and workers from Zhejiang villages dominated the silk-weaving factories.[42]

If there is a single theme underlying the clustering of people from certain places in certain sectors of the economy, it is that the Shanghai social landscape reinforced the basic differences in the rural economies north and south of the Yangzi River. Workers from poverty-stricken Subei consistently did the lowest-paying, most physically taxing, and dirtiest work in Shanghai. From the time the foreign concessions were created and Shanghai began to grow in importance as a commercial center and port, migrants from Subei had done the coolie work that others were not willing to do. Most of the men who were not rickshaw pullers were construction, transport, or dock workers. Some were night soil or garbage collectors. Some men from Yangzhou became barbers, whom Shanghainese looked down on.[43]

This division of labor according to native place was apparent even in professions that employed workers from both Jiangnan and Subei. A striking example of how regional stratification applied to women is prostitution. The highest class of prostitutes, called *zhang san* (long threes)—a name derived from the customary three dollars a customer paid for a drink with them—lived in lavishly furnished brothels and catered only to Shanghai's wealthiest businessmen and officials. They were mostly from Jiangnan. By contrast, girls from Subei, many of whom had been kidnapped from their villages, filled the ranks of the lowest class of prostitutes, called *ye ji* (wild chickens). Usually led by an older woman, they wandered the streets of Shanghai's red-light district (the area near the intersection of Fuzhou and Tibet roads), soliciting customers.[44]

As industrial development accelerated in the years following World War I, a large number of factory workers were needed, but in general people from Subei did not constitute a significant portion of the industrial work force. When Subei migrants, whether male or female, did secure jobs in factories, they were almost always the jobs that were considered the least desirable. This division of labor was especially obvious in the tobacco industry: though most of the workers were from Ningbo and only a very small percentage were from Subei, those from Subei made up the majority of the unskilled laborers, who were hired only on a temporary basis.[45] There was an analogous situation in the silk filatures. In the late 1920's the head of the YWCA Labor Bureau, Cora Deng, was especially struck by this stratification that placed Subei women in the worst jobs. Describing her visit to a silk filature, she wrote:

Just as we got to the middle of this passageway we came to a door on the right hand side leading to the skeining department. . . . The workers in this department look much better off than those in the other departments. They wear very good clothes and look like girls from more refined homes. They work only six or seven hours a day, while getting seventy cents per day, the highest wage in the factory.

I learned from other girls that most of them are relatives and friends of the staff or of the management. Here you see in action the Chinese family idea of caring for its own members first!

Then we came to the peeling and selecting departments. The two departments share one room with a partition of lattice work in the middle. The room looked dark and smelled filthy. The windows could give them better light if they only cleaned them. . . . According to what I learned from the head of the department most of the workers in these departments come from country places north of the Yangtze River. . . . The work in these departments does not require much skill, and wages are comparatively lower than others—the highest being fifty cents, and only twenty cents for beginners—so naturally the places are filled with these northerners [Subei women] . . . who are willing to accept lower wages.

The head said to us, "These northern women are rude, dirty and have no ambition to do better work."[46]

In the silk industry, as in the tobacco industry, the workers from Subei were a small minority; most workers came from Zhejiang. In fact it appears that only in the cotton industry were a large proportion of the women workers from Subei villages.

Information from cotton mills about the origins of women in each department is insufficient to make an absolute distinction between the kind of work done by Subei people and that done by Jiangnan people. But a general statement can be made about the jobs assigned to women from Subei: usually women from the north, considered strong, robust, and accustomed to dirt, were channeled into the mill workshops where the work was most arduous and dirty. Often they did the jobs that in earlier stages of industrialization had been performed by male workers, jobs that women from Shanghai proper or Jiangnan were not willing to do.

During the 1920's, when women were hired primarily in the reeling, spinning, and weaving departments, those from Subei were most likely to be found in the reeling workshops. Reeling paid least and was much more difficult than other tasks done by women. Li Cishan, the writer for *New Youth* who surveyed industrial conditions in Shanghai in 1920, noted that "since women from Jiangbei [Subei] are physically stronger and more robust than local women, most of them work in the reeling department."[47] This impression is corroborated by a sample of women workers from one of the Nei Wai mills. Of 59 women from Subei villages who entered the mill between 1920 and 1930, 34 began in the reeling department.[48]

The other operation apparently dominated by Subei women was roving. As was explained in Chapter Two, in the early 1920's the first two stages of roving were done by male workers; only the third was done by women. During the depression of the early 1930's, women began to replace men in the first two steps of the roving process. But it was not *any* women who were hired for this job; rather it was specifically Subei women. "This was because natives of Shanghai were not willing to do that work," a mill engineer explained. "The wages were not necessarily the lowest, but the work was rough. In roving there was more dust and the air was not very good. Since the work was hard, Subei people were more able to do it."[49]

Women who were not from Subei, on the other hand, were concentrated in the weaving department. Even as late as 1946, more than two-thirds of the women from Jiangnan and Shanghai who entered the Shanghai Number Fourteen Mill began in the weaving department.[50] Weaving jobs generally required more skill and paid better. Moreover, many Jiangnan women who began their careers as workers eventually became supervisors, or even secretaries or bookkeepers in the mills. Whereas very few women who entered the mills before World War II had had even a year of schooling, those who did, almost without exception, were from Wuxi, Changzhou, or Shanghai.[51]

Thus, although women from Jiangnan, Subei, and Shanghai might have worked in the same mills, they did not enter the work force as equals. Nor did the mills act as a melting pot. Working in different workshops, they had little contact with each other during the working day, and this segregation extended to their lives outside the mills as well. Women from Subei generally lived in straw hut settlements. Surveys of these shantytowns, whether in Xiaoshadu, in Caojiadu, or in Yangshupu, indicate that the overwhelming majority of residents came from Subei. It was rare for workers from Subei to trespass into neighborhoods dominated by migrants from Jiangnan.[52]

Segregation was only one aspect of the relationship between women from Jiangnan and Subei. Prejudice, contempt, and hostility were other aspects. Language reflected the attitude of women from Jiangnan toward migrants from north of the river. Of the two names for people from northern Jiangsu, *Subei ren* (*ren* means "person") was considered neutral, if not polite. More often, however, Subei people were called *kompo nin*, the Shanghai pronunciation of *Jiangbei ren*. Calling people *kompo nin*, whether they were actually from Subei or not, was (and still is) considered an insult. A speaker of Shanghainese who wanted to insult someone even more sharply might say *Kompo zhuluo* ("You Kompo swine!").

Attitudes toward dress were an equally vivid expression of the contempt shown women from Subei. With a more prosperous place of origin and perhaps some education and a better-paying job, it is not surprising that a Jiangnan woman looked very different from her Subei counterpart. "Outside the factory there is a great variety in dress," the authors of a major study of Shanghai's workers noted in the late 1930's.

There are some women who dress fastidiously, especially women who are relatively educated. They are often called the "student group" because many of them wear a long dress with a high neck and a slit skirt, and leather shoes. In the winter, when they go outside, they wear a woolen overcoat, and insert a fountain pen. It's just as if they were students. This applies mostly to women of districts in Jiangnan who like to dress up this way.[53]

It is doubtful that most women workers from Jiangnan villages dressed so extravagantly. Even those who did not flaunt long dresses, wool coats, and fountain pens tended to make their clothes of more "tasteful" blue, black, or gray material. The bright red and green garments, colorfully embroidered shoes, and pink stockings worn by Subei women in Shanghai were an eyesore to these southern sophisticates. Their attitude, of course, was not due to purely aesthetic considerations: to Jiangnan women, bright colors came to be associated with the relative backwardness and poverty of the Subei women with whom they worked. "Even today," one woman recalled, "if you buy a piece of red cloth people will say, 'That's like a Jiangbei person. It's so ugly!' "[54]

Verbal abuse sometimes escalated to physical assaults. It was not unheard of for a woman from Ningbo, while waiting for a ferry after work, to shove a fellow worker from Subei with whom she had argued at work into one of the many canals that crisscrossed Shanghai.[55] Subei women were not always on the receiving end of these assaults. "We Subei people really knew how to make trouble," a woman from Nantong boasted. She then recalled the time a woman from Subei had dumped a bucket of night soil onto the head of a woman from Shanghai who was walking to the mill one morning.[56]

Antagonism between women workers from different areas can be understood as part of a larger problem of regional rivalries among all workers in Shanghai. Street brawls between the so-called Shanghai clique, the Anhui clique, the Jiangbei clique, and the Ningbo clique were commonplace occurrences in the 1920's and 1930's.[57]

This rivalry was not simply one of workers from one area fighting those from another. It had another dimension—specifically, that of workers from a poorer area pitted against workers from a wealthier one. This phenomenon seems to have been common to the development of working classes, whether in China, in Western Europe, or in the United States. Although the Subei women who came to work in the mills were not immigrants from a foreign country, their role in the cotton industry is nonetheless analogous to that of the Irish immigrants in the cotton mills of Lowell, Massachusetts, in the mid-nineteenth century. The relationship between Yankees and Irish immigrants described by historian Thomas Dublin in his study of the female work force of Lowell is strikingly similar to that between Jiangnan and Subei women in Shanghai. Like the Subei women, the immigrants who came to the Lowell mills were fleeing famine in Ireland. The Irish lived in distinct neighborhoods, dressed differently, and spoke a different language. In the mills they were concentrated in the least desirable workshops. Tamara Hareven has found a similar rift between immigrants from famine-struck Quebec and native workers in the cotton mills of Manchester, New Hampshire, in the nineteenth century.[58]

These divisions need not be based on migration across national boundaries. A woman who worked in a Japanese textile mill in the late nineteenth century recorded in her diary the hostility of women from the "well-bred" families of castle towns and those from poor, backward mountain villages. "The girls came from all over Japan," she wrote.

The ones from Shizuoka were daughters of former retainers of the shogun. They were quite well bred, spoke in the Tokyo manner, and were charming girls. . . . The girls from such places as Komoro, Iiyama, Iwamurata, and Susaka were well bred. In general the people from castle towns had pleasant appearances. It may make people angry when I say this, but the mountains and rural districts were not as advanced as they are now; the people from these areas had somewhat backward manners, and often they were less refined in speech and upbringing than the castle town girls.[59]

And as in Shanghai, where calling people "Subei folk" meant that they were poor and dirty, in that Japanese mill calling someone a person from Shinshu implied that she was backward and ill mannered. If there is a common element in these cases, it is the contempt of workers from economically richer areas for those from poorer, often disaster-ridden, districts.

In twentieth-century Shanghai the politics of imperialism served to intensify the antagonism among women mill workers. Women from Subei were willing to work in Japanese-owned mills, even when it was considered unpatriotic to do so. In some cases this was not due to any choice on their part, but was rather a result of the Chinese mill owners' preference for workers from Jiangnan. As one mill engineer who had worked in Chinese-owned mills said, "In cotton spinning we tried, as much as possible, to use natives as workers. Why was this? It's hard to say. If you say that Subei people are not good workers—this is not nice to say. It is just that there are certain social attitudes. It's easier to talk to natives, easier to handle them. Subei people are harder to handle. . . . Perhaps it's a historical problem."[60]

Despite this preference, some women from Subei succeeded in securing jobs in mills owned by Chinese capitalists. They usually did so by altering their dress to disguise their origins. Often this disguise was part of the initiation rites of their careers in Shanghai: those who had come earlier might have warned them about the discrimination they would face when they applied for work, and have instructed them on how to avoid it. One YWCA social worker finally made sense of a phenomenon that had puzzled her for some time. Knowing what she did about their families' financial circumstances, she could not comprehend how some Subei women acquired fashionable Shanghai clothing so quickly. A girl from the Subei countryside explained that a friend from the same village had promised to provide an introduction to a job in a Chinese-owned mill, warning the newcomer, "You cannot go to the factory looking like such a country bumpkin. First you have to go get your hair cut and make a long *qi pao* [a dress]. You must buy a new pair of shoes. Make your pants shorter, and [your] stockings longer. Otherwise the managers will treat you with disgust."[61]

Despite the thinly disguised preference of Chinese managers for local women, the managers were often unable to control who obtained jobs and who did not. During the 1920's and 1930's, as will be discussed later, most women obtained their jobs through introductions to Number Ones. Job allocations depended at least as much on social networks among women employees as on the policies and preferences of management.

In this light it is significant that many Subei women preferred to work in Japanese mills.[62] When a Chinese member of the YWCA staff was helping to find work for cotton mill workers who had lost their jobs because of factory closures in 1932, she discovered that the majority of the women from Subei were not willing to work in Chinese-owned mills. "Most people do not understand the situation very well, and think that these are [Subei] people who have no conscience at all and are traitors to China," she wrote. "But if you persist in asking them precisely why they are not willing to work in the mills owned by our own people, or better yet, if you have the experience of trying to take them to get a job in a Chinese-owned mill, you definitely will not continue cursing them."[63] While accompanying women from Subei to Chinese-owned mills she found that the mill managers made little attempt to hide their sentiments. The writer was deeply impressed by the compelling words of one woman from Subei: "Japanese people are just as polite to us [Subei] people as they are to the Shanghainese. They treat us like human beings. Every day when we go to work they nod their heads to greet us, and smile. But in Chinese mills, they just treat us like trash. They swear about how terrible Jiangbei people are."[64] The YWCA staff member went on to reflect:

Truthfully speaking, our cruel behavior toward [Subei] people is no different from the way imperialists treat our coolies, and it is no different from the way in which American people treat black slaves. We oppose imperialist exploitation of our people; we oppose Americans making slaves of black people. But what about our treatment of [Subei] people, who are our own countrymen? Furthermore, we are always accusing [Subei] people of not being patriotic. But is it patriotic to always discriminate against [Subei] people, to curse them and beat them? If we are going to talk about loving our country, we had better begin by loving our fellow countrypeople![65]

As anti-Japanese sentiment intensified during the thirties, contempt for Subei people crystallized. Although there is no indication that the majority of workers from Jiangnan or from Shanghai left their jobs in Japanese mills to protest the Japanese stranglehold on Shanghai, southerners perceived Subei people to be traitorous because they continued to work for the Japanese. "They are acting as traitors to China," one reporter exclaimed. The accusation of collaboration with the Japanese fueled the contempt of the natives for their Subei co-workers.

In other words, political circumstances made the divisions between workers from different areas more acute in Shanghai than elsewhere. To the extent that this division between workers from Jiangnan and those from Subei inhibited the development of solidarity between women mill workers, it aided management attempts to control the labor movement. There is no evidence, however, that these divisions were the product of a conscious management strategy. To understand how this segregation of workers from different places was preserved within the mills, we must look at how women got their jobs.

Making
CHAPTER FOUR # Connections

No matter what a mill's official policy was, the crucial factor in hiring situations was *guanxi* (connections). Although the mills had established procedures for recruiting and hiring workers, management was often unable to enforce them.

Tang Hai's survey of Chinese labor conditions in the mid-1920's described three recruiting systems: the British system, the Chinese system, and the Japanese system. In British enterprises, such as the gigantic Yi He Mill, a compradore hired foremen, who in turn hired workers and issued wages. The Chinese system was essentially the same: foremen recruited workers, but there was no compradore, and management, not foremen, issued the workers' wages.[1]

The Japanese mills, according to Tang Hai, had also used the foreman system but by the mid-1920's had replaced it with a personnel office that hired workers according to their skill.[2] They had sent a group of Chinese women workers to Japan to study production technique and subsequently established an apprenticeship (*yangchenggong*) program for training new women workers.

The Right to Hire

Since the Japanese were the most ambitious in attempting to implement a formal recruiting and training system before the war, it is instructive to examine how their system actually operated. Beginning in 1922 many Japanese-owned mills, such as Ri Hua, Da Kang, and Nei Wai, established an apprenticeship program. The system as they envisioned it involved recruiting teenage girls, providing them room and board in factory dormitories, and then training them in the workshops. When Da Kang opened its second mill in 1922, mill agents posted the following announcement:

Construction of the No. 2 factory is completed. Three thousand experienced workers and unskilled female laborers are needed by the roving, reeling, and spinning departments. Workers will be treated well, and will be given free professional training.

The factory is sending recruiting agents to different towns, and those who are interested in engaging work should take advantage of this opportunity. . . .

Those who seek employment must be at least thirteen years of age. They must be examined for their height, weight, and eyesight. As for height, they must be at least four feet three inches. Those with an evil appearance or whose temperament is coarse and violent, those who are deaf and dumb or despondent, those with bound feet, and those who have been fired by other factories are not eligible for employment here. Upon entering this factory, they will undergo a trial period for two weeks.[3]

In form, at least, the Japanese had the ingredients of a rational hiring procedure: anyone was free to apply for a job, and only qualified applicants were hired. But in practice it was not always easy to implement this system. The Chinese foremen and forewomen (Number Ones) often had their own ideas about how workers should be hired.

Despite the use of advertisements, recruiting agents, and personnel offices, the reality was that foremen and forewomen controlled the hiring system, and they refused to relinquish this power. A strike at a Japanese-owned Ri Hua cotton mill in March 1926 illustrates the situation. This strike, according to the editors of the *North-China Herald*, was "being waged over the right of the laborers to dictate to the management with regard to the employment of labor."[4] The sequence of events leading to the strike was reported as follows. In mid-February nine women workers, accused of being troublemakers, were fired from the reeling department. When the forewoman of that department proposed to hire a particular woman to fill one of the empty slots, the personnel office objected. It claimed that although the woman had previously worked in a Chinese-owned mill, she had never worked in a Ri Hua mill and thus had no reliable work record. The forewoman did not back down but continued to insist that the office hire her candidate. "The fact is," the *North-China Herald* editors commented, "that the foremen and forewomen are collecting 'squeeze' from the workers on the promise of employment, so that a worker having paid for a job expects to get it or there will be trouble for the 'squeeze' taker. . . . What is so remarkable in this situation is that the workers will back up the forewomen."

The already tense situation became a crisis when the management proposed another candidate for the job. Still refusing to hire the woman recommended by the forewoman of the reeling room, the management accepted an apprentice recommended by the forewoman of the blowing department. "As soon as the apprentice entered the Reeling Room, the forewoman of that room kicked up a frightful row," the *North-China Herald* reported, "She threw bobbins all over the place, and shouted to her people to leave. The strike was on. . . . They got into the mill yard and created what looked like an incipient demonstration. The Chapei Police Station was called as well as an Emergency Squad from the Gordon Road Station. . . . Order was immediately restored and the place closed down. Three thousand laborers are now out on strike in this mill."[5]

Disputes over hiring did not commonly prompt several thousand workers to declare a strike. Nevertheless, in Japanese-, Chinese-, and British-owned factories, forewomen considered it their right to decide who should get jobs in their workshops. In the years before the War of Resistance, securing jobs through connections with the Number One was the rule, not the exception, for women workers. A survey of one of the largest Japanese enterprises in 1925 indicated that 64.3 percent of the women workers were introduced by the Number Ones, 32.8 percent were formally recruited, and 2.9 percent applied independently for their jobs.*

*Udaka Yasushi, *Shina rōdō mondai* (Shanghai, 1925), p. 329. Conflicts between foremen in the workshops and a central personnel office over the prerogative to hire labor are not unique to the Shanghai mills. Tamara Hareven's research on cotton mills in Manchester, New Hampshire, finds an almost identical situation: attempts by the newly established employment office to centralize hiring were hampered by "the

And as long as they could supplement their regular salary with the bribes received from workers who purchased their jobs, these forewomen were not willing to permit a personnel office to usurp the hiring function.

MAKING CONNECTIONS

Getting a job through an introduction usually meant, as one woman worker put it, "going through this person who knew that person who knew another person who knew the Number One."[6] Sometimes it required nothing more than asking friends and relatives if they knew of any jobs. "When my mother wanted my sisters to start working," one mill worker recalled, "she asked someone she used to work with to make the arrangements. At that time, if you wanted to find work for your children, you had to go through relatives or people you knew. They would see if there were jobs where they worked."[7] Sometimes finding work required a much more concerted effort, involving circuitous connections. "How did I get the job there?" one woman asked rhetorically. "My third-youngest sister worked in a cotton mill in Hangzhou. Her Number One helped her get a job in the Da Feng Cotton Mill in Shanghai. It was Japanese. I would often go visit my sister and got to know the Number One there and the overseer. The overseer knew the foreman at Shen Xin Number Nine Mill, and introduced me there."[8]

These connections were almost always made through networks built on kinship relations or ties between people from the same native place. Since people from a particular village tended to congregate in the same streets and alleys of the working-class districts, a woman turning to her new neighbors in Shanghai for help was most often perpetuating native place ties rather than forming new relationships. Occasionally, however, securing an introduction to a Number One involved the gradual formation of new networks. One woman, for example, got a job in the weaving department of a Yong An mill

overseers' traditional autonomy in the hiring and firing of workers and [by] the workers' own customary reliance on friendship and kinship ties in obtaining jobs or transfers." Tamara Hareven, *Family Time and Industrial Time* (Cambridge, Eng., 1982), p. 42. This problem of contending with the power of foremen in American industries in the late 19th and early 20th centuries is also discussed in Nelson.

through the introduction of a classmate from a YWCA literacy school.[9]

Some women simply could not find a relative, neighbor, or friend to help get them a job. As a final resort they might turn to local hoodlums, who gathered in working-class neighborhoods hoping to make some money from this business of "making connections." "If you didn't know anyone to introduce you," one woman remembered, "you could find local hoodlums who had connections with the foremen in the mill. They would be your guarantor. They were in the neighborhood, and everyone knew who had the connections. You had to give them five dollars for this." Some had to borrow money to pay this fee.[10]

Relying on a stranger to serve as go-between could be a risky undertaking, especially for village women hoping to make the connections before leaving home. Some enterprising criminals used the pretext of introducing village women to a factory to lure them to Shanghai, only to sell them on arrival to brothels. The story of two sisters from Wuxi exemplified this vulnerability. The two sisters never managed to get the mill jobs that their go-between had promised them. Persuading them to give up their jobs in the Wuxi mill, she brought them to Shanghai and then used them for other purposes. The *North-China Herald* related their story:

The girls came and Mrs. Chang lodged them in a house which she occupied with a paramour on Burkhill Road. On the third day after their arrival Mrs. Chang asked the elder girl to come with her to the market where she was going to buy vegetables. The girl was glad to go and see something of the city. They were away an hour, or so, and when they returned, the younger sister was missing. No one knew where she had gone, but they all assured the elder girl that a person lost in Shanghai was like a needle at the bottom of the sea; never found again. This almost broke the girl's heart and she threw herself on the bed and wept bitterly. She sobbed all day and at night, after she had fallen asleep, they introduced a man into her room whom she was unable to get rid of.

Next day she still sobbed for her sister and some of the neighbors, taking pity on her, told her that Mrs. Chang's paramour had sold her sister to a family that lived not far away. They advised her to go to the police station and ask for help. . . . She took this advice and the police promptly apprehended Mrs. Chang, her paramour and the man who had forced his attentions on the elder girl. From these they learned where the younger girl was to be found, went to the address given and apprehended the woman who had made the purchase.

The two girls, now reunited, were sent to the Door of Hope [an orphanage]. The case came up for trial and Mrs. Chang and her lover were each sent to prison. The woman who had bought the younger girl pleaded that she had a son for whom she wanted a wife and purchased the girl with no evil intention; she was to have been her daughter-in-law. The judge chose to accept this explanation and discharged her with a caution and the two girls were sent under escort, back to their home in Wusih.[11]

In a similar case, albeit with a more typical ending, a male passenger on a boat from Taizhou to Shanghai befriended two young girls who had left their home hoping to find jobs in a Shanghai mill. Hearing that he was the cook at a Yong An cotton mill and could help them get jobs there, they went with him to his factory dormitory. During the next few days he assured them that he was making arrangements with the Number One; instead, he sold them as child brides.[12]

LOOKING OUT FOR NUMBER ONE

For those who had not been led astray in their attempts to make connections with a Number One, finding the appropriate go-between was only the first step in securing a job. The next, and most crucial, was obtaining the Number One's approval. Persuading a Number One to grant a job to a person introduced to her usually required sending her gifts. These presents most often took the form of food or drink: eggs, ham, wine, or if the woman's family lived on a farm near Shanghai, fresh produce. Money was rarely used as payment. One woman described her first meeting with a Number One in a cotton mill as follows:

When I started to work I had to send all kinds of things to the forewoman. The person who had worked with my mother told her where the forewoman lived. After finding out where she lived, my mother . . . had to borrow money to buy things to send as presents. We went to take the things there ourselves.

The first time I went with my mother, so the forewoman could

have a look at me. The forewoman did not live too far from us. . . .
Her house was a little better than ours, since her wages were a bit
higher. But she was not rich or anything. She was older than my
mother.

I wore better clothes, because if the forewoman saw that your
clothes were too ragged, she would not want you. The first time she
said I was too small, and would not hire me. My mother told her we
were really poor and couldn't get along, but she still did not agree.
My mother went back a second time, and sent her more things. Then
she agreed.[13]

After being approved by the Number One, there was usually one hurdle remaining: passing the factory's height test.
Young girls who feared they were too short devised methods
of increasing their apparent height. The most common was to
add something under their feet. "My mother was afraid they
would say I was too short," one worker said, "so what could
she do? She attached wood blocks to the bottom of my shoes,
so I would be taller. And then they hired me."[14]

Once she was approved by the forewoman and had satisfied
the height requirement, a woman could begin work. Because
the Number One made virtually all decisions about hiring and
firing, about the number of machines a woman operated on a
particular day, and even about allocating high-quality thread,
it was important to curry her favor. Consequently a worker's
gift-giving relationship with the Number One did not end
upon being hired. On the Number One's birthday, at the time
of the Spring Festival, and on other holidays the workers
would give her presents. In return they received job security.
Some women workers cemented their relationship with the
Number One by pledging loyalty to her as their "godmother"
(*bai guofangniang*). With the Number One as her godmother, a
woman could expect full protection. And of course she could
expect to send her godmother presents.[15]

This practice of pledging loyalty to a protector was not
unique to women mill workers: male workers pledged loyalty
to "godfathers." When he visited the Shen Xin Number One
Mill in 1925, one reporter was struck by a ceremony in which
male workers pledged loyalty to protectors. Near one of the
walls in the blowing room stood a table that held a wooden

board about a foot long, three inches wide, and four inches thick. Two candles burned at each end of the board, and in the middle of the board was an iron cup containing several sticks of incense. Two men who appeared to be in their early twenties lit the incense, bowed their heads three times toward the wall, and finally turned to kneel in front of an older male worker three times.[16] The significance of this practice in the mills is that it formed bonds of loyalty and obligation between workers and their foremen and forewomen, relationships that militated against the development of allegiances between workers based on their shared predicament.

Having secured a job for herself, a woman often sneaked daughters or friends into the mill so that they could learn the skills necessary to qualify for a job. The story one woman told of entering a mill in 1918 is typical. "When I first worked in a mill I went secretly," she recalled.

I used my cousin's work card to enter. My cousin could just tell them her work number. Since she had worked there a long time, they knew her anyway. I went on the night shift because there were [only two] guards on duty then. Whenever the overseer came through our workshop, I ran to hide in the bathroom. . . . After one week there was a test for new workers. Then I had to send presents to the Number One. I sent glutinous rice and a chicken from the countryside. Friends coming from home brought them to Shanghai for me.[17]

So long as the girls who slipped in to learn a skill hid whenever the overseer toured the workshops, management did not necessarily know about the unofficial laborers in the mills. Only the Number Ones knew. For the Number Ones it was advantageous—and extremely profitable—to allow women workers to bring in friends and relatives to learn skills. Those who obtained their training under her supervision would join the ranks of women indebted to her, from whom she could expect to receive gifts. As Morris David Morris pointed out in his study of Bombay's cotton mills, where people called jobbers played a role analogous to that of the Shanghai Number Ones, so long as jobbers commanded bribes, it was in the jobbers' interests to supervise as many workers as possible. Moreover, the more frequently workers took time off and had friends fill in for them, the greater the number of bribe payments the jobber could receive.[18]

Under these circumstances the most desirable workers were not necessarily the most skilled but rather those who could offer the most attractive gifts. The workshops were filled with women who had bribed, and therefore had *guanxi* with, the Number Ones. Not until after World War II did mill managers make significant headway in establishing control over the recruitment and training process in their factories.

Yangchenggong: Creating a New Class

The apprentice bureaus represented the aspirations of the mill managers, especially those who had studied textile production and industrial management in Japan, Britain, or the United States, to implement a modern recruiting and training system in the Shanghai mills. Some mills had tried to institute such a system in the mid-1920's and early 1930's, but when they were not defeated by the objections of foremen who resented this intrusion on their power to hire workers, the gangs often usurped this power[19] (see Chapter Five).

The end of the war and the ensuing departure of the Japanese from Shanghai provided an opportunity for the mill managers to assert control over the recruitment of new workers. First, the huge Japanese mill complexes were turned over to the China Textile Reconstruction Corporation, and Chinese managers and engineers filled staff positions formerly held by Japanese. Second, because many mills had ceased operations, operated at a very limited capacity, or moved to the interior during the war, the size of the Shanghai work force had been drastically reduced. Hence, when the mills reopened in the winter of 1945, they had to recruit large numbers of new workers.

The old workers and the new managers did not agree on how to fill the jobs. When thousands of former employees staged massive demonstrations demanding that they be rehired, the mill owners, forced to compromise, allowed them to register for the vacant positions. However, both the mills owned by Chinese capitalists and those taken over by GMD bureaucrats instituted apprenticeship bureaus to hire and train new workers. Although the ostensible motive for recruiting apprentices was to train a modern, skilled work force, the managers' hope of using apprenticeship programs to control the escalating workers' movement was only thinly veiled in their public statements about the system. The editors of a survey of the Shanghai Number Six Cotton Mill complained that during the war, the workers had been contaminated by many "evil customs" of the enemy, and the result was that some

do not follow discipline and are irresponsible. By admitting workers on the basis of examination, and then adding conscientious training and strict management, we can produce the polite, healthy, clean-spirited, responsible, and disciplined modernized workers of tomorrow. This will create a new atmosphere and new strength in the factory. It will cause those who are evil to be ashamed, those who are ignorant to study, those who commit wrongs to reform. This will make ours a great industry that can contribute to the reconstruction of our country.[20]

In light of the almost uninterrupted series of strikes by mill workers taking place at the time of this survey, it seems likely that most of the workers described as harboring evil customs, committing wrongs, or failing to follow discipline were in fact union activists.

To recruit suitable apprentices mill managers used some of the same methods they had used in the past, such as posting announcements and contacting relatives. One manager at a Chinese-owned mill recalled writing letters to his relatives who were still in Zhejiang, telling them that his mill needed workers and explaining the requirements. "I told them that we preferred graduates of primary school, but actually if they had *guanxi*—if they were friends or relatives of the management—then they could be accepted without having graduated from primary school."[21]

The recruits were not all from the managers' home cities or villages: there were as many from Subei as from Jiangnan.[22] If the literacy requirement was enforced, however (and interview data indicate that it was), the recruits, whether from Jiangnan or Subei, were probably not the daughters of the poorest peasants. "The apprentices all had some education," one older worker recalled. "They were not from the poorest families of the villages. They were from the middle class. There were some from Subei—from the parts of Subei that were already liberated—and the families that were originally better off were in trouble, so they left."[23] More research must be done to determine whether there was, as this worker has suggested, a relationship between the land reform that followed the establishment of liberated zones by the Communists and the emigration of wealthier peasants.

Destruction of the rural economy during the war likely prompted women from well-off families to migrate to Shanghai and seek mill work. An apprentice named Jin Bao told a meeting of women workers held by the YWCA in 1947 that she came from Ningbo, where her family had lived comfortably until the Japanese occupation, when her parents were killed and their property destroyed. She then came to Shanghai and passed the test given prospective apprentices at one of the GMD-owned mills.[24]

The factors, such as family conflicts, that had caused women from families with comfortable incomes to leave home in the 1920's and 1930's continued to induce women to leave their villages and apply for the apprentice programs. Another apprentice at the same YWCA meeting said that her family's circumstances too had been good until her father lost his job because he insulted his boss. Her mother, unable to tolerate her unemployed husband's temper, killed herself by eating raw opium.[25]

ADMISSION TO THE PROGRAM

Admission to the apprenticeship program was based on examinations, which only about one-tenth of the applicants were able to pass. The procedure for testing at the Shanghai Number Six Mill was typical. On the morning of the tests applicants came to the factory and lined up in the alley for the first round. A supervisor measured each girl and asked her age: apprentices had to be between four feet six inches and five feet four inches tall, and between fifteen and seventeen years old.[26] Those who met these preliminary requirements were allowed to enter the factory, where the supervisor administered literacy tests. Each girl filled out a registration form and read a text out loud.

Each applicant was then given a series of tests designed to determine her ability to do mill work. The first was a dexterity test, which required her to place pegs in the holes of a peg-board for one minute, first with her right hand, then with her left. Next were tests to check her vision and hearing, and a physical exam to determine her exact height and to ensure that she was in good health. Finally there was an interview. Often conducted by the factory manager himself, the interview was meant to glean information about the applicant's family circumstances, her purpose in seeking work, and her temperament. "The test would take all day," one woman who passed the grueling series remembered. "When I went in it was eight in the morning, and we were there until four in the afternoon."[27]

When an applicant who had not been eliminated the first day arrived the second day, she was informed that she had to have a photograph of herself and a guarantor. The guarantor "had to be the owner of a store. But not just any store. If it was just a one-room store, that wasn't good enough. It had to be a big-ger store. The owner of the store would have a chop, and he would put his seal on the form. Usually we wouldn't know the store owner ourselves. We would go through relatives and friends to find someone. You'd have to send him a present— wine or medicines."[28] The guarantor had to fill out a form, stating his name, native place, age, and relation to the person being guaranteed, and he had to affix a half-inch photograph of himself. Finally he had to sign a statement guaranteeing that he would assume financial liability if the recruit left before the two-year apprenticeship period was expired.[29]

On the third day, when she had submitted the sealed guar-antee and photograph, the supervisor of apprentices asked her once again to state her name, age, height, and weight. The supervisor compared these responses with the information re-corded the first day, to prevent substitution.[30]

THE TRAINING PROGRAM

Those who were accepted then embarked on a two-month training program, designed not only to teach them a particular skill but to cover subjects ranging from textile production to national politics. Technical training took place in special sections of each workshop; lectures on supplementary topics were held in classrooms inside the factory complex.

The young apprentices were gradually eased into the routine of working a ten-hour shift. For the first two weeks they spent only six hours a day in the workshop, followed by four weeks of eight hours a day, and finally two weeks of nine hours a day. The hours remaining after work were by no means free time or rest time. Apprentices had to attend classes about production safety, factory rules, and health. They were taught how to keep diaries and write letters, and were instructed in mathematics and morality. Once or twice a week the assistant factory head paid a visit to these classes to speak about current events, human relations, or the relation between their own mill, the cotton textile industry, and national reconstruction.

In the workshops the apprentices were taught by experienced workers who had been appointed to serve as instructors. In theory the program of instruction gradually increased the apprentices' accuracy and speed, as well as the number of machines they could operate. What actually happened sometimes departed from the intentions of the management. One woman, for example, complained that the "old hands" assigned to teach the apprentices made only a token effort to do so. "I have to be extremely careful to treat them well, to wash their clothes and buy things for them. And if I indicate even the slightest sign of resistance, they even beat me. But worst of all is that they won't teach us anything."[31] The instructors may have been trying to undermine the apprenticeship system, or they may simply have been attempting to reap some benefit from their position as instructors. Much to the managers' chagrin, some of the most enthusiastic instructors were CCP members; they were extremely anxious to be assigned to this position so that they might educate and recruit the apprentices.

At the end of the two-month period the apprentices had to take another test. Those who passed were assigned to a regular shift, and from then on they had to alternate between night shifts and day shifts, like the rest of the workers. Although their formal training was finished, they were considered apprentices for two years and had to live in an apprentice dormitory during this time, no matter where their family lived. "At night they would close the doors at nine, and if you came back after that you couldn't enter," one former apprentice in Shanghai remembered. "Then they would contact the Number One and she would dock your wages."[32] When they went to the factory or classroom from the dormitory, apprentices were required to walk in a double line. On their one day off per week, they participated in organized recreation programs, including group singing and sports; every third Sunday there was an assembly at which the manager enjoined workers to dedicate themselves to successful production at the mill.

To complement this discipline imposed by management, the personnel office set up a "self-governing society" for the apprentices. This society consisted of small groups of twelve to fifteen members, who selected a group leader to assume responsibility for their good performance.[33]

Aside from producing a more efficient, more easily managed work force, the apprenticeship system appealed to managers in one other way: using apprentices cost them less than paying skilled workers. During the two-month training period the apprentices received room and board plus four to six *jiao*, considered a subsidy rather than a true wage. After that apprentices received six to eight *jiao*, but a set amount was deducted for the meals they ate at the factory cafeteria. Finally, after the two-year period had been completed, the apprentice-graduates could choose to stay in the dormitory or move out, and they earned the same wage as other workers.[34]

Although most mills admitted several hundred apprentices in the years following World War II, the apprentice system did not completely supplant the former system of hiring based on connections. "Sometimes the Number Ones would circumvent this official system," one manager recalled. "They would bring in friends and relatives and teach them work. . . . There were some girls who couldn't pass the *yangchenggong* test. Then they would go through the Number One, send her presents, and try to bribe their way in. This still happened after 1945."[35] In their smart factory-issued dresses and hats, apprentices must have seemed a privileged group to other women

workers who lacked the financial resources and thus the education necessary for admission to the program. Ironically,
Subei women, who accounted for a large percentage of the
yangchenggong, were now treated contemptuously by their fellow workers not because of poverty but rather because of their
wealth.

The apprentices of the post–World War II era represented
the elite of the Shanghai work force. Management's goal was
the creation of a free labor market, one in which managers
were free to hire workers who had proved themselves qualified, rather than being forced to hire those who had *guanxi*
with the Number Ones. The number of apprentices indicates
the extent to which mill managers succeeded in controlling the
recruitment and training of labor. The limits to their success
were symbolized by the presence of another group of women
workers in the mills: the contract laborers.

CHAPTER FIVE   Contract Labor

In the early 1930's Xia Yan, one of the founders of the League of Left-Wing Writers, was living in the Yangshupu district of Shanghai. Some of his friends, intellectuals who were recruiting members for trade unions, used his house to change from their long Chinese gowns or Western suits to blue cotton workers' outfits on their way to meetings with the laborers. From these friends he learned of the living conditions of the many young women who were contract workers in the city's cotton mills. Unlike other women workers, who were relatively free once they passed the factory gates, these women appeared to be the prisoners of labor bosses who traveled to villages and purchased teenage girls from their parents. With an "X" or a thumbprint on a sheet of paper, the girl was contracted to work for the boss for a fixed number of years.

Xia Yan was appalled by what he heard about this contract labor system, and "in bitter indignation determined to expose this hell on earth." As he set about investigating the conditions of contract workers, he too shed his gown for workers' clothing. He went to work on the night shift in a mill for several weeks. A young woman who was a member of the Communist Youth League and worked in a Japanese mill collaborated with him, trying to talk to the contract laborers in her workshop and to find out more about the circumstances of their recruitment and their lives in Shanghai. Many of them suspected that someone so curious about their conditions must be a spy, and they refused to talk to her.

Attempts to visit contract laborers' living quarters were

even more frustrating: there were very strict rules, and visitors were rarely allowed beyond the "Japanese gendarmes and sentries and thugs employed by the labor contractors." Xia Yan successfully sneaked past the guards twice before they spotted him and brought his investigation to an end. In 1936, using the information he had gathered, Xia Yan wrote the short story "Contract Labor," the most detailed contemporary report about the contract labor system.[1]

Several others tried to investigate the system during the early 1930's, but they too found the secrecy surrounding the system difficult to penetrate. Cora Deng, "having been told more than once by workers how badly treated are the girls under contract labor," wanted very much to find out more about their predicament. Like Xia Yan, she found the police guarding their dormitories a formidable obstacle, but finally, "through a long list of personal relations," she managed to pay a visit to one of the contract labor dormitories. Even then she had to dress and arrange her hair as if she were an older peasant woman related to one of the contract laborers.[2]

Sociologist Chen Hansheng also attempted to study the contract labor system. In 1930, shortly after becoming a member of the Social Science Research Institute, he began an investigation of the system in the Japanese run cotton mills of Shanghai. He had not worked on the project long when Chai Jiemin, then the head of the institute, instructed him to curtail the project because "there are people who oppose this work." Chen abandoned the research, left Shanghai, and set about studying the rural economy, the work for which he is better known.[3]

From then on, although the plight of contract laborers became a cause of social reformers and a rallying cry of Communist organizers, no one attempted to publish anything new about the system. Not until after Liberation, when there was a large-scale movement to document the pre-Liberation experiences of urban workers, did the contract labor system enjoy a revival in print. Xia Yan's story became a popular pamphlet; contract laborers were interviewed and their recollections compiled and issued in booklet form. The conditions under which contract laborers lived and worked even became the theme of an opera and later of a movie. In these popular portrayals the contract labor system assumed legendary dimensions. The squalid existence of the contract laborer was often described as typical of the experience of Shanghai's pre-Liberation women cotton mill workers and cited as an illustration of the brutal conditions resulting from foreign domination of the cotton industry and of capitalists' inhuman exploitation of the workers.

An examination of the historical record, however, suggests that the contract labor system cannot be ascribed either to brutal capitalists or to imperialists. By reconstructing the system and then tracing its development during the first half of the twentieth century, with particular attention to the forces that gave rise to it in the Shanghai cotton mills, this chapter will show that the contract labor system was instead a product of the power of the Green Gang in Shanghai.

"Plucking Mulberry Leaves"

In Shanghai during the 1930's the business of buying and selling young girls was referred to colloquially as "plucking mulberry leaves." The men and women who engaged in this business—at times there were as many as 5,000 of them—were part of the underworld of hoodlums and gangsters who controlled commerce in everything from drugs, fish, vegetables, and night soil to human labor.[4] Those who plucked mulberry leaves could sell their harvest as prostitutes, servants, child brides, or child workers in the cotton mills.

The contractors who made a business of going to villages, buying peasant girls, and bringing them to Shanghai to work in cotton mills belonged to an intricate network of cliques. Commonly known as the Green Gang, this network controlled most of the social, economic, and legal institutions of Shanghai. Although almost all accounts refer to labor contractors as "Shanghai local hoodlums," very little is known about their social origins or the process through which they became contractors. Like the women they purchased, most were probably originally peasants who had come to work in Shanghai.[5]

Some found that buying and selling young girls was more lucrative than working as a coolie in Shanghai. In one case that reached the Shanghai courts, "a coolie confessed that, for a wage of twenty cents small money a day and his food, he was accustomed to prowl about the streets of Wusih and entice young children from their homes by offers of sweets and other delicacies. The children were then brought to the Shanghai market."[6] Other contractors were the husbands or wives of Number Ones. For instance, the husband of a woman called The Blind One, a Number One at a Yong An cotton mill, was a labor contractor; eventually she too became a contractor.[7] Contractors made more money than Number Ones. The more successful contractors also practiced usury and ran teahouses, bath houses, and hairdressing shops, and their appearance reflected their relative wealth. One labor contractor was described as "a man over thirty years of age, wearing a black silk jacket and a pair of black silk trousers, all padded with silk wool. He was tidy and clean and looked well fed."[8]

There has been no systematic study of the geographic origins of contract laborers, and since the system was often clandestine and obscure even to the mill management, there are not likely to be records that would make such a study possible. Still, some general comments can be made about recruitment patterns; for instance, there were areas where contractors did not go. Many of the areas that furnished large numbers of women workers (described in Chapter Three) were not sources of contract labor. There seem to have been no contract laborers from Wuxi, Changzhou, or Ningbo and very few from places such as Haimen that were just across the river from Shanghai. In the overwhelming majority of documented cases, the contractors went to one of five places: Yangzhou, Taizhou, Taixing (all in Subei), Shengxian, or Xinchang (both in the Shaoxing region).[9] These regions were poor enough that people were willing to sell their daughters, but they were not necessarily the poorest regions. Had there been a direct correlation between poverty level and recruitment, more contract laborers would have come from the Yancheng-Funing and Gaoyou-Xinghua areas. That this was not so suggests that social connections, rather than economic considerations alone, determined the contractors' choice of recruiting centers.

We can only speculate about these social connections. If we assume, as most contemporary observers did, that most contractors were affiliated with the Green Gang, then the little that is known about the origins of the gang might help explain the areas they visited. We know, for example, that the Shaoxing, Yangzhou, and Taizhou areas were all centers of Green Gang activity during the late Qing dynasty. Furthermore, the gang boss who controlled the kidnapping racket in Shanghai, Gu Zhuxuan, was himself from Subei.[10] In other words, the origins and the social networks of the gang seem to correlate with the favored regions for recruiting contract labor.

BUYING

The first step in the process was for a contractor to pay a visit to his or her home village. There the contractor looked for teenage girls, usually from fourteen to eighteen years old, who could be lured to Shanghai.[11] In some cases the contractor posted an announcement in the village and then signed contracts with those who responded. This was how one woman from a village near Xinchang was recruited. "In 1945 a labor contractor came to our village to look for workers," she recalled.

It was the first time one had come. Afterwards there were more, but I was in the first batch. We had no idea if he came from one particular factory or where he came from. We just knew he was looking for workers. He was also from Zhejiang but not from our own village. He had connections with people at the village office. He had posted an announcement on a wall in the center of town [with] an address where you should go if you wanted to register. We couldn't read. Other people in our clan told me about the announcement. They said, "Your family is hard up. You can go register to work in Shanghai."[12]

More frequently, however, the contractor would talk to friends and relatives, determine which families were in particularly dire circumstances, and then pay them a visit. "The year

I was twelve a recruiter by the name of Gong came from Shanghai," one woman from Taixing recalled. "Every day he would be at houses of young girls, talking about how good their life in Shanghai could be."[13] Sometimes a child-daughter-in-law (*tongyangxi*, a girl whose parents had arranged a marriage for her and had then sent her to live with her fiancé's family) was sold to a contractor by her parents-in-law[14] (see Chapter Seven for a further discussion of the practice of *tongyangxi*).

The prospective recruit's family was promised that she would have meat and fish for dinner every day, a house to live in with other girls, a job, a chance to learn a skill, and a day off every week to see the skyscrapers, double-deck buses and other "strange, amusing, foreign sights of Shanghai."[15]

Aside from selling their daughters to labor contractors, a family's alternatives might have been few. Young girls could do farm work, such as tending cows and pigs or picking weeds, or they could either wash clothes for neighbors or do housework for the landlord, as their mothers did. It is doubtful that any of these was as lucrative as a wage-paying job in Shanghai.

Selling young women to contractors was not a completely new phenomenon, nor was it simply a result of industrialization. Instead it was an extension of the tradition of selling and indenturing women as future daughters-in-law, brides, or servants. Sue Gronewold's remarks about prostitution in China can be applied to contract labor as well: "a thriving market in women already existed and all women were to some extent regarded as merchandise."[16] In other words, although the contractor may have been a new figure in the rural social landscape, the practice of selling young girls was an old and familiar one.

Once the parents had agreed to sell their daughter, they signed a contract written on a sheet of white paper or on a small crumpled scrap.[17] A typical contract read as follows:

The undersigned, X, because of present economic difficulties, on this day wishes to hire out his daughter, Y, to recruiting agent of the name Z, who will take her to work in a cotton mill in Shanghai. The hiring payment will be [$30] for a period of three years. The money will be paid in three annual installments of [$10], to be paid in March of each year.

From the time she enters the factory, the girl will owe full obedience to the recruiting agent, and must not violate his instructions. In the event of her abscondence or death, the undersigned takes full responsibility. If she should fall ill, the recruiting agent will be responsible. Throughout the three-year contracted period, the girl will be clothed and fed by the recruiting agent. If any working time is lost, the girl will have to make it up at the end of the contracted period. After the contract expires, the recruiting agent has no further responsibility for the girl.

I hereby agree to this.[18]

Some contracts added a clause forbidding the use of the child for immoral purposes. One of the parents, who usually did not know how to read or write, would make either a thumbprint or an "X" at the bottom.[19]

Although a fee of $30 for three years seems to have been a fairly standard price, there were many variations in the terms of the contract, depending on the age of the girl. Girls were often divided into three types: old (paid as much as $50 for three years' work), medium ($40 for four years), and young ($30 for five years).[20] Sometimes contract conditions were negotiated, as the price of food at a market would be haggled over. "The contractor told my mother that he wanted to recruit me and that he would provide food and clothes," one woman remembered. "My mother agreed and said, 'For two years give me fifty dollars.' The contractor haggled: 'Fifty dollars for three years.'"[21] The agreed-upon price, called the family allowance, was rarely paid in full in advance. Usually it was divided into three payments, as set forth in the sample contract reprinted above, the first being the smallest and the last the largest, to ensure that the girl continued working for the duration of the contract. For the period of time contracted, the wages paid to the girl by the factory belonged to the contractor.[22]

For teenage girls who had lived all their lives on a farm or in a small town, the arrival of the contractor from Shanghai, the discussions that led eventually to a signed contract, and her departure with the contractor for the city must often have seemed an extremely rapid sequence of events. "After we registered there wasn't much time," said the woman who had responded to an announcement posted in her village. "We had to leave within a week. The contractor didn't even look us over before we left. He just took whoever was willing to go. Fifteen of us came together."[23]

Some contractors brought groups of as few as ten girls to Shanghai; others recruited as many as a hundred at a time. Often a group consisted of girls from several neighboring villages. Since the contractor paid the cost of transportation to Shanghai, he or she naturally sought the cheapest means possible, for example, in the freight cars of a train or the cargo compartment of a boat. One woman later described her experience leaving the village: "The next day [the day after signing the contract] was the first time I ever left our village. I left dreaming I'd be able to eat. We got on a boat for Shanghai. There were eleven other girls with me. On the boat we twelve girls were in the cargo compartment. The recruiter, staying in a room above, would sometimes come to talk to us. But the farther we got, the less he had to say."[24]

SELLING

Because contractors were not employed by particular cotton mills, they did not always know in advance which mills would hire the girls they recruited. Upon arriving in Shanghai, contractors faced the urgent task of securing jobs for the contracted girls. Some notified the hiring agents at various mills and arranged for them to look the girls over and choose whomever they wanted. One girl described this process as follows: "When we first arrived in Shanghai we slept in an empty lot next to the train station. The boss went home. The next morning he came back. Then hiring agents from different mills came to look at us, and they would decide who they wanted."[25]

On other occasions a contractor, like an ordinary job seeker but on a grander scale, had to present a gift to a factory's Number One before securing work for the girls. The contractor sometimes deducted the price of the expensive gift from the amount of money owed the girls' parents.[26] On still other occasions a contractor brought recruits to Japanese mills, where job seekers lined up at the factory gate each morning, and entered them into the lines. Girls under the supervision of a contractor might have had some advantage in getting jobs: the contractor would first fix their hair, dress them up in pretty clothes, and put rouge on their faces so that they would stand out in the crowd. A contractor might also give them high-heeled shoes so that they would appear tall enough to reach the bar at the gate that represented the minimum height requirement.[27] During their first few days in Shanghai, some girls were taken from mill to mill by the contractor in the hope that if one was not interested in hiring them, another would be.

But there were always some girls who were not hired. Since the contractor would have to send money to their families, simply abandoning them was not an attractive alternative. The contractor usually found some other employment for the girls. Some, rejected because they were too small, were kept by the contractor to be servants until they grew big enough to get a mill job. One girl who spent several years doing housework for the boss wrote the following melodramatic account of her daily chores:

Every day at three o'clock in the morning the boss's wife would wake me up to draw the bellows and make the gruel for the morning shift of contract workers. If I'd do it too slowly, she would pull my hair or knock my head with her knuckles. After they had eaten, I would have to wash six or seven toilets and the high spittoon in the boss's house. Sometimes before I had finished, the boss's wife would yell at me to come wash diapers.

At 6:00 A.M. I would go to the market with the boss's wife. I would walk behind her, carrying a basket. She would go from this stand to that one, buying the leftover vegetables that no one else wanted. Then when we got back I'd have to wash them. By this time it would be 9:00. . . . The night shift contract workers would have eaten and gone to sleep, but no one . . . paid attention to whether or not I had eaten. She'd tell me to just eat whatever was left in the tub.

At lunch and dinner time the table in the boss's house would be full of meat and fish. I would have to stand beside the table and serve them food. Then I would go take care of the workers' food. Afterwards I would clean the dishes, and then I could eat whatever leftovers there were.

After eating, the boss's wife had nothing to do, so she would just play mah-jongg all day. I would have to stand behind her and massage her back while she played. Sometimes she would play till eight or nine at night, but even when she'd go to bed my duties were not over. Until she fell asleep I would have to massage her legs and waist.

Most nights I would not go back to the contract workers' room till eleven or twelve o'clock. Then I'd look for a place to sleep. Because there were not many plank beds, and lots of people, and because I was just a servant, I did not have a real place. I would just squeeze in between the other girls and use the corner of their quilt. Or, more often, because the girls would be so crowded and their quilts too small to cover them and me, I would just look for some empty space on the floor and spread out my cotton padded jacket to sleep. . . . Often I had no sooner found a place to sleep, closed my eyes and fallen asleep, than the old wife would call me to get up and start the fire.[28]

Since many of the household chores were done by the contracted girls who did have mill jobs, it was not necessary to keep more than one or two as house servants.

Another possibility was to try to get the unemployables other factory jobs, even if they paid less than mill work. Some contract workers, for example, were employed in silk filatures, but that work was seasonal. Once the season ended, so did the girls' wages, and the contractor had to look for a new way of employing them.[29]

A more common alternative was to send them to work as prostitutes. Like contract laborers, prostitutes were systematically recruited from the countryside, and there may not always have been a real distinction between the bosses who recruited prostitutes and those who recruited mill laborers. The distinction, if it existed, was further blurred because the people recruiting prostitutes often lured women to Shanghai on the pretext that they were taking them to work in the mills. The story of two such swindlers who recruited eight girls from a village near Shaoxing is typical of reports that appeared in the Shanghai newspapers throughout the early 1930's. Apparently the girls were told they would have jobs in cotton mills, but on arriving in Shanghai several were taken immediately to a brothel in the French Concession and sold as prostitutes. When the case went to court, one swindler was accused also of having arranged to sell one of the girls as a child bride.[30]

Local restaurants and teahouses were another place where

contractors might seek employment for the young girls they had purchased. It is not clear how widespread a practice this was; references are most numerous in connection with girls from Shengxian. This district, famous by the early 1930's for its peasant troupes that performed Shaoxing opera, was also a district that furnished many contract laborers. "Those who went to Shanghai to become female workers naturally had many opportunities to sing," one writer noted. "At first they would just sing for each other. When the labor contractor heard them he picked out the best of the young girls and took them to sing in restaurants where workers gathered."[31] As Shaoxing peasant operas became increasingly popular, contractors began to recruit girls specifically for performing in Shanghai restaurants, and later in theaters.

Since the people who contracted girls to work in cotton mills were all part of the underworld, it is not surprising that the "plucked mulberry leaves" were peddled from one enterprise to another. The brothel bosses, the teahouse owners, and the labor contractors were connected through their membership in the Green Gang.

"GUARANTEED RICE"

Inside the mill the contract laborers were treated like other workers. Because they had come directly from the countryside and had no prior experience working in a cotton mill, they began work on the same terms as apprentice workers and in fact were usually assigned to the machines reserved for training apprentices. Like apprentice workers, contract laborers underwent a period of training during which they were paid substantially less than skilled workers. The length of this training period varied. In some cases workers would "study till they mastered the technique" and then be eligible for higher wages. More commonly they were required to remain apprentices for six months, even though most could master the skills much sooner.[32]

One difference between contract laborers and the ordinary workers and apprentices hired directly by the mill was that contract laborers did not keep their wages. "When it was time to get paid, the Number One would give us a receipt, saying how much we should get," one woman explained. "Then we would go stand in line at a window and they would give us the money, which we would give to the boss."[33] In some of the more progressive mills, the factory would give its contract laborers two or three *jiao* at the end of the year for spending money.[34] But the biggest difference between the experience of a contract laborer and that of an ordinary woman worker was outside the factory. Every aspect of her life was controlled by the contractor. She had no options—she lived where the boss told her to live, she ate the food he or she provided, she left the dormitory only when the contractor allowed her to.

Some of the more prosperous contractors had their own dormitories. A contractor named Huang from Taixing reportedly had one house next to the Japanese-run Da Kang Cotton Mill in eastern Shanghai, where a hundred contracted girls lived, and another next to a Chinese-owned mill in western Shanghai, housing another sixty or seventy girls. He lived in a separate house next to the dormitory in east Shanghai, and one of his relatives managed the dorm in west Shanghai.[35]

Most contractors, however, rented rooms for their contract laborers from the mill owners. No sooner had mill owners begun constructing dormitories than the gang tapped this new source of income. A social worker who investigated the problems of housing for working women in 1933 noted that a large portion of company housing was "monopolized by those people who made a business of contract labor."[36] Contractors sometimes rented entire blocks of dormitory space. That was the case at the Japanese mill in Yangshupu that Xia Yan visited and later described:

The compound is oblong, enclosed by a high red brick wall and intersected into two long narrow strips by a cement road. It is split up as neatly as a dovecote: eight rows on each side with five buildings in each, making altogether eighty two-story buildings. . . . These loft houses have no front entrance. Their front door is like an ordinary back door. Over each is a wooden slip three inches long on which are written in Japanese-style Chinese characters the name and place of origin of the contractor [who rented the rooms for his workers], like "Chen Dongtian, Taizhou," or "Xu Fuda, Yangzhou." Pasted on the doors are lucky tokens cut out of red paper, woodcuts to keep away ghosts and evil spirits, or mottoes on faded red paper expressing such pious sentiments as "Virtue is its own reward" and "Honesty pays."[37]

The contractors paid about four or five dollars a month for one room, in which they could house anywhere from fifteen to forty girls. Two girls almost always shared a single sleeping space: a girl on day shift would sleep there at night, and a girl on night shift during the day. Cora Deng recorded her impressions of the inside of a contract laborers' dormitory:

This particular contractor rented from his mill owner five ordinary two storey tenement houses where he managed to house his own family together with more than ninety contracted girls. The first house we visited had on the first floor a big sitting room which, clean, tidy and fairly well furnished, looked like a lower middle class living room. Being the contractor's private living quarters, naturally it is not open to the girls under contract for use. . . .

[The contractor] took us to see the dormitories, but we were so carefully guided and shown, that we saw only, as I was told afterwards by a worker, the best part of his place. This particular dormitory is on the second floor of the second house. It is just a big room without partitions of any kind. On the floor there were two rows of sleeping places, four on each side. Each of them had some straw underneath a mat. Some had old rags as bedding while others did not even have rags. When he was asked whether some of the girls' bedding was taken out to be aired in the sunshine (it happened to be a very good sunny day) the contractor answered, "Some girls have taken out their bedding to be aired, but some, being used to sleep without any bedding in the country, can get along without any." There were eight sleeping places, but the people occupying them were sixteen in number, because two girls, one using it during the day and the other at night, shared one bed. . . .

There was no furniture of any kind, not even broken stools or worn out tables. This explains why the floor was full of basins, bundles, and the wall was decorated with dresses, towels, shoes, stockings and what not, hanging all over the walls. One was impressed as being in the steerage of a boat![38]

A contractor usually hired thugs to guard the dormitories and to accompany the girls to and from the factory. For the most part the laborers were not allowed to leave the dormitory or factory premises except during the Spring Festival and on specified days about once every two weeks. Even on those occasions they were accompanied.[39]

The contracts signed by the laborers' parents stipulated that the contractor assumed responsibility for providing the girls' food; in fact, the contract labor system took its popular name, *bao fan* ("guaranteed rice"), from this stipulation. But the less contractors spent on laborers' meals, the more profit they made, so they usually provided no more than the minimum level of subsistence. The only real meal the girls ate was lunch, which the contractor often sent to them at the mill. Lunch consisted of dry rice with vegetables on top—usually dried turnips and discarded vegetable leaves and stalks, as well as salted cabbage. The girls were treated to meat or fish only on holidays. Breakfast and dinner were a thin congee made from Indian rice and miscellaneous grains or leftovers such as soybean dregs. Xia Yan watched the girls prepare for breakfast: "After the mats and tattered bedding downstairs have been bundled out of the way, the girls take down two tables which have been hooked to the wall during the night. A dozen or more bowls and a handful of bamboo chopsticks are slapped down on these tables, and the girl doing duty as cook puts a tin bucket of thin, watery congee in the middle."[40]

Cooking was only one of many chores the contract laborers were expected to do when they were not at work. In addition to washing and mending their own clothes, which usually consisted of no more than two sets issued by the contractor, they had to wash and mend the clothes of the boss's family. They had to sweep the floors, empty and clean the wooden chamber pots, and take care of the boss's children.[41] If the boss was a man, they were sometimes expected to provide sexual services as well and were beaten if they did not comply. Cases of contract laborers being beaten and raped by their bosses appeared frequently in the Shanghai newspapers during the 1930's. The story of Tao Kougu, an eighteen-year-old girl from Taizhou, was typical of hundreds of others. She lived and worked in west Shanghai under contract to a 32-year-old man also from Taizhou. According to Tao, one morning she had not gone to work at the mill because her feet were swollen and sore. She was in the dormitory house resting. At 6:00 A.M. the contractor "burst into the room and forced me onto the bed, and then raped me. He covered my mouth so that I could not utter a sound. For the next two days he . . . would not let me go out anywhere. He raped me two more times after that."[42] Another article reporting a similar occurrence noted that "every day there are instances of arguments and fights between the labor bosses and recruited girls."[43]

Given this combination of inadequate food, crowded living quarters, and physical abuse, it is little wonder that contract laborers were frequently ill. The most common illnesses were tuberculosis, beriberi, and various skin diseases. Because there was no medical care, problems that were initially minor ones often became quite serious. "When we'd finish the day's work our feet would be swollen and we'd get big blisters," one woman recalled. "Even after several months they would not heal. There was nothing to do but use straw paper and cotton rags to bind them up. My feet still have scars. Of ten apprentices, nine had infected feet."[44]

Although the extremely poor health of these contract laborers usually passed unnoticed by the world outside their dormitories, the girls' illnesses sometimes attracted the attention of the mill managers, or even the local police. In 1939 the Shanghai police charged a contractor with mistreating a girl who was later found, in two independent medical examinations, to be suffering from chronic malnutrition and tubercular glands. She came to the attention of the police when she tried to escape from the contractor. According to the police report, "her contractor pursued her, overtook her on a wharf, and attempted to force her to return. She resisted, and in the struggle police attention was drawn to the incident. The man was charged under Article 286, Section 2, of the Chinese Criminal Code, 'for that on divers dates between October 1938 and July 1939, at XXX Cotton Mill Quarters, [he] did for the purpose of gain maltreat one named Tsu Mei Ying.'"[45]

Very few girls, however, were so fortunate as to attract official notice. If they were sick they usually continued to work, not only because the contractor forced them to do so, but because they would later have to make up any work days they missed. For every one day of work they missed, they had to

add two or three days of additional work at the end of the
contract period; in rare cases they had to add as much as one
month per day missed. Hence very few girls were freed from
their contracts at the time originally specified. Many of those
who had originally contracted for three years ended up working for four or five years before the contract was officially
terminated.

Many girls, like Tsu Mei Ying, did try to escape before their
contracts expired. Slipping past the thugs hired as guards was
not easy, and even if a girl could manage to flee beyond the
dormitory walls, there was a great likelihood that she would
eventually be found. A girl who escaped successfully would
immediately be blacklisted by her contractor, and since most
contractors had *guanxi* with the Number Ones in the mills, it
was not difficult to prevent her from being rehired.[46]

"TAKING RICE"

When the contract, including any extensions imposed, did
finally expire, many girls still could not sever their ties to the
contractor. Some stayed on under a slightly different arrangement called *dai fan*, or "taking rice." Under the *dai fan* system,
which in theory was an improvement over the contract labor
system, a worker was not bound by a contract and was entitled
to keep her salary. From her monthly wages she paid the contractor a set amount, usually seven or eight dollars, for room
and board. In reality, though, she continued to live, work, and
eat under the same conditions as before.*

Considering the brutality to which contract laborers were
subjected, it may seem peculiar that they stayed on after the
requirements of their contracts had been fulfilled. Their alternatives, however, must have been few. At the time their commitment ended, though they had worked for three or more

---

*In some cases of "taking rice" the contractor went to villages and recruited
women to come and work in Shanghai. Then the difference between "taking rice"
and "eating guaranteed rice" was that no contract was signed and there was no period
of contract. The contractor would simply promise the girl that if she came to Shanghai
he or she would help her get a job, and that she would have room and board for $7 or
$8 a month. "Chinese Labor and the Contract System," *People's Tribune*, 5 (1933), no.
8: 410; Sun Baoshan, "Shanghai fangzhichangde baoshenzhi gongren," *Huanian zhoukan* 1 (1932), no. 22: 466; Du Shipin, ed., *Shanghaishi daguan* (Shanghai, 1948), pt. 3,
p. 65.

years, they had no money of their own. Most were still teenagers, and many had no relatives in Shanghai to turn to for
help. If they wanted to continue working in Shanghai, staying
on with the contractor might well have been the only arrangement they could afford.[47] Often, the contractors forced them
to stay, presumably hoping to extract a portion of their salary
for as long as possible. One woman remembered that "after
seven years the boss said to me, 'If you want to keep working
then you had best keep living with me and eat *dai fan*. You pay
me eight dollars a month for food. If you don't live here, then
you won't be able to work.' Having had seven years of experience, I knew that all the bosses collaborated . . . so I ended
up being a *dai fan* at his house."[48] Many other women recalled
being forced into a similar predicament.

Not only the women who had been recruited from the countryside and had served as contract laborers had a *dai fan* arrangement. Many young, single women workers already in
the city eventually contracted for room and board with labor
contractors, probably because they offered the cheapest arrangement available. Furthermore, since the contractor and
the boarders in most boarding places all came from the same
village, some girls might have perceived the arrangement as a
kind of surrogate family. Finally, because contractors controlled much of the job market and factory housing, there
might have been little choice for girls who wanted to get work
in the mills. One woman tells of coming to Shanghai to work:

I heard other people say that if you were starving in the village the
only thing to do was to go to Shanghai and look for work. That way
you could not only solve the problem of supporting yourself, but
also send money home to support your family. This possibility stuck
in my mind until finally I was able to get the introduction of someone
from the same village to come to Shanghai and work in a cotton mill.
I roomed and boarded at his place. There were many other girls like
me boarding there. Probably all were introduced into the factory by
him, since he was a labor boss in the cotton mill.[49]

Once a young woman began boarding at a contractor's
house, several conditions made it difficult to move elsewhere.
If the girl had just arrived in Shanghai and had never worked
in a mill, she had to work first as an apprentice for several
months. During this time she earned only a few dollars a

month, and she consequently could not pay the eight dollars charged for room and board. The contractor would lend her the money but would charge a high interest rate, refusing to let her leave until she had repaid her debt.[50] Another problem was that without the contractor's continuing assistance, she might lose her job. This was especially true of people who were simultaneously foremen or Number Ones and keepers of boarding establishments. One woman who had wanted to leave a boarding establishment remarked, "But if you don't eat his rice, then you won't have any work. There are already too many unemployed people in this society—so where else would I go to get work?"[51]

One should not conclude that being contracted from the village or entering a boarding establishment once in Shanghai was always tantamount to life imprisonment. Most contemporary accounts, as well as the recollections of contract laborers compiled after Liberation, describe the most extreme cases of victimization by the contractors. For at least some women, the job introductions and the inexpensive room and board provided by contractors from their native villages were a source of support when they arrived in Shanghai and had no one else to turn to. Some girls depended on a contractor for no more than a temporary arrangement, one they abandoned once they had begun to develop a network of relationships of their own in the city.*

PROFITS

Whether operating a *bao fan* or a *dai fan* system, the labor contractors made a handsome profit from their business of plucking mulberry leaves. A contractor operating a *bao fan* system would pay about $5 a month for food and rent for one girl. The girl, once her apprenticeship was over, would earn a minimum of $12 a month; in one year the contractor would earn $84, and in three years $252. Subtracting $10 for expenses incurred in the process of recruiting and the $35 (more or less) paid to the parents, at the end of three years the contractor

---

*For instance, one woman originally from a village near Shengxian described coming to Shanghai in 1945 and boarding at first with a boss—also a Zhejiang native—at the Shen Xin No. 9 Mill. After six months, when she began to receive full wages, she went to live with a co-worker from the same village. Interview with Zhang Xiaomei, Shanghai, Feb. 25, 1981.

could have accumulated $207 for a single girl. And since most contractors had from ten to one hundred laborers, the contract labor business was indeed lucrative. In three years a contractor who had ten girls could make $2,070, whereas an ordinary foreman in a mill would have earned only about $1,080—just about half as much.* As a report of the Shanghai Municipal Council concluded, "if the contractor has from eight to ten girls, his or her living is by no means unsatisfactory for an unskilled and unlettered person." Or as Sun Baoshan put it, "No wonder many contractors have two or more wives!"

Many accounts of the contract labor system brand it one of the many ways the "capitalists even more severely exploited the workers." But though the system was clearly profitable for the labor contractors, it was not so obviously beneficial to the mill owners and managers. There is no evidence that contract laborers were any cheaper than other women workers from the mill owners' point of view. While contract laborers were being trained they could be paid the reduced wages of apprentices or child workers, but once they qualified for the wages due a skilled worker, it was obviously in the interest of the contractor to press for that amount since his or her income depended on it. Furthermore, how productive could the contract laborers have been? If most contract laborers lived and worked under conditions at all resembling the ones outlined above, then one can imagine them to have been weak, if not downright ill, and probably less efficient than other workers in the mill.

It appears that the mill owners perceived this to be the case. In the mid-1930's there were frequently conflicts between mill owners and contractors, conflicts that usually focused on the contract laborers' health. Contract laborers often arrived at the factory workshop either pathetically ill or bruised from beatings. The Number Ones sometimes tried to persuade the con-

*These figures are approximate, based on several different estimates of the expenses incurred by a contractor. Of course the amount paid to the contract worker in the form of wages was important in determining how much the contractor earned. Since contract workers worked in different departments and in different mills, there was a great deal of variation. See Shanghai Municipal Council, *Annual Report, 1938* (Shanghai, 1938), p. 41; Sun Baoshan, "Shanghai fangzhichangde baoshenzi gongren," *Huanian zhoukan* 1 (1932), no. 22: 431; Shanghai shehui kexueyuan, jingji yanjiuso, *Yongan fangzhi yinran gongsi* (Beijing, 1964), p. 90.

tracted girls to request several days of sick leave, but the girls knew that they would have to make up any lost time. Xia Yan told of a letter to the editor of a Shanghai newspaper written by a man who, having nothing better to do one day in October 1935, dropped in to listen to court trials in Caojiadu. That particular day there was a case concerning a contract laborer from a cotton mill who had been accused by her contractor of stealing gold earrings and some clothing, and then fleeing. In the course of the trial some extenuating circumstances emerged: the previous month the contractor had demanded that she have sexual relations with him, and when she refused he beat her until her eyes were swollen shut. At work the mill managers told her to take sick leave and go home, but the contractor did not agree.[52] According to the young mill worker with whom Xia Yan discussed the problems of contract laborers, cases like this were fairly typical.

In the late 1930's one large cotton mill studied the work efficiencies of three types of women workers: those who lived with their own families, those who lived on their own in factory dorms, and those controlled by contractors. Based on the results of the study, the general manager realized that "the contract system is not good, producing as it does apathetic, lethargic workers." He subsequently took measures to limit the number of contract laborers and insisted that the contractors pay for the laborers under their control to eat in the factory dining room, "where good food is available at reasonable cost." The Industrial Section of the Shanghai Municipal Council even concluded that "self-interest on the part of management of this mill will ultimately drive out the system."[53] If the mill owners were as disenchanted with the contract labor system as these accounts suggest, one cannot help wondering how the system originally got a foothold in the cotton mills and why it continued for so long.

Many contemporary observers attributed the development of the contract labor system to Japanese mill owners. In Cora Deng's account of a visit to a contract laborers' dormitory, she described the system as one peculiar to Shanghai's Japanese mills; articles with titles such as "Contract Labor in the Japanese Cotton Mills in Shanghai" appeared in newspapers and magazines. Several factory engineers, looking back at the system, commented, "Contract labor—oh, that was something they used in the Japanese mills," or words to that effect.[54]

If the system had been confined to the Japanese mills, then the explanation offered by many historians might suffice. The Japanese, they said, unfamiliar with Chinese language and customs, had no choice but to depend on local hoodlums to recruit their labor, and so long as production continued they did not care how the workers were treated.[55] Unfortunately, the matter is not as simple as this version suggests. There are no systematic records indicating the number of contract workers at particular mills at particular times. Nonetheless, the scattered data available make one point clear: the contract labor system was by no means confined to the Japanese-owned mills. To be sure, large numbers of contract laborers worked at Japanese mills such as Nei Wai and Da Kang, but there were also contract workers at the British mills during the 1930's, particularly the Yi He Mill. Most striking is the evidence of contract labor at Chinese-owned mills, both at the Shen Xin mills, considered to have the most backward management techniques, and at the Yong An mills, considered to be the most modern. Some observers claimed that the Chinese-owned Shen Xin Number Nine Mill at one point had more contract laborers than any other Shanghai mill: 1,200 of 3,000 workers were said to be contract laborers in 1936.[56] Could it be, as some have suggested, that the contract system started in the foreign-owned mills and spread to the Chinese ones?

Traditions: Foreign and Chinese

To understand the extent to which the nationality of mill owners determined the patterns of the contract labor system's development, we must look at the traditions that might have given rise to the system in the first place.

FOREIGN

Because so many accounts of the contract labor system attribute its origins to the Japanese,[57] we begin by asking what might have prompted the Japanese to adopt this system in Shanghai. There was in fact a history of contract labor in the Japanese domestic cotton industry, but the question remains whether the Japanese capitalists who established factories in Shanghai considered this a system worth copying. What we know of the history of the contract labor system in Japan suggests that they probably did not.

The contract labor system began in Japan in the 1890's, when the rapid expansion of the cotton industry created a severe labor shortage. The mills no longer could rely on people who lived nearby but instead had to begin a recruitment program. "As its demand for labor skyrocketed," wrote Takejiro Shindo,* "the cotton industry was compelled to initiate serious efforts for the procurement of labor by appointing recruiting agents to work exclusively for channeling female operatives into the mills."[58] It was not easy to convince the parents of a teenage girl to allow her to leave the village and go to work in an urban factory. Mill owners therefore found it advantageous to employ recruiting agents who had come from those villages themselves and not only were familiar with rural conditions and peasants' attitudes but also had networks of relatives and friends to draw on.

In this way there developed a group of men and women who made a living by recruiting female laborers from the countryside and selling them to factories desperate for workers. These contractors, often people with criminal records, were also involved in recruiting prostitutes, geisha, and teahouse girls. Like the contractors of Shanghai they often lured women to the city by promising high wages and boasting of the luxurious life of the city, and then housed them in dormitories, restricted their activities, and frequently forced them to work as waitresses or to perform "demoralizing acts."

By the early twentieth century the system was in such ill repute throughout the Japanese countryside that contractors were hard pressed to persuade women to go with them. Commenting on the system in 1925, Shunzo Yoshisake wrote:

The irresponsible promises of the recruiting agents, given simply to entice the women to work, the disagreeable manner of their persistent attempts to persuade them, their violent and insulting acts, and other injustices have had a decidedly negative influence. Again, the country folk see many sudden changes in their friends and receive

*Shindo was a former chairman of the board of directors of the Toyo Spinning Co. of Japan, which owned several mills in Shanghai.

bitter disillusionments; they hear of the risks to life and health in factory work; an innocent country girl, who left home full of health and vigour, soon returns with wrecked health and haggard face, or news comes of her utter moral ruin and degradation.[59]

The situation was so extreme that in 1926 one village formed a union of men and women workers, headed by the mayor, to maintain certain standards of working conditions for the women who were recruited from that village to work in urban factories.[60]

By the 1920's the problem had become so acute that legislation was enacted to control the abuses of the recruiting system. The Regulations Concerning the Recruitment of Workers, passed in December 1924, required licensing of all people engaged in recruiting workers and guaranteed that "in the case of women workers their chastity is protected, while in the case of men . . . their freedom and security should be ensured."[61] This law apparently brought the system under control.

The history of imperialism abounds with examples of factory owners leaving areas where laws have been enacted that require them to treat workers according to certain standards, leading to a rise in the cost of labor. The absence of enforceable labor laws in China and the low cost of labor must certainly have appealed to Japanese investors, but these factors would account for the importation of the contract labor system only if it had truly proved profitable. But the Japanese contract labor system was clearly not one that had achieved unqualified success. Furthermore, though there is ample evidence of contract labor in Shanghai's Japanese-owned mills by the 1930's, there is no record of Japanese mills using this system during their early years in Shanghai. In other words, although a contract labor system existed in Japan, it does not appear that Japanese managers used this system when they first opened mills in Shanghai.

CHINESE

During their early years of operation in Shanghai, it appears that Japanese mill owners, like their British and Chinese counterparts, adopted recruiting systems shaped primarily by traditions prevalent in China. A cluster of related hiring systems developed, with names sometimes so similar that they have been mistaken for one another. Moreover, the contract labor system itself did not exist in the Shanghai mills until the late 1920's, although earlier recruiting systems included parts of it.

The system most often confused with the contract labor system (*baoshenzhi*) is the contract work system (*baogongzhi*). The contract work system, which had existed long before the contract labor system, continued to exist alongside and sometimes in conjunction with it. In the contract work system the owner and the manager of an enterprise relinquished all decisions concerning production to a foreman, who was paid a flat fee for producing a certain amount of the finished product. The foreman determined how many workers should be hired and how much they should be paid, but he usually hired several subordinate foremen to handle the recruitment of workers. Much has been written about the use of this system in the Chinese mining industry.[62] In Shanghai the system was most prevalent at the docks, where all workers were hired by contractors who paid the workers only 20-40 percent of the rate paid by the shipping firm;[63] it was also used by the Shanghai Public Works Department, the French Tramway Company, and some oil and tobacco companies.

Shanghai's cotton mills used the contract work system extensively from an early time. In 1916 an observer from the United States Department of Commerce, Ralph Odell, described in his survey of China's cotton mills a typical contract work system in use at the International Cotton Manufacturing Company, originally a German enterprise. He noted that all the workers at this mill were employed and paid by a contractor, who was in turn paid by the manager according to the number of pieces produced.[64] At times some Chinese-owned mills, such as the Heng Feng Cotton Mill and several of the Shen Xin mills, also used the contract work system.[65]

This system was distinct from, but compatible with, the contract labor system. A contract labor system could be used within the contract work system; that is, the subordinate foremen who actually recruited the workers could go to villages, sign contracts with parents of teenagers, and put the girls to work in the mills. Or the subordinate foremen might have had connections with a person engaged in such a business. But just as frequently, the workers were recruited by advertisement, or lived in the Shanghai suburbs and were not provided room and board by the foremen. Most important, this system was instituted by the mill management.

Managers of mills that did not use the contract work system sometimes appointed their own recruiting agents. Before the 1930's these agents sometimes brought women from other places to work in Shanghai mills under conditions similar to those of the later contract labor system; however, the recruiters were members of the mill staff, not local hoodlums. One such case, which appeared in the Changsha and Shanghai newspapers in 1920, involved the Hou Sheng Mill, owned by a Chinese capitalist originally from Hunan. According to an interview with a Mr. Huang, the foreman responsible for hiring female workers, the general manager had requested that 50 jobs be reserved for women to be recruited from Hunan, where "due to repeated military engagements and inflation . . . people's lives were rough."

The women who were recruited did not necessarily sign a contract, but they were expected to work for three years because, as Huang explained, the mill had "invested" in these women. When the women left Hunan each was given a leather suitcase, a washbasin, and a basket. "The factory had to pay for all of this," the foreman explained. "We must insist that the women work for three years before leaving. Otherwise we fear that they do not really want to work for us, but only want to use this as a pretext to find other means of earning a living." During the three years they worked, the women were paid eight dollars a month from which five dollars was deducted for room and board. They were housed in a dormitory constructed especially for them. At the end of three years those who wanted to continue working could do so; those who wanted to leave could leave.[66]

Insofar as the women were recruited from outside Shanghai and were brought to the city with the understanding that they would work for three years, their situation resembled the guaranteed-rice system, but insofar as they were paid a monthly wage that they were entitled to keep (minus a fixed amount for room and board), it approximated the taking-rice arrangement. Nevertheless, this instance of recruiting 50 women from Hunan, intended as a trial to determine the suitability of Hunan women for mill work, was initiated and executed by the mill manager. The women were beholden to the factory managers, not to local racketeers.

Similarities may also be seen in the *yangchenggong*, or apprentice, system. The purpose of the training bureaus created during the 1920's, when women workers were replacing male workers in many operations, was to provide very young girls with several years of training before they were put to work.[67] In this system mill agents went to villages, usually not too far from Shanghai, and recruited teenage girls. Before final acceptance into the training program, the recruits were required to pass a very simple literacy test, a physical exam, and a dexterity test, and then to provide a guarantee that they would remain at the mill for three years. During that time they were housed in factory dormitories. The Nei Wai mills recruited a group of these girls in 1923, as did the Yong An mills in 1925.[68]

As with the contract work system, contract labor could have been grafted onto the apprentice system: local labor contractors could have made deals with the mill agents responsible for finding and hiring the apprentices. There is little evidence that this occurred, although it is difficult to rule out the possibility entirely since in post-1949 historiography the terms "contract labor system" and "apprentice system" are often confused or used interchangeably. The confusion was perhaps generated not only because the systems are similar, but also because during the 1930's and 1940's what was referred to by the locals of Yangshupu as contract labor (*baoshengong*) was called trained labor (*yangchenggong*) by the workers of Xiaoshadu. Many post-1949 accounts of the labor movement describing attacks on the contract labor system during the May Thirtieth Movement, in light of sources from that era, seem actually to have been referring to attacks on the apprentice system. The workers attacked the apprentice system because many of their jobs were threatened by these young trainees.

The Green Gang and the Contract Labor System

Although there were several systems that resembled contract labor, on close scrutiny there is no direct evidence that the contract labor system existed before 1928, either in foreign- or in Chinese-owned mills. The system is not mentioned in contemporary newspaper or magazine accounts describing work conditions and strikes, although if it had existed at that time, there are several documents and publications in which we might expect reports to appear. *New Youth*'s 1920 special labor issue included articles discussing every imaginable aspect of labor problems, yet not once did it refer to the contract labor system. References to contract labor were similarly absent from the report of the Child Labor Commission of 1924, Tang Hai's and Udaka Yasushi's studies of China's labor problems, both written in 1925, and the works of other major Chinese observers of labor problems, such as Chen Da and Ma Zhaojun.[69] Finally, although the description of the contract labor system above is drawn from many different sources, most of them either were written during the 1930's or are recollections of women who worked in cotton mills at that time. It is of course possible that the contract labor system existed all along but did not strike these observers as something unusual enough to deserve special discussion or a name of its own. Or perhaps there was a contract labor system but it involved only a small number of workers.

In 1930, however, the system became a newsworthy phenomenon. It was extensive and distinct enough to be given the name *baoshenzhi*, which had not appeared before, and extraordinary enough to attract the attention of social scientists such as Chen Hansheng, who organized a team of researchers in that year to investigate the system. There was a sudden proliferation of articles in the daily papers about girls from villages struck by flood or famine being bound by contracts signed by their parents, who received a pittance for the promise of three years of their daughters' labor. The fate of these girls once they arrived in the city was as newsworthy as the conditions under which they were recruited, not only because they were sent to live and work in the squalid conditions described above. What many reporters found most distressing was that, subsequent to their arrival in Shanghai, these girls frequently lost their virginity, because they either were raped by the contractors themselves or were passed on to other hoodlums.

Thus, although there might well have been recruitment from the villages before the 1930's, it had taken on a new aspect by that time. A woman worker was no longer simply a laborer recruited by someone who provided a mill with workers and perhaps worked as a foreman himself. She was now the possession of a contractor who was part of a criminal network of racketeers. This meant, for example, that it was easy to blacklist girls who tried to escape and to sell girls not marketable in mills as maids or as prostitutes. The contractors now were part of, and had *guanxi* with, an extensive network of mulberry leaf pluckers.

Before 1930 there were capitalists who needed workers, there were foremen and forewomen who often did the work of recruiting, and there were women who left their villages to work in the Shanghai mills. But what was significantly different during the 1930's was the underworld element: the emergence of the contract labor system coincides almost exactly with a radical increase in the power and scope of activities of the Green Gang. The story of contract labor is therefore not simply a story of impoverished peasants, wealthy capitalists, and imperialists but is just as much a story of the Green Gang of Shanghai and how it cornered the cotton mills' labor market.

THE GREEN GANG

The Green Gang is perhaps the most elusive element in the political and social history of Shanghai. On the one hand it is described as omnipotent; on the other hand, it appears only between the lines in accounts of industrial development. The Shanghai Green Gang has been described as embodying "the characteristics of the Society of December Tenth as utilized by Louis Bonaparte, the Russian Black Hundred, and the modern Chicago variety of racketeers and criminal gunmen."[70] The gang boasted members from all echelons of Shanghai society.

At the top level were the so-called Big Three: Du Yuesheng, Huang Jinrong (called Pockmarked Huang), and Zhang Xiaolin. The rank and file, numbering as many as 20,000 in the early 1930's, included many politicians, GMD labor leaders, degree holders, journalists, policemen, and military officers, as well as most factory foremen and labor contractors. A history of the relationship of the Green Gang to the financial and political institutions of Shanghai is beyond the scope of this study. What concerns us here is when and how the gang came to play a powerful role in one of Shanghai's largest industries, not only among workers and foremen but among owners and managers as well.

In this context the events of 1925-27 may be particularly significant. Following the May Thirtieth Movement an increasing number of workers joined the radical Shanghai General Union. They engaged in continual strikes, demanding an ever-expanding list of improvements in their work conditions, from a minimum wage and a paid day off every week to freedom of speech and of association. The power of the labor movement was dramatically displayed during three uprisings in 1926-27, when workers battled to seize control of Shanghai from the warlords. The first two failed, but by March 1927, after the third, workers controlled the Chinese-owned parts of Shanghai and had established a provisional municipal government.

Alarmed by these events, the Shanghai business community turned to Chiang Kai-shek for assistance in opposing the labor movement. That the capitalists forged close connections with the GMD is only part of the story of the struggle to quell the workers' movement during the late 1920's. GMD officers and soldiers did not hunt down labor leaders and worker activists, or infiltrate the unions. The GMD turned these jobs over to the Green Gang, headed by Du Yuesheng. Virtually no other group could undermine the power held by the Communists in Shanghai at that time. Shanghai's treaty port status partially accounted for this predicament: Chinese troops and police were not allowed to enter the foreign concessions, where most mills were located. Even if the official institutions had had the organizational strength to contend with the CCP, foreign domination would have rendered them impotent. In this context an organization such as the Green Gang could assume wide-ranging powers.[71]

Delegated the job of destroying the Communist-led labor movement, Du Yuesheng created the Society for Common Progress. "Located in the French Concession, the association mobilized and equipped thousands of gang members. At a given signal these men rushed out of their sanctuary and overwhelmed the Communist workers. . . . By its intervention, [Du's] group managed to redraw the political map."[72] From 1927 on, the Green Gang became a political power that all contenders had to take seriously.

As most studies have lamented, the gang was extremely effective in destroying the labor movement. But they did not do this job for free: the mill owners became vulnerable to the gang's determination to claim a share of the profits to be made from industrial development. This sense of vulnerability was expressed by a mill engineer, speaking of the early 1930's:

> At that time, when capitalists opened factories, they hoped that there wouldn't be strikes or anything in the factory. . . . All the guards at the factory gates were gang members. When you wanted guards, you would contact the gang, and they would send people. That way the gates were secured, and if there were any problems or disputes with workers, we'd go get these "old heads" at the gate. And if we did not use them, then they would come and damage the factory.[73]

If the mill owners did not comply with the gang's demands to control certain aspects of mill operations, it was not simply two or three dissatisfied gate guards who came and attacked the factory. Those guards could mobilize the forces of a massive network to do more than slight damage to a factory.

Damaging the physical plant was only one of many techniques used by the gang to keep the mill owners in line; attacking, kidnapping, or even murdering those who offended them was not unheard of. The fate of a certain Yih Dai-mien might have been a lesson to others. Yih, from a family of compradores, was the insurance department compradore of Probst, Hanbury and Company. In 1929 he had "recently become a joint manager of the Oriental Cotton Mill and had made dras-

tic changes in the management of this mill," when the following account of his murder appeared in the *North-China Herald*:

> Another grave outrage took place early on May 31 in Avenue Road
> when three men shot and killed in cold blood . . . Mr. Yih Dai-mien,
> who had just left his residence, 85 Carter Road, in his motor car. The
> compradore, who, it is thought, was perhaps kidnapped for revenge,
> put up a strenuous resistance within 500 yards of the house. Deserted
> by his chauffeur, who jumped from the car when the shooting began,
> he struggled against three armed men, until so weakened by the loss
> of blood occasioned by his wounds, he sank to the floor of the car.
> The gang, not wishing to have a wounded man on their hands, de-
> serted the car and their victim.[74]

The report did not specify what Yih had done to offend the
gang. But it is possible to speculate: in the late 1920's instituting reforms in mill management almost always meant replacing labor bosses and foremen, who had local influence but no
training, with professional engineers who were usually graduates of schools such as the Nantong Textile Institute. When
these professionals began work in the mills, they encountered
fierce resistance, most often manifested as threats, beatings,
and other intimidation.[75]

Demanding control of the labor market was only one issue
in the use of violence against capitalists during the late 1920's.
Parks Coble's study of Shanghai capitalists documents the
Green Gang's reign of terror over Shanghai capitalists, beginning in 1928. Chiang Kai-shek, desperate to raise funds for his
government, enlisted the assistance of the Green Gang to extract money from the capitalists. Kidnapping wealthy businessmen or their family members and holding them for ransom became a routine affair in the 1930's.[76]

THE SYSTEM EXPOSED

In January 1932 the problem of contract labor briefly commanded the attention of more than just the readers of newspaper crime pages and industrial engineers plagued by the
problems of developing a modern and efficient work force. As
one editor commented, "It was not until two days ago that
baoshenzhi, this new term, became known in local society. Actually it has a history of more than one year, but those who are

immersed in Shanghai's pleasure world of music and women never paid any attention to this evil system."[77] Hundreds of contract laborers emerged from semicovert imprisonment into the limelight. Their working and living conditions, as well as the realization that they were village girls who had been bought by contractors, scandalized Shanghai.

When the Japanese attacked Shanghai in 1932, labor contractors were in a precarious position. Many had houses in Zhabei, the area most severely damaged in the attack, and they were forced to flee to the International Settlement. Furthermore, many Japanese mills stopped production, putting large numbers of contracted girls out of work. Unlike other unemployed workers, who had to fend for themselves during times of unemployment, contract laborers were still entitled to housing and food provided by the contractors, even though they were not receiving wages. The contractors found a way out of their predicament by taking advantage of the refugee relief agencies set up in the International Settlement to deal with the thousands of people rendered homeless by the Japanese attack. Apparently the managers of the relief agencies quickly discovered this situation, and when they began to investigate, found more than a thousand contract laborers scattered in various refugee camps. As soon as the factories reopened, the labor bosses showed up to reclaim their contracted laborers and put them back to work in the mills. "The first step," one writer proclaimed, "is to notify the relief agencies not to let people come and take these children away. We must think of a method to rescue them from the contractors."[78]

Ironically, though the events of 1932 led to the exposure of the contract labor system, they also contributed to its expansion. At the time of the Japanese attack in January, thousands of women workers fled the city and returned to their home villages. When the cotton mills began to resume production in the spring, the contractors had an opportunity to secure control over even more workers than before. In addition to trying to reclaim the women they had deposited in the refugee camps, they could go to the countryside and bring back more workers. That the political situation, particularly the anti-Japanese boycott, may even have made dependence on labor contractors necessary for Japanese-owned mills to resume operation is suggested by a report about the partial reopening of thirteen Japanese mills in April 1932:

According to the local Chinese papers it is reported "that the Japanese cotton mills have provided 20 foremen with huge sums of money to proceed secretly to Taishing, Yangchow and other inland places to recruit laborers. Our workers should not be allowed to work with the Japanese at the present moment when the whole nation is unanimously resisting Japan. . . . We therefore request that the various *hsien* governments be instructed to prohibit strictly such labor conscription to avoid all pernicious consequences."[79]

It was just after the Japanese attack that Xia Yan was able to work in a mill himself, and his observations attest to the increase in the number of contract laborers. "Whereas the number of workers has diminished," he wrote, "the percentage of contract labor in the total work force has shot up. Thus twenty-four out of thirty-two girls working at the drawing frame of a mill in Yangshupu are contract labor."[80] Indeed, there is dramatic statistical evidence of the expansion of the contract labor system during the thirties. When Sun Baoshan conducted his survey in 1932, he estimated that in all Shanghai mills there were approximately ten thousand contract laborers.[81] By 1937 an investigation conducted by the YWCA concluded that there were some 70,000–80,000 contract laborers in the city's mills.[82]

As had happened five years earlier, when the Japanese attacked Shanghai in 1937 the factories had no sooner shut their doors than the contractors sent the girls to refugee camps. One woman, after visiting a refugee house, wrote:

All the refugees there are women and children. You can go and have a look. Whether they are yellow-faced young mothers still breast-feeding their infants, or sickly older women whose hair is already very thin, or malnourished pale young girls—as soon as you ask them you will find out that they are all women workers who, under enemy fire, have fled from the Japanese cotton mills.

Among these people there is a group of young girls who are 12 or 13 to about 17 years old. They especially attract people's attention. Some look like their hands have never been washed. Some have bound feet. At a glance one can tell that they have only recently come from the village to the city. If you try to talk to them they won't open their mouths. They are afraid you are going to trick them. These girls are all contract laborers.[83]

This time the Shanghai Municipal Council was alarmed by the condition of these young women, conducted investigations of its own, and ultimately concluded that

there is nothing contrary to law in an entrepreneur undertaking to obtain work for another and being remunerated for this service. The custom is widespread in China. There is, however, something which calls for the attention of authorities when large groups of girls are removed from country surroundings and from the home of their parents (even if at the instigation of parents), and are placed in the control of another who profits unduly out of the work of the girls. Mill managers may not be aware that some of their employees are in the hands of middlemen. Entrepreneurs who go to the country often do so as an enterprise of their own. Though mill managers may not be a direct party to the poor conditions of lodging and poor food to which the girls are subject, they must nevertheless be aware of these. Whether the responsibility for conditions lies with the contractor or the mill management, it is obvious that a large group of adolescents are in a situation where they need the protection and supervision of authorities.[84]

During this time several women's organizations sponsored a meeting to develop a plan for rescuing those contract laborers who were at least temporarily free of their bosses. They first requested that all relief agencies investigate the numbers of contract laborers in the refugee houses, stressing that the girls should not be sent back to their villages because the bosses might come for them or their parents might sell them again. They proposed that the contract laborers be identified and then be gathered together in several refugee houses reserved especially for them, where they could be taken care of and provided some education. Those who attended this meeting even envisioned sending these girls, "who have neither family responsibilities nor the demands of rich material life," to the interior to do organizational work against the Japanese invaders.[85]

On a more sober note the members of the women's organizations realized that implementing these plans might be difficult. Housing, feeding, and educating the contract laborers would require a large amount of money, which could not be obtained by soliciting contributions from a few people. More important was the fact that the contractors, even though they might have temporarily relinquished control over the girls owing to the circumstances of war, still wielded tremendous influence in the lower echelons of Shanghai society. Although the outbreak of hostilities may have been a temporary blow to the hoodlums operating in the cotton industry, their colleagues were making inroads in other sectors. News reports in late 1937 condemned the resurgence of racketeering along the Shanghai waterfront since the beginning of war and expressed concern that gangsters were expanding their sphere of influence to the Shanghai Municipal Council's pontoons along the Bund. "Here by duress," one article noted, "they have gained a monopoly on the wharf coolie labor market and are charging exorbitant rates for working cargo. The danger of violence has frightened away other coolie labor."[86] No one expected the labor bosses to readily give up their power; nor did anyone doubt that they would strongly resist any attempts to eliminate their influence in the mills.

THE MILL OWNERS ATTACK

The Shanghai Municipal Council and women's organizations were not the only ones trying to eliminate the contractors. In many cases the mill managers themselves sought to make the most of the retreat of the contractors to undermine their power. The best-publicized campaign by the managers against them took place at the British-owned mills, which had reputedly had one of the largest concentrations of contract laborers. The managers had actually succeeded in replacing the contract system with "direct employment" in the spring of 1937 at the smallest of their mills. The procedure had not been easy: their initial efforts resulted in two successive strikes. The workers, who appeared to be striking against the elimination of the contract system, were presumably induced to strike by the bribes or threats of the contractors. Ultimately the company succeeded in replacing the contractors with a labor manager it hired to take direct responsibility for hiring workers.[87]

Successfully instituting a modern, professional management system did not necessarily ensure that the labor bosses would be kept at bay. "Even where it would appear that a more modern arrangement exists," Eleanor Hinder wrote in 1942,

where there is a personnel department with an employment manager directly in the employ of the company, the management may not be a completely free agent in the handling of its affairs. A "gang" may influence the relations between the employer and his workers. There may be in the district a gang leader, a *lao tou-zi*, or "old head," with considerable authority. If there is a difference between the management and the workers, the management may have to accept the mediation of the *lao tou-zi*, who may even be responsible for having fostered the dispute. Moreover the management may have to employ workers whom the *lao tou-zi* sees fit to recommend. The *lao tou-zi* may be powerful within a trade instead of a district. For example, the real employment manager of several large textile mills in the Settlement is stated to be one *lao tou-zi*. The personnel managers and even the management of these enterprises appear to bow to the influence of this powerful "boss."[88]

Under these circumstances, it did not seem to matter that a mill ostensibly employed its workers through a contract work (*baogongzhi*) system or a modern personnel department; nor did it seem to matter whether the factory was owned by Chinese, Japanese, or British capitalists. They all used contract laborers at certain times. The only difference was whether or not the management knew about the system. When all hiring and firing and wage paying was in the hands of a foreman, the managers might not have known. When it was under the direction of a personnel department, they probably did know but were powerless to eradicate the system.

The contract labor system appears to have been at its zenith in the years before the War of Resistance, but as long as the gang continued to wield power, the system could not be destroyed. No investigations of the contract labor system were conducted between 1937 and Liberation, and there are absolutely no figures suggesting the numbers of women workers still owned by the bosses after this date. But reports of scattered cases continued to appear. The recollections of contract laborers published after Liberation include accounts of women recruited in the late thirties and early forties. The Japanese invasion certainly produced circumstances conducive to the persistence of the system—poverty, the destruction of the outlying areas, and thousands of orphans left to the care of whoever would take them. An overwhelming majority of cases turned over by the police to the Child Protection Section of the Shanghai Municipal Council were those of orphaned children with nearly identical histories: "Parents died in the war. The child was taken by a neighbor and sold."[89]

There are accounts of women contracted even after the war. That these were not merely isolated cases is suggested by a general survey of Shanghai's social conditions published in 1948. The section about women laborers consists of little besides a discussion of the contract labor system, which appeared to be operating exactly as it had in the thirties. "This kind of contract labor system for women workers, all the way up to the present, has continued to exist," the 1948 survey reported. "But because the factory authorities and unions are trying to make reforms, the number of women involved is beginning to gradually decrease."[90]

Regardless of the descriptions by earlier writers, then, contract labor is not a system that was prevalent in the early twenties before being destroyed during the workers' uprisings of 1925-27, to reappear only occasionally. It can be seen as a product of the May Thirtieth Movement but, again, not for the reasons that others have suggested. Although mill managers may have sought to undermine the labor movement by employing these well-controlled workers, the significance in this context of the workers' movement, beginning May 30, 1925, is that mill owners opted for an alliance with the Green Gang in order to control the workers. As a result the gang emerged with unprecedented power.

This power developed just when mill owners were trying desperately to eliminate outdated management systems (see Chapter Four); it was an era when trade journals seemed obsessed with introducing the modern management techniques being used in the United States and Japan. Yet the managers were in the stranglehold of the gang, to whom they remained indebted. The contractors, at the height of their power controlling as much as two-thirds of the female cotton mill work force, made the development of a free labor market unimaginable. The capitalists were no more free to buy the labor they chose than the workers were to sell it.

The significance of the contract labor system hence is not that it represents a system of extraordinary exploitation resulting from foreign domination of the cotton industry. Rather it represents the vulnerability of both women workers and mill owners, Chinese as well as foreign, to the Shanghai Green Gang.

CHAPTER SIX   The Working Day

In July 1963 an exhibition at the Shanghai Number Two Textile Mill opened to the public, with a banner strung across the top of the doorway to proclaim the title of the exhibition: "The Angry Indictment by the Workers of the Formerly Japanese-owned Cotton Mill."* The exhibition hall was divided lengthwise into two large rooms. One room was devoted to portraying incidents in the history of labor struggles in the mill, including the slaying of Gu Zhenghong by Japanese guards, the event that triggered the May Thirtieth Movement in 1925. The displays in the other room evoked the lives of women workers before Liberation.[1]

Photographs lined the walls. One depicted women and children tending machines in a dust-filled workshop; another showed an overseer beating a woman worker, who had collapsed on the floor. The caption posted next to this photo quoted a retired worker: "To the Japanese owners and managers, beating Chinese workers was everyday fare. They would swear at us [and say], 'In Shanghai it is very hard to find one hundred dogs, but to find one hundred workers is very easy.' To the Japanese, we Chinese workers were not even as good as dogs." Other pictures showed the turnstiles the women passed through as they were searched for stolen goods before leaving the mill, and the mud-floored straw huts in which many cotton mill workers lived.

In the center of the room was a glass display case containing

---

*The mill consists of what was, before 1945, the Japanese-owned Nei Wai nos. 5, 6, 8, and 12.

the articles women workers used every day. A set of clothes included a frayed pair of blue cotton padded pants, a long-sleeved shirt, and a work apron with a white number printed on the front. Next was a small, partially disintegrated bamboo basket with a handle on the top, the kind women used to carry their rice for lunch to the mill. A sign next to several bamboo sticks explained that in the Japanese mills workers had to request such a chit from the overseer in order to go to the toilet. A white chit granted permission to urinate, and a red one to defecate. The items in this display became symbols of pre-Liberation working-class life. Similar displays appeared in other mills, as well as in museums and cultural palaces, and they served as the basis for many popular historical pamphlets. These displays and pamphlets were designed to provide class education for those too young to have witnessed the poverty and oppression endured by pre-Liberation urban workers.[2]

The daily life of female cotton mill workers was quickly reduced to five or six clichés, repeated in every exhibition, book, or "speak bitterness" speech:* before Liberation women were beaten by the Number Ones; before Liberation women worked long hours for little pay; before Liberation women ate nothing but rotten vegetables; before Liberation women did not have the freedom to go to the toilet; and before Liberation women were subjected to body searches. In short, the lives of women workers were characterized as "worse than the lives of beasts of burden."

Factory records, textile journals, contemporary social surveys, newspaper reports, and oral history interviews all corroborate these clichés. Yet these records also suggest that working life was much more complicated and varied than this simple portrayal suggests: it takes the features of the most poverty-stricken women, namely women from Subei, during the most difficult period, the Japanese occupation, as representative of all women throughout the period called pre-Liberation, which in fact spans several decades of changing conditions. Three major flaws of this condensed and simplified portrayal

---

*"Speaking bitterness" was part of the class education movement of the late 1950's and early 1960's. Workers and peasants were encouraged to tell audiences about their bitter experiences before Liberation.

concern the blurring of time distinctions, the glossing over of differences between workers, and the tendency to present women as passive victims.

First, although there was very little discernible change in the standard of living and the substance of daily life between World War I and 1937, the years of the Japanese occupation of Shanghai did result in extraordinary hardships. Many workers, for example, ate little besides whatever garbage they found in the streets. Japanese foremen assaulted Chinese women workers in the mills; Japanese soldiers assaulted them on the streets. However, the years of the occupation represent only a small portion of the period from World War I to Liberation. Conditions before 1937 and following the surrender in 1945 offer a significantly different, and probably more typical, picture of working-class life.

Second, these generalizations overlook the important differences in daily life determined by a woman's age, position in her family, and economic status. The experience of a young girl who lived with a mother and grandmother was very different from that of a married woman who lived with her husband's family and perhaps had children of her own to care for while she worked. Likewise, the daily life of a poor migrant woman from a Subei village was substantially different from that of her Jiangnan co-worker. There were indeed women from Subei who lived in mud-floored straw huts and had only one ragged set of clothing to wear. But (as we have seen in Chapter Three) there were also women, particularly those from Wuxi and Changzhou, who wore long gowns and high heels and had money to spend on cosmetics and elaborate coiffures.

Finally, these portrayals present the women as passive, ever-suffering victims, subject to constant beatings by foremen and Number Ones, to humiliating body searches, to unbearably long work hours. There is little in their daily lives to glorify or romanticize, but women did find ways to survive. We find, for example, women taking naps by their machines or in yarn bins when they were supposed to be working, and arranging for relatives or neighbors to substitute for them when they needed a day or two off. The routine of working a twelve-hour shift at the mill, to which were usually added the demands of household chores and child care, left little time for social activities. Nevertheless, an occasional performance of local opera or a visit to a Buddhist temple to pray and burn incense was a central event of the working day for many women in Shanghai.

It is with an eye to how they mitigated the hardships as well as to the hardships themselves that we try to reconstruct the daily routine of the women who worked in Shanghai's cotton mills.* This daily routine represents the social reality from which their consciousness of themselves as women and as workers eventually emerged.

Beginning the Day

A cotton mill worker's day began at 4:30 A.M. The streets were still dark, silent, and deserted, except for an occasional cart carrying mounds of fresh vegetables or a quartered pig. These carts were pulled by peasants from nearby villages, taking their produce to the morning markets in Shanghai.[3]

A worker most often did not have a clock. If she lived close to a mill, a shrill whistle blown at 4:30 woke her up.[4] But most depended on the chickens they raised, which were brought into the kitchen at night. "We would get up when we heard the crow of the roosters," Chen Zhaodi recalled. "Usually they were about right, but not always. Sometimes, since we did not know what time it really was, we would get to the mill way too early. Anyway, we never dared to sleep later than the cock crow."[5]

As she crawled out of bed at this predawn hour, a woman had to be careful not to disturb the four or five others sleeping in the same room, which was probably no larger than ten by fifteen feet.[6] She slept on a wooden bed covered with a mattress made of rice straw, an indigo-print cotton sheet, and in winter a cotton padded quilt. Year round, a dark blue mosquito net hung over the bed to keep out the mosquitos and the ever-present flies.[7]

*The description of the working day that follows portrays the life of cotton mill workers during the period before 1937. Conditions during the Japanese occupation and after 1945 will be discussed below.

Before leaving for the mill, she had to dress, wash, and eat breakfast. Her first task was to fetch water. She went to the nearest public water outlet—either a tap installed at one end of the lane, or, more commonly, a well or nearby creek.[8] "I would have to walk about ten minutes to get to the place where we could draw water," Wang Luoying remembered. "We would go twice a day. When we brought it back we would put it in a wood tub in the house, and then we would be very sparing when we used it."[9] If there was a hot water shop nearby, she could pay a cent or two for a kettleful of boiling water; otherwise she boiled it herself.[10]

Preparing the stove was the next morning job. Wood chips, cotton stalks, and straw were put in the bottom compartment, then covered with a layer of coal briquettes. Once lit, during the half hour or so it took the coals to heat, someone would sit next to the stove and fan it to keep the fire going.[11] For this reason the stoves, usually cylindrical and made of tin, were called beat-air stoves. During the winter they offered the only source of heat.[12]

About 5:00 A.M., while she was outside squatting next to the stove and tending the fire, the night-soil collector made his rounds. Since there was no plumbing people used chamber pots, which they emptied into buckets kept outdoors. The buckets were collected every morning by men who came around pulling a cart and yelling, "Empty your toilet! Empty your toilet!" as they passed through the lanes and alleys of Shanghai's working-class districts.[13]

After her pot of water boiled, a woman used some of it to wash and the rest to make *pao fan*—cooked rice warmed in boiling water. Instead of taking time to cook a fresh pot of rice in the morning, she always cooked rice at night and used what was left over to make *pao fan*, the standard breakfast fare of the Shanghai worker. Sometimes she added a bit of bean curd, pickled turnip, preserved greens, or salted fish.[14] After breakfast she put another portion of cold leftover rice into a bamboo basket and carried the rice to the mill to eat at lunchtime.[15] Embarrassed to be recognized as mill workers, some women wrapped their rice baskets in newspaper before setting out for work.[16]

Getting to Work

At 5:30 A.M. the whistle at the mill blew a second time, to signal workers who lived nearby that it was time to leave home. They would get to the mill on foot, a means of transport jokingly called taking the Number Eleven bus.[17] Those who lived farther away had to set out much earlier. Wang Fuying, whose family lived in Baoshan Xian, spent an hour each morning walking to the Yi He Mill in Yangshupu. One foreigner living in Shanghai in 1916 was deeply impressed by the sight of a young worker who had to walk for two hours each morning in order to reach the mill gate:

She starts to the mill each morning at four o'clock, as it takes her two hours to walk there. . . . Many a time when the moon is shining the child mistakes its bright light for dawn and sets out at three or earlier. The walk is not so bad in pleasant weather, lonely only until she joins crowds of other mill folk moving in the same direction. But what of the chill days in winter, with a bleak wind blowing, rain falling, and roads treacherously slippery with mud? It is hardest for the women who have bound feet.[18]

Fearful of attacks by street hoodlums, women never walked to the mills alone. "At first, when I was still very small, my father would take me there every day," Wang Fuying recalled. "Later I would go with my brother and sister."[19] Girls in their teens or twenties made arrangements to walk to work with their friends. "Oh! We would *never* walk alone," Chen Zhaodi exclaimed. "We always went together. There were three of us who lived on the same street. You come to my house and wait for me, or I go to your house and wait for you. We would meet and go together to work. Otherwise it was not safe."[20] For many women the walk to work required crossing Suzhou Creek, the Huangpu River, or one of the canals that crisscrossed Shanghai. When they came to the bank, they boarded a small paddleboat. There were frequent accidents on these boats, such as one that occurred on a winter night in 1921:

Two nights ago there were more than ten male and female workers from Zhabei. They boarded a paddleboat at Suzhou Creek to go to do night work at a certain cotton mill in the western district. There were many people, and the boat was small. When the boat was paddled to the middle of the river, suddenly there was a big wind and waves. The boat turned over and all the workers fell into the water. People living in houseboats along the river immediately went to save them, but five or six had already been swept away by the waves.[21]

Overturned boats and drownings were even more frequent on the Huangpu River, where the presence of large steamships made the trip across especially hazardous for small paddleboats.

Women who could afford it paid about one *yuan* a month to ride to work on a wheelbarrow. "The Shanghai wheelbarrow is mostly used for freight," Mary Gamewell noted. "But because of its cheapness it is a favourite passenger vehicle with a certain class of Chinese, especially the women and children going to and from the mills. Often eight or ten crowd on, sitting sideways with their feet hanging down. Once eleven women and girls were seen on one, pushed along by a single coolie."[22]

The women making their way to the mills in the morning wore a variety of clothing. Often their dress reflected the styles and customs of their home villages. The clothing women wore also depended on how much money they and their families could afford to spend on it. Some family budgets were so tight that the women owned only two sets of clothes—one set for winter and one for summer. Each year when summer began, they would sell their winter clothes to a pawnshop to get some extra money; at the onset of winter they would reclaim their padded clothes and pawn their summer set.[23]

Some women approaching the mill gate wore clothes that were much more refined, even "pretty and fashionable"; some wore earrings or rings.[24] At the Yong An Number Three Mill in Yangshupu so many women were dressing in a manner considered too extravagant that the management published dress regulations in 1939. These rules forbade women to wear high-heeled leather shoes to work and prohibited permanent waves and rouge. "These practices compromise sanitation conditions in the mill," the management explained.[25] On the other hand there were mills, particularly those owned by Japanese, where dressing well was a prerequisite for obtaining a job, which meant that some women had to spend beyond their means to purchase clothes. A YWCA secretary who lived in a mill district explained:

Every morning, very early, you can see hundreds of women workers, each one dressed very neatly, wearing rather pretty clothing. Some people would certainly think they are quite satisfied. But that is not so. There was a woman worker who once told me: "Dressing so smartly is not something we do willingly. It is because the managers in the mills, if they think we are not good-looking, or are dressed shabbily, will not only dislike us, but will even kick us out. So we would rather not eat well, and not have other things we need. But at least we must dress well."[26]

Converging on the mill gates, then, were women hobbling on bound feet, women wearing cloth shoes, and women wearing high heels; women wearing black or striped trousers and faded green or blue jackets and women decked out in long gowns; old women with buns and young women with braids, short bobbed hair, or even a permanent wave. Some had traveled an hour or two and some had left dormitories next to the mills only minutes earlier; some had walked and ridden ferries and some had ridden wheelbarrows.

At mills that employed contract labor, women congregating near the mill gate would be joined by lines of contract laborers being led by their boss from their dormitory to the mill. "These two groups seldom speak to each other on the road," Xia Yan observed when he worked at a Japanese mill. "Perhaps the workers from outside hold aloof because of the dirty, country ways and queer accents of the village girls, whom they despise."[27] For the same reasons, women from Shanghai or cities of Jiangnan usually did not speak to those from Subei, even if they were not contract laborers.

There was one more element in the crowd that gathered at the mill gate. A cotton mill employing more than a thousand workers on a single shift provided an abundance of potential customers for enterprising street peddlers of all varieties. Most sold snacks: noodles, noodle dumplings stuffed with pork, soup with glutinous-rice-flour dumplings, sweet cakes, glutinous-rice cakes, or *da bing* (round, flat wheat cakes). If a woman had time and money she could pay several coppers for a bowl of noodles to eat for breakfast before entering the mill. Some bought *da bing* to take in and eat while they worked. The food stalls probably attracted the most customers, but there were also peddlers selling cosmetic goods such as small wood combs, packets of powder, and pocket mirrors.[28]

At the Mill

At 5:45 A.M. a third whistle blew; the enormous iron gates swung open and the workers streamed in. Although the day shift did not begin until 6:00 A.M., each worker was required to enter the mill fifteen minutes early so that she would be at her machine and ready to take over the moment the night shift ended. This way the machines could run continuously.[29] Anyone who arrived late was fined. At the Shen Xin Number Five Mill, a worker who was five minutes late paid three cents, one who was ten minutes late paid five cents, and one who was fifteen minutes late paid ten cents.[30]

As a woman passed through the mill gate, she had to show her work card to the guard stationed there, to prove that she was employed at that mill. Often a woman who held a regular job at a mill helped her sibling or relative sneak in, to learn the skills involved in textile production. The use of work cards did not entirely prevent this practice. A woman gave her work card to the person she was sneaking in and told the guard at the gate that she had lost her own card. Some even asked for a new card and then changed the name on the original card so that the trainee could continue to use it. This trick was so common that some mills imposed a fine on those who were caught: five cents for losing a work card; three cents for altering the name.[31]

After entering the mill each worker handed her work card to an attendant, who gave her a numbered stick in return. Having collected all the workers' cards, the attendant took them to the pay department, where the cards were stamped with a seal as proof that the person had come to work. The stamped cards were sent to the workshops, and the Number Ones handed them back, in return for the numbered sticks.[32]

By the time a woman reached her workshop, she had only a few minutes to put on her "grease clothes" (slang for work clothes). A few mills, such as the Japanese-owned Tong Xing Mill, had uniforms issued by the plant management. The majority of mills, however, did not have regulation clothes. They required only that a woman put on a work apron, which had a number printed on the front and ties in back. She usually sewed a pocket or two onto the front for bobbin cases, scissors, or other instruments used on the job.[33]

At six sharp a fourth whistle blew. Night shift workers stopped their work and went to change their clothes while the day shift workers immediately took over the machines.

IN THE WORKSHOP

Conditions inside the mills varied from plant to plant. An American factory inspector, Charles Moser, described the workshops of one of the largest Chinese-owned mills as "dirty, badly lighted and full of lint collected on machinery and windows."[34] In general, the Japanese mills impressed observers as being cleaner and better maintained than those operated by Chinese or British owners. Mary Gamewell described the structure of a Japanese mill "that represents the very latest thought in building and equipment" in Shanghai as follows: "The brick walls are lined with cement, the floors are reinforced concrete, while the saw-tooth roofs, with glass on one side, admit an abundance of light."[35]

Whether the owners were Chinese, Japanese, or British, certain features were common to workshops in all mills, namely noise and dust. The dust was most conspicuous in the hot, humid air of the spinning workshops. "In the roving and spinning rooms, countless wisps of cotton fluff in the air are visible to the naked eye," Xia Yan observed.

The girls who sweep the floor push piles of fluff before them. Though sweepers go up and down, up and down between two rows of roving machines, the cotton fluff still drifts on the floor like snowflakes. In the blowing and carding rooms it is of course even worse. . . . In these rooms, no matter what you are wearing, in a very short time you will be covered with white. Cotton fluff flies about . . . as if some devil were in it, getting into your eyes, nose, mouth, ears, and every pore of your body, sticking to your hair and eyebrows. . . . In a twelve-hour working day it is estimated that on the average they breathe in .15 grammes of cotton fluff.[36]

The rows and rows of spinning machines generated such a din that a worker could not make herself heard unless she shouted, or spoke directly into the other person's ear. In the weaving room the noise was even worse: to the background roar of the motors was added the rhythmic clash of the shuttles going back and forth on the looms. Here even shouting was futile. Supervisors carried whistles with them at all times for issuing instructions to the workers.[37] To reduce the supervisors' need to compete with the noise of the machinery, some mills had a "slowly revolving six-sided drum suspended from one of the beams in such a position that it was visible in all parts of the shed, and on each side were painted in the fewest possible characters simple instructions to the operatives."[38]

WORK RHYTHMS

What a woman did from the time she took over the machine at 6:00 A.M. until a night shift worker relieved her at 6:00 P.M. varied from workshop to workshop and from job to job. In the spinning room, for instance, there were women piecers, doffers, and sweepers, and each had a slightly different work routine. Since piecing was one of the most common jobs in the mill, we will look at how a woman who worked as a piecer spent her day.

For twelve hours a day the world of a piecer was an aisle several feet wide between two rows of spinning frames. Because her head was a foot or two short of the top edge of the frame, she could not see the rows and rows of frames on either side of her. She recognized her frame by the number painted on its end, just above the switch operating the motor. For most of the day she stood facing the frame. Beside her were several women assigned to other portions of the same frame, and behind her were the women tending the frame on the opposite side of the aisle. Her frame was divided into several sections, or staffs, each consisting of six spindles. A piecer was assigned responsibility for a certain number of staffs and was paid according to the number of staffs she tended. In most mills a piecer tended at least twelve staffs, and some could handle as many as twenty-five or thirty.[39]

Tending a staff involved primarily fixing the threads that broke as they wound onto the spindles. Whenever she saw a broken thread the woman ran over to that spindle, grabbed the two loose ends, twisted them around her index finger, and rolled them against her thumb to form a knot. The knot had to be very small; otherwise it would appear as a defect in the cloth that was eventually woven from this thread. After forming the knot the piecer snipped the extra thread with her scissors. A novice took a full minute to perform this motion, but to get a job, a piecer was expected to be able to join six broken threads in a minute, or one every ten seconds.

A piecer spent most of the day trying to keep up with snapping threads. Sometimes she noticed a broken thread only moments after fixing another; occasionally several threads broke at once. The frequency of breakage depended on the humidity and the quality of the raw cotton and of the machines.[40] Sometimes women in the spinning room spread sand on the machine belt to slow the rate at which it revolved, thereby decreasing the frequency of thread breakage.[41]

Every half hour or so a piecer used a small brush to wipe off the thread bits that had accumulated on the face of the machine. Twice a day, at nine in the morning and at two in the afternoon, she had to do a more thorough cleaning of her area. Since cotton dust was constantly drifting in the air, after several hours a thin layer of white dust covered every exposed part of the spinning machine. A piecer used her brush to dust the ring plate and the lappets in front of her.[42]

Several times during the day a male worker oiled the spinning frame. As the spindles filled with thread, doffers passing through swiftly removed the full spindles and put them in a large container. They put full containers in the aisle, and male movers periodically came to take them to the winding and weaving departments.

The Number Ones responsible for the workers in one section of the spinning room spent the day walking back and forth, making sure that everyone was working; an overseer was responsible for the entire spinning room. The extent to which these supervisors actively disciplined the workers varied from mill to mill. "In some cases," a British mill inspector observed, "one saw overlookers walking about with a little cane with which they tapped the hands of any young operatives not doing their work well."[43] Sometimes they were harsher, beating workers who made mistakes in their work.

The small percentage of male Number Ones in the spinning room often combined sexual harassment with routine discipline, flirting with the women workers and patting them on the face as they made their rounds through the workshops.[44] A woman who did not submit to their advances risked punishment or even firing. Since the work a woman was assigned in the workshop depended entirely on the whims of the Number One, she could scarcely afford to jeopardize her relationship with him. "In the spinning room we had this situation," Wang Luoying recalled. "One of the foremen was male. Then if there were young girl workers who did not have a mate, he would want them to be his mate, and sleep with him. If a girl went along with him he would give her more comfortable work. . . . If you did not go along with the male foreman, he could give you lousy and hard work. Because of this situation some women just left the mill to go somewhere else to work."[45] The Shanghai daily newspaper frequently reported stories similar to that of a woman worker at the Japanese-owned Dong Hua Mill: an overseer propositioned her, she refused, and he beat her badly, causing serious injuries.[46]

A REST

Relations between women workers and the Number Ones were not uniformly antagonistic. Sometimes, for example, when women workers needed to rest, the Number Ones collaborated with the operators. In all Japanese mills the overseers retired to the tearoom at 9:00 A.M. for an hour break. If the Number One in her department was sympathetic, a piecer could take advantage of the overseer's absence and rest. The worker walked to the aisle as soon as the overseer was gone and turned off the motor running the spindles on her frame. The bobbins of roving instantly stopped whirling and the thread feeding the spindles froze in place. Either the Number One or one of the other operators would stand guard, watching for the overseer to return, and then signal the workers to resume production. They knew that if they were caught they would be fined or fired.[47]

Even if the overseer did not leave the workshop, a piecer, perspiring and tired from several hours of dashing back and forth through her aisle to join broken threads, could still take an unofficial rest break. Scores of young girls brought into the spinning room by friends or relatives were grateful to be given an opportunity to practice piecing while she sat down for a rest.

By this time the piecer may have wanted to use the toilet. Every workshop had a lavatory, but (as explained earlier) a worker was not allowed to use it without first obtaining a bamboo bathroom chit. A worker who wanted to use the toilet waited for the Number One to pass her spinning frame and then requested one of the chits. There were a fixed number of chits, and if others were using them she had to wait until the next time the Number One came by.[48]

At the lavatory door she encountered a female guard who checked the chit before allowing her to enter. The guard was also supposed to make sure that the woman was not trying to take scraps of cotton or yarn into the bathroom to use as a sanitary napkin; if she caught a woman doing this, she was to report the incident to the mill management immediately.[49] The guard made sure that the woman did not spend too much time inside, for many women prolonged their stay in the bathroom in order to rest. If the guard performed her job diligently, she would periodically burst into the bathroom to see that women were not chatting or combing their hair. Women caught combing their hair in the bathroom paid a fine of one day's wage.[50]

Learning to arrange for unofficial breaks—by turning off the machine, by calling a trainee to substitute, or by going to the bathroom—was part of adjusting to mill life. One woman recalled being appalled by the lackadaisical attitude the more experienced workers showed in taking time off. On her first day in the mill, she wrote,

my foot started to hurt, and my waist was aching. I saw that there were . . . people who were secretly sitting on the floor to rest. I was too scared, and had to just put up with standing at my machine and watching for broken threads. Finally I really could not stand it any longer, and decided to take a risk. I motioned to Axi [the woman who had introduced her into the mill] to go with me to the bathroom. I sat down on the *matong* [toilet box], and then I did not want to get up again. Axi was still sitting there, and I did not want to be the one to suggest that we get up, even though I had finished urinating long ago. For ten minutes I sat there, and it seemed like I was asleep when Axi finally roused me and we returned to the machines.[51]

The only official rest period for workers was lunch. At most mills they were allowed a half hour to eat, usually beginning at 10:00 but sometimes not until noon.[52] Although there were canteens in most mills, they were only for overseers, office staff, and managers; workers ate at their machines. When it was time to eat, they took their baskets of cold rice with a bit of bean curd, salted fish, or vegetable on top to a hot water outlet and held them under the tap, letting the boiling water pour onto the rice, filter through, and drip out the bottom. Having thus warmed their food, they returned to their machines and ate.[53] In Japanese mills the machines were switched off during lunch. In most Chinese and British mills, however, the machines did not stop during lunch, so the women alternated: while one group ate, the other group tended their own machines and the machines of those who were eating.[54] There were frequent complaints that these conditions were not sanitary, and hence the management of the Yong An mills was commended for allowing workers to use the rice-steaming box in the canteen, which could hold more than fifty baskets at once.[55]

Every mill had a number of women who had recently given birth, and these women used the lunch break not only to eat their meals but to nurse their babies as well. Some mothers occasionally gave their infants opium so that they could work while their babies slept in the workshop.[56] "In many mills," the Shanghai Child Labor Commission reported, "rows of baskets containing babies and children, sleeping or awake as the case may be, lie placed between the rapidly moving and noisy machinery."[57] Other young mothers carried their babies on their backs as they worked. The advantage of these arrangements, which were ostensibly forbidden by most mill managers, was that women could nurse their infants without interrupting their work: some women workers, "while feeding their children at the breast, continue to work at the machines."[58]

For the majority of mothers, who left their babies at home, making arrangements for nursing was a much more complicated procedure. Someone from home had to bring the child to the mill for nursing. "After I gave birth," one worker recalled, "every day my mother would bring the baby to the factory gate at noon so I could nurse it. . . . I would eat and nurse my child at the same time."[59] Before 1945 none of the mills had nurseries; however, several mills set aside a "nursing room." A family member still had to bring the child to the mill, but instead of standing at the mill gate, they could, at the stipulated time, bring the child inside the mill and meet the mother in the nursing room. Afterward whoever had brought the child carried it back home, and the worker returned to her machine.[60]

SPINNING TILL SIX

After lunch there were no official breaks. A piecer continued to tend her machine, and the afternoon was a repeat of the morning: the tedium of work punctuated by routine cleanings, visits of the oiler, sweepers, bobbin movers, and supervisors, and an occasional trip to the bathroom.

The workday ended as it had begun. At 5:45 a worker from the other shift arrived and prepared to take over the machine; at 6:00 a whistle sounded, ending the twelve-hour shift.[61] The day shift piecer prepared to leave. She changed out of her grease clothes, and before leaving the workshop might quickly comb her hair, brush on some face powder, and peek in a small pocket mirror.[62]

As a worker reached the exit she had to be searched before leaving the mill premises. At the exit of a cotton mill there was a barricade to prevent workers from rushing out and avoiding the search. The barricade, made of wood or iron, was either a zigzag maze or a revolving turnstile that only one worker could pass through at a time.[63] In several mills workers were encouraged to surrender whatever scrap materials they might be trying to pilfer from the mill before entering the barricade. One American commercial agent described "red boxes attached to pillars near the barricade, a large white hand pointing to the opening in the boxes, and underneath an inscription to the following effect: 'Have you something in your pocket? Ask your heart. You do not want to steal. If the answer is Yes, put it at once into this box.' In about fourteen days every box is full of all kinds of waste, bobbins, bits of cloth, etc."[64]

Whether or not she had voluntarily returned filched materials, a worker had to join the single-file line to pass through the barricade. Men and women formed separate lines; female guards searched the female workers, and male guards or Sikh policemen searched the men.[65] Waiting in line to be searched added as much as an hour to the time a worker spent inside the mills. By the time she left the mill, with a layer of white cotton fluff stuck to her hair and clothes, she had been there close to thirteen hours.[66]

GOING HOME

When she left the mill, a woman often had to contend with male workers who saw this time as an opportunity to have some fun with the women. "Whenever the Wing On Cotton Mill at Markham Road dismisses workers in the evening, men workers always tease and make fun of the women workers, resulting often in fights," a daily paper reported in 1935. "Pootoo Road and Gordon Road police stations in the neighborhood make it a practice to detail special police at such times to maintain order and prevent trouble. Yesterday the police had to use force to disperse a crowd of men workers who were troubling women workers. In escaping from the police a girl worker accidentally fell into Soochow Creek, and was drowned before she could be rescued."[67]

The hoodlums who roamed the working-class districts presented a more serious threat. Most of them belonged to neighborhood gangs: the Black Tigers, the White Tigers, the Number One Dragons, and so on.[68] "You could tell hoodlums by their dress," a woman who had worked in a cotton mill recalled. "The male hoodlums wore Western suits and overcoats and long Chinese-style gowns with the sleeve cuffs rolled up.

They usually had tattoos on their arm. And they wore a hat."[69] These hoodlums were constant antagonists in the daily lives of women mill workers.

Sexual harassment was the most obvious threat they posed. "Hoodlums would wait at the mill gate, and if you were a pretty woman they would force you to sleep with them," recalled Rong Peiqiu, formerly a Number One. Other hoodlums loitered in the streets, then flirted with and pursued women as they made their way home from the mill. Even homes were not a haven from these neighborhood toughs. One woman had caught the attention of a particular hoodlum several days in a row as she walked home. At nine o'clock one night, when everyone else was out, he broke into her house and raped her several times.[70] Powerful hoodlums, such as the western district's famous Wu Fangzhang, often used coercion to make women their mistresses. One woman remembered having to temporarily quit her job at the mill when the pressure to leave her husband became unbearable.[71]

But sexual abuse was only part of the problem. Women who were wage earners were a source of income not to be overlooked by the neighborhood gangs. Hoodlums invented a variety of schemes to claim a share of the money women earned in the mills. Some sound imaginative, if not far-fetched, yet so many women recall similar experiences that it seems safe to conclude that they were a common part of working-class life.

One method of extortion was to accuse a woman and her husband of committing adultery and then force them to pay to redeem their innocence. This could happen as in the following scenario. A woman walked to work with her husband, and because it was raining they huddled close together under a single umbrella. As they approached the mill a hoodlum suddenly blocked their way, hurling accusations at them. "That's my wife," he exclaimed, "and you are trying to go off with her!" In order to resolve this "misunderstanding," the couple had to pay the hoodlum a sum of money. If they refused to pay he forced them to go to the police station, where he insisted to the police officers that the woman was his wife. Since hoodlums usually worked in collusion with policemen (who were themselves usually gang members), there was little possibility of obtaining justice. Both the police and the hoodlum could extort money from the couple, in exchange for which they would be released.[72]

Another trick hoodlums used to collect money from both male and female workers was to insist on compensation for alleged bodily harm. For example, as a woman walked home from work, a hoodlum intentionally bumped into her and, accusing her of having injured him, insisted that she pay. Or he might trip a woman, accuse her of having damaged his shoe, and demand compensation for the cost of repairing the shoe. The purchase of groceries provided an opportunity for yet another variation of this practice: as a peddler ladled pickled vegetables into a container for the woman, a hoodlum might intentionally fall against the peddler's arm, causing salty water to drip onto his clothes. The woman purchasing the pickles would be held responsible for the damage and have to pay.[73] Finally, there was a method called "stripping a sheep." A hoodlum would grab a woman and steal her clothes, which he could then sell, and often would seize the opportunity to rape her as well. (Stealing the clothes of a child was called "stripping a frog," and when the victim was an adult man, it was called "stripping a pig.")[74]

Compared with these practices, the most common method of extorting money from women, that is, to simply ask for it, must have seemed almost civil. "On any occasion they could think of—holidays, marriages, births, birthdays, or funerals—the gangsters would send invitations to everyone in our neighborhood," a worker explained. "When you received an invitation you had to send them money, or else they would come and beat you up. We usually sent one or two dollars, about one-fifth of a month's wage. It was not just one hoodlum who sent them. We received invitations from lots of them."[75] Those who did not comply were instantly reprimanded. When a woman worker named Yang Meiying failed to satisfy a hoodlum's request for money, he sent several of his underlings to pay her a visit. "They pulled my hair, and took some of it out. This kind of thing happened all the time."[76]

Most of these activities were obviously in the purview of male hoodlums. But not all hoodlums were male. "Oh, lots and lots of hoodlums were women!" one woman exclaimed.

"You could tell which women were hoodlums," another woman added. "They dressed very well. They wore silk, not cotton, and they ate much better than us. They wore long silk gowns and gold necklaces."[77] Some female hoodlums were moneylenders; others ran brothels. Many kidnapped young girls and sold them to brothels. "One of the commonest crimes in Shanghai is kidnapping," Mary Gamewell reported during her visit in 1916. "Most of the kidnappers are women, and the nefarious business is so lucrative that a large number are engaged in it. Kidnappers grow bold as well as wily, picking up children at play on the street, or off on errands, and even beguiling or snatching them away from their very doors. . . . Pretty little girls are always easily disposed of, either in brothels or in private homes as slaves or future daughters-in-law."[78] Many of these kidnappers belonged to the Green Gang, which since the early twentieth century had included women as well as men.[79]

Developing ways to protect oneself from the gangs was the key to survival in Shanghai's working-class neighborhoods. Many women "pledged sisterhood" with their friends, promising to protect one another while going to and from the mill (see Chapter Eight). Often, however, the assistance of other young women was not adequate to contend with the hoodlums. Many workers found that actually joining the gangs or establishing formal relations with a gang leader was the only effective form of defense against harassment. "Male workers would find a male hoodlum and women workers would find a female hoodlum," Zhu Fanu recalled. "When male workers pledged to a hoodlum it was called pledging to an 'old head,' and when women workers did it, it was called pledging to a godmother or pledging to the wife of a hoodlum. When you found the person who would protect you, you would send him or her presents. Then if another hoodlum ever bothered you, you could go tell your patron and he or she would take care of you."[80] As we saw in Chapter Four the person chosen by a woman worker to be her pledged godmother was often the Number One in her workshop. By choosing her Number One a woman could protect both her job and her personal safety.

Equally fearful of male and female hoodlums, a woman worker was always escorted home. A young girl was sometimes picked up by her mother at the end of the workday. "Until I was thirteen," Gu Lianying recalled, "every evening my mother would pick me up at the mill and walk home with me."[81] A woman often had a parent, sibling, or other relative working at the same mill; she almost always had friends from the same hometown to rely on. "When we'd get off of work we'd walk together, to go home. We did not see much of each other after work, because everyone would just go home and that would be that until the next day."[82]

By the time a woman arrived home, it was already seven or eight in the evening. Since she would have to get up at four or five the next morning, she went to bed by nine or ten o'clock. The evening, then, consisted of only two or three hours—little time for much besides eating, washing, and getting ready for bed.

Preparing dinner, the main meal of the day and the only freshly cooked one, was not a simple procedure. Most of the vegetables had to be purchased each day.[83] There were no big central markets in the working-class districts; instead, peddlers carrying wares on shoulder poles went from lane to lane, offering fresh vegetables, fish, and bean curd. The variety of vegetables depended on the season, but Chinese cabbage, onions, garlic, sweet potatoes, and turnips were almost always available, and in the spring there were soybean pods, spinach, celery, clover, string beans, and tomatoes as well. Bean curd products, available all year, were more usual working-class fare than meat.[84]

Having purchased a basketful of vegetables, the women then had to clean them. Sometimes they used water they had brought home earlier in the day; otherwise they went to get another two buckets. Many women simply took their vegetables to the neighborhood tap, well, or creek and washed their produce and picked away the stems there in the company of their neighbors. Once all the ingredients were prepared, they put some coal briquettes into the stove, waited for it to heat up, and then cooked the rice and one or two other dishes.

Not every female mill worker was responsible for preparing dinner. Whether a woman was expected to cook depended primarily on the composition of her household, and her position in the family. If, for example, she was a young girl whose mother no longer worked at the mill, the mother most likely would have shopped and prepared dinner before the girl even arrived home from work. In many households a grandmother did the cooking. But if a young wife or an adopted daughter-in-law lived with her in-laws, she would be expected to do the cooking, even if the mother-in-law was not employed outside of the home.[85] Sometimes no particular rule, other than convenience, dictated who did the cooking; in some cases it was more convenient for a male member of the family to do it. One woman worked in a different workshop of the same mill as her husband. "Whoever had time or got home first would do the cooking," she recalled. Others related a similar practice.[86]

Of course, some women had no family in Shanghai. Many who had migrated to Shanghai by themselves rented a space in some friend's house and arranged to eat their dinner on a contract basis. Often a working-class family that wanted to make some extra money cooked enough food for seven or eight other people, and a group of young single workers would pay six or seven dollars a month to eat dinner with them.[87] Some stopped for a very quick meal at an "open air cafeteria," usually consisting of a table with a bench on each side, set up along a main street of a working-class neighborhood. At the end of the table there were two coal stoves with pots: one pot contained steaming rice and the other had a vegetable dish with a bit of meat or fish.[88]

After they had eaten dinner and cleaned up, the day was over for most women. "After dinner we wouldn't do much," a worker named Shi Xiaomei recalled. "Lights—well, it cost money to use electric lights. So we didn't have light. We would just go to bed early."[89]

Night Shift: The Working Night

Despite attempts at government regulation and the steadfast opposition of social reformers, mill owners persisted in operating twenty-four hours a day. Although most aspects of the working night were the same as those of the working day, the two shifts were not identical. One difference was that on the night shift women slept fewer hours outside the mill but more hours inside the mill.

As we have seen, night shift workers arrived at work at 5:45 P.M. and began work at 6:00. They worked until midnight, when they had a quarter-hour or half-hour break for dinner.[90] The stretch from one or two in the morning until the shift ended at six was the most trying, and many workers took naps for part of this time. "To anyone who has never seen night work in operation, a visit to a factory round about 4:00 A.M. is a revelation," Agatha Harrison wrote during her visit to Shanghai in the mid-1920's. "Judging from the sleeping, or half asleep workers, one wonders how, apart from every other consideration, night work can be a paying proposition."[91] The fact that so many women took naps did not necessarily reduce productivity. Usually while one woman rested, another took over her job, and then they switched.[92]

Aware of the reality on the shop floor, management in some mills took measures to help workers stay awake through the night. Most mills at least gave night shift workers a *da bing* and a *you tiao* (a long, twisted piece of dough, deep-fried). At the Yong An mills, which enjoyed a reputation for exceptional modernity, "the factory would give us each two biscuits to eat, and then at 3:00 A.M. everyone would get a cup of coffee, so that we would not fall asleep."[93] Despite such preventive measures, few women stayed awake to work the whole night through.

For some women, being able to sleep a greater portion of the time made night work preferable to day work. One Chinese YWCA worker, pleading the cause of abolishing night work in the Shanghai mills, was astonished when she learned of this preference among women workers. "Those who see the social implications of night work for women and the effects on women themselves and society at large, feel that night work for women should be prohibited," she wrote in 1928. "Yet the working women seem to prefer night work. When questioned for a reason, a little girl said in her innocent way, 'I prefer to work at night because the foremen do not watch us closely as they do in the day,' and a woman said, 'It gives me chances to attend to other duties, both social and domestic.'"[94] One worker's recollection made night work sound almost pleasant. "When we did night shift we had free time during the day," Gui Jianying remembered. "We would go see movies, or go window-shopping, or lie on the bed and read."[95]

Night shift workers did have more ways to spend their hours off than day shift workers did. But not all were enthusiastic about this extra time for social and domestic duties. Ideally, after finishing work at 6:00 A.M., a woman returned home, ate breakfast, and went to sleep around nine or ten in the morning. In theory she could sleep until four in the afternoon; in reality, however, sleeping during daytime hours was not always feasible. Since women workers lived in small rooms shared with several other family members, the noise level must have made sleep difficult. A graduate student at Shanghai University who studied the conditions of women factory workers in Yangshupu in 1930 found that few managed to sleep more than a few hours during the day. Explaining the circumstances they might encounter during the day, she related the following incident:

I know a girl worker who is an adopted daughter-in-law in some people's house. One morning I went to visit her at 11:00 A.M. She still had not gone to sleep. After the night shift she had come home, and then had to make food for the rest of the family to eat, and wash clothes. Just when she had been ready to go to bed, suddenly two or three male workers came along. They had come to play cards with her husband-to-be. They sat on the bed and played, gambling too. Their noise filled up the entire room. The girl said to me, "Last night I worked all night, and I had hoped to sleep today. But with this racket, how can I sleep?"[96]

The combination of inadequate sleep and long shifts during the night in humid, dust-filled workshops took its toll on the workers' health. One survey showed that seven out of ten female cotton mill workers who had been on the night shift every other week for two years suffered from tuberculosis.[97]

The Workweek

Except for those who worked in the weaving room, female cotton mill workers alternated day and night shifts. Most mills changed shifts once a week; on Sundays the machines stopped and workers on both shifts had the day off.[98] A woman beginning a week of working on the day shift would enter the mill at 6:00 A.M. on Monday morning and work for six consecutive days. She would be free from Saturday evening until Sunday evening, when at 6:00 P.M. she would begin a week of night shift work.[99]

This was the prescribed routine, but it was not always followed. Often the weekly schedules varied according to fluctuations in the cotton market. When business for yarn and cloth was good, for instance, the mills would try to increase production as much as possible, and one way to do this was to reduce the number of hours the machines were idle on Sundays. To maximize production, management often implemented "Sunday work": those working the night shift Saturday night were required to work until nine or ten o'clock Sunday morning, and those who normally would have been expected to begin work at six o'clock Sunday evening were instead required to begin work at two or three in the afternoon. Each group thus worked fifteen or sixteen consecutive hours. In addition to the extra dimes of wages they paid for the extended hours, most mills gave every worker three *da bing* as remuneration.

The Chinese-owned Xin Yu Mill in western Shanghai became known for practicing the most extreme form of Sunday work. Its requirements were similar to those of other mills in that the night shift workers were released at ten in the morning, and the next week's night shift workers started at 2:30 in the afternoon. However, during the late 1930's, when business was especially good, the mill announced that whichever group of workers in the roving and spinning departments arrived at the mill first on Sunday would get a bonus. The Number Ones would receive one *yuan*, and each of the workers would get two *jiao*. Groups of workers hoping to earn the bonus arrived at the mill at nine to take over as the night shift left, and worked continuously for 21 hours, until 6:00 A.M. the next day.[100]

During times such as the depression of the 1930's, when sales slumped, cotton mill owners reduced the weekly work hours. Workers were given what they called the big weekend, with an extra day off. When there was a big weekend, day shift workers finished their week's work at six on Saturday evening, and the mill was closed Sunday day and night. They did not begin their week of night shift work until Monday evening.[101] Of course, the workers' wages reflected this reduction in work time. Some mills implemented this system during especially hot weather, even in prosperous times.

The so-called big weekend was a moderate form of reduced operations; mills hit especially hard by the depression were forced to curtail operations even more drastically. In 1935 the China correspondent for the International Labor Organization reported that most mills had suspended night work altogether. The British-owned Yi He and Gong Yi mills were open three days per week, the Yong An mills three to five days a week, and the Shen Xin, Xin Yu, and Tong Yi mills four days a week.[102]

A woman's workweek did not always conform to the schedule announced by the mill. Often, for a host of reasons (illness, child care, or family problems) women took days off. The one woman's attendance record that is available shows the extent to which the work year could be abbreviated: she was absent from work 193 days in one year, missing 45 days after giving birth, 74 days while caring for her husband, who suffered from tuberculosis, 28 days while caring for her ailing mother-in-law, 10 more days after her mother-in-law's death, and 36 days while caring for her sick child.[103]

Some young women, presumably those with families not entirely dependent on their income, occasionally took a day off for a reason no more urgent than getting together with friends. "Sometimes these young women workers would rather have a day to relax and have fun than earn a day's wage," one journalist commented.[104] This happened so frequently that almost all mills either imposed fines on those who missed days of work or issued bonuses to those who had perfect attendance records. At one Japanese mill, for example, a woman who did not miss any days of work in a year received a bonus of four *yuan*, one who missed one or two days received two *yuan*, one who missed three or four days received one and a half *yuan*, and one who missed six days received one *yuan*.[105] In some Chinese-owned mills the bonus was calculated with every wage payment, that is, every half month. At the Yong An mills a woman who had a perfect attendance record for two weeks received the equivalent of one day's wage as a bonus. One who was delinquent was fined. In addition to being docked the wages for days not worked (there was no paid sick leave or vacation time) a woman who had missed two days of work was fined the equivalent of a half day's wage; and missing three days of work cost her a full day's wage.[106] Some mills made the penalties even stiffer during the summer months, when women frequently skipped work because of illness and hot weather. They were docked as much as one or two *yuan*, and in some cases they risked being fired for excessive absences.[107]

One final routine that punctuated the workweek of female cotton mill workers was religious observance. Most women workers were Buddhists, although belief in Buddhism meant different things to different women.[108] Some women, like He Ningzhen, were vegetarians. "When I was very young," she recalled, "I had learned to chant all the Buddhist texts. That was because there were all those old women who were picking tea leaves in the hills near our home in Zhejiang. So when I went to help my mother pick tea leaves, I learned from listening to them. Then when I came to Shanghai and worked in the cotton mill, I still never ate any pork or beef. I just ate vegetables."[109] Others abstained from meat only on the first and fifteenth days of each month.

On these days they also would burn incense. "Whenever it is the night of the fourteenth or thirtieth day of the lunar month," one guide to Shanghai noted, "you will undoubtedly be able to hear Pudong women on the streets, yelling that they have incense sticks to sell."[110] Although some women made these offerings in their home, many women liked to go to the local temple, and they often left the mill for several hours to do so. In the 1940's some mills, such as the Shen Xin and Yong An mills, set up small temples with a statue of the bodhisattva Guan Yin on the factory premises. A visitor to the large Shen Xin Number Nine Mill was shown the mill's temple on a tour of the women's dormitory. The mill manager told him that on the first and fifteenth days of each lunar month, as many as two hundred women had been leaving work to go to the Hong

Temple, but by constructing a temple at the mill the management had been able to "eliminate the trouble of so many women leaving the factory to go burn incense and at the same time reduce the factory's losses. It is good to let them go stand in front of the Buddhist idol to grieve and gain some consolation," this visitor was told.[111]

In addition to these visits to Buddhist temples, at least until 1945 there was another biweekly event in the routine of most women workers: payday. Payday was distinguished from ordinary workdays in several ways. First, of course, workers received their wages. Second, because many workers were superstitious, sorceresses would go into the workshops on payday, knowing that workers had cash. They would offer for a fee to use their spiritual powers to tell a worker her fortune, to exorcise devils, or to perform rituals to reduce her future misfortunes.[112]

The final distinguishing aspect of payday took place at the factory gates, where usurers called stamp moneylenders gathered. Usually either local hoodlums or Sikh constables, stamp moneylenders charged interest rates of up to 120 percent a year. This form of usury took its name from a stamp the moneylender would put on the folder that represented the loan contract each time the borrower paid an installment of the debt. On payday, knowing that the workers had cash on hand, the moneylenders came to the mills to try to force them to make payments on their debts as they left work.[113]

Those who managed to retain the money they had been paid were vulnerable to hoodlums, who saw in payday a welcome opportunity to win some cash. In western Shanghai in the early 1920's, there was a hoodlum named Deng Haizhou whose band of underlings specialized in making off with women's wages.[114]

"Rest Days"

Ordinarily, as we have seen, after six days working on one shift in the mill, a worker had a rest day. Although she did not have to go to the mill that day, she did not necessarily use the time to rest.

Laundry and bathing were usually a woman's first order of

business on her day off. Washing clothes required more water than what could be stored in the tub in her house, so on Sundays she took her family's laundry to a public water source. When Lamson surveyed a working-class neighborhood in Yangshupu, he observed that "on Sundays the water [in the wells] is dirtier than other days because it is at that time that the women workers have time to wash their clothes. They do their washing near the wells because of the convenience in drawing the water. Dirty slops are poured on the ground nearby and some of this seeps back into the well."[115] Laundry was women's work. A woman often did the laundry of single male workers in her neighborhood as well as her own family's, thereby earning a few extra coppers.[116] After finishing the laundry for her own family, a young woman worker sometimes had to go to her Number One's home and help her do chores such as washing clothes, mopping the floor, and looking after her children.[117]

Although the tasks involved in cleaning a house were time-consuming, many women also took time for visiting. Most women had relatives in Shanghai, usually in the same neighborhood, and Sunday was a time for family visits. Young women who were not yet married and whose household responsibilities were therefore relatively light often went to see friends. "After working a long time, then you would start to have friends," Gu Lianying remarked. "And on Sundays, if you had time, you could go visit their house. Maybe I started that when I was seventeen or eighteen. All my friends were cotton mill workers."[118] Sometimes they went to a nearby park. More often they would get together and stroll along the shopping streets, window-shopping as they talked. The area around the Big Clock Tower in Xiaoshadu and the circle at Five Corners in Caojiadu were favorite places for young women workers to congregate on Sundays.

Occasionally groups of women workers would go to see performances of local opera. "We used to love to go see Subei operas," recalled Chen Zhaodi, a worker originally from the Binghai district of Subei.

Would women go? Why it was mostly women who went! Not only did we go see the operas, but sometimes we would sing them in the mill workshops. There were two opera troupes that performed in the western district. We would go in the evening, from seven to eleven. It was hard to buy tickets. They cost several *jiao*. We almost never went with our husbands or children. It was usually some of us women who worked together who would go. But I would not tell my family where I was going. My mother-in-law would never have let me go. I just went secretly.[119]

Those who could not afford tickets gathered outside the door of the theater to listen to the singing. Women workers from Shanghai and cities of Jiangnan also liked to hear performances of local opera, but they were not interested in Subei operas. Native Shanghainese, for example, were willing to pay a little bit more for a ticket to hear Suzhou opera at the Bright Moon Teahouse on Ferry Road in west Shanghai.*

Another place workers visited on their day off was the so-called Great World of the Western District. Unlike the famous Great World amusement center on Tibet Road, its namesake was a makeshift operation resembling a temple fair. Every Sunday thirty or forty shacks were set up in a vacant lot, some featuring snacks such as noodles, soup, or cakes; others, juggling and story-telling. There were three stages for Peking opera performances, two for Subei opera, and one for Suzhou opera.[120]

Whether women went to the Great World of the Western District, to opera performances, to a shopping district, or to friends' or relatives' homes, they rarely left their own neighborhoods. "No matter what we were doing we would always be in Yangshupu," Gu Lianying said. "We almost never went into the city."[121] Although Yangshupu and most other working-class districts were technically part of Shanghai, many women thought of these places as distinct villages. To them

*The extent to which pride and prejudice based on regionalism were manifested by operagoers was made most clear to me when I naïvely asked an old woman worker from Subei whether she ever went to see performances of *Yueju*. (*Yueju* is the kind of opera that originated in the area around Shaoxing.) An older male factory official present at the interview indignantly interrupted to explain to me that "they [people from Subei] did not go to see *Yueju*. Most people in this mill are Jiangbei people, and so they would not go to see *our Yueju*. *Yueju*—that's something for us Shaoxing, Ningbo, and Yuyao people to see. Subei people did not go to that. People like Chen Shifu would go to see Jianghuai operas."

Shanghai meant the banks and business offices along the Bund, and the department stores and shops lining Nanjing Road. They had little reason to visit these downtown areas, and moreover, there were no buses or even paved roads connecting some working-class districts to "the city."[122] Only on holidays did some women venture into downtown Shanghai.

Holidays

Each mill had its own holidays. Almost all included three days off for the Spring Festival (the lunar New Year), a day off for the Dragon Boat Festival (on the fifth day of the fifth month of the lunar calendar), and a day off for the Mid-Autumn Festival (on the fifteenth day of the eighth month). Several mills also observed Sun Yat-sen's birthday (November 12) and Independence Day (October 10).[123]

The Spring Festival was the holiday involving the most extensive preparations and festivities. "No matter how poor you were, everyone celebrated Spring Festival," Chen Zhaodi recalled.* Most workers spent the first three days of the new year visiting relatives or entertaining guests. Even workers with little or no money bought foods that they otherwise never ate: chicken, duck, and New Year's cake. To entertain guests many also served tea, peanuts, melon seeds, candy, and Shaoxing wine or sorghum liquor.[124]

For those who were Buddhists, going to a temple was part of the New Year festivities. Some walked as far as the Long Hua Temple, in a suburb on the southern edge of Shanghai. "We used to believe that if you went to the Long Hua Temple three years in a row and burned incense," Xu Shumei recalled, "then you would have a better afterlife."[125] More commonly workers went to the Temple of the City God at the center of the old Chinese city.

---

*Interview with Chen Zhaodi, Shanghai, Apr. 11, 1981. During the 1930's, the Nationalist government declared New Year to be the first three days of January. Some mills subsequently switched their New Year holiday to conform to this edict. They found, however, that whether or not the lunar New Year was an official holiday, workers took three days off, so they reverted to the traditional practice. See Augusta Wagner, *Labor Legislation in China* (Beijing, 1938), p. 43.

At the city temple there were sixty idols, one for every age from one to sixty. You would go to the one for your age that year. My mother and I went every year at New Year. At that time there were so many people there that you could not move an inch. You really did not have to walk. The crowd was so thick that you would just get pushed along by the other people. Sometimes there were so many people burning incense at the temple that the idols would catch on fire and burn![126]

Another New Year ritual was visiting a fortune-teller, who predicted the events of the coming year. "The fortune-teller was a blind person," Xu recalled. "He sat on the sidewalk and beat a gong with a hammer to attract people." Almost inevitably the first prediction was dreadful, but for an additional fee the fortune-teller could be persuaded to provide a more optimistic forecast.[127]

The Spring Festival was one of the few times when workers might venture to the downtown districts of Shanghai and visit the famous amusement halls. "It took about an hour to walk there from our house," remembered a woman who went with her father and older brother each year during the Spring Festival. "You could eat and see all kinds of performances. And once you bought a ticket to go in, you were entitled to stay until they closed, way after midnight."[128]

Celebrations of the Mid-Autumn Festival and the Dragon Boat Festival in summer were less elaborate. At the time of the Mid-Autumn Festival, workers went to special stores to purchase candles, incense, and moon god statuettes. "You could buy big or little statuettes, just depending on how much money you had," Xu said. On the eve of the holiday it was customary to arrange a plate with apples, pears, a moon cake, soybeans, and perhaps a fish head, and place it in front of the household's moon god statue, with burning incense sticks on each side of the statue. The next day family members ate whatever had not been devoured by the gods. Those women who agreed to forgo the holiday and work at the mill were given two moon cakes. At the time of of the Dragon Boat Festival, they were rewarded for choosing to work with two *zongzi* (bamboo leaves filled with glutinous rice and pork and folded in triangles), the traditional food eaten on that holiday.[129]

One further aspect of a worker's celebration of holidays might be to express gratitude to, or to ingratiate herself with, the Number One of her workshop and the leader of the local gang. When there was a holiday a woman often purchased gifts, usually food or spirits, to send as a gift to her patrons.

The working day for women in the Shanghai mills was long, demanding, and in some ways brutal. After twelve hours of operating a machine in a hot, dusty, and noisy workshop, many returned home only to face the chores of maintaining a household. Women workers, however, did not experience the daily routine as lonely, isolated individuals, nor were they completely passive victims of capitalist exploitation and industrial poverty. Part of a mill worker's experience was learning to manipulate the contours of the workday: a worker often took naps while a friend or trainee took over her work, she knew how to slow down the machines, she pretended to lose her work card so a neighbor could take her place at work while she took several days off—and still she collected a bonus for perfect attendance.

In order to do these things a woman depended on her co-workers. This dependence was perhaps most urgently felt after work, when a woman who walked home by herself was vulnerable to attack by hoodlums. Out of the need for mutual aid and protection, as Chapter Eight will show, emerged the first spontaneous organizations among women workers. But working in a gigantic factory that employed several thousand workers of varied origins did not radically transform a woman's social relationships. The number of people with whom she had contact during the course of a day was very small. After entering the mill she went to her workshop and spent most of the day in the area to which she was assigned. She might leave the confines of that area to go to the toilet or to get hot water to pour over her rice at lunchtime, but she almost never had occasion to visit other workshops.

Hence she did not feel a sense of identity with all women workers; in fact most relationships of work sharing and mutual assistance described in this chapter were based on the traditional connections of native place previously discussed in

Chapter Three. A woman who visited her friends on Sundays or who went with them to parks or to operas was perpetuating the bonds forged between people from a common hometown who stuck together to survive in a complicated, and in many ways threatening, urban environment.

Although the large metropolis of Shanghai must often have overwhelmed a woman who came from a rural village, the world in which she lived her daily life was small and self-contained. The routine of the workday required that she go no farther than the mill, and when she had time off she almost always visited friends and relatives in the same neighborhood or sought entertainment in a nearby theater. She had almost no contact with workers in other districts or with the world of downtown Shanghai. In many ways she lived the life of an "urban villager," raising chickens, purchasing food from street peddlers, washing vegetables and laundry in a group gathered at a neighborhood well or creek, just as peasants did in the countryside. She insisted on preserving her traditional religious practices, even if this meant defying mill rules. It was with her fellow urban villagers in Shanghai—those who lived in the same alley or worked in the same workshop or went to the same temples or operas—that a woman mill worker found ways to survive in the industrial world of Shanghai.

CHAPTER SEVEN   Working Lives

Although a woman may have spent more days working for a cotton mill than in any other occupation, cotton mill work usually represented only one part of her work history. She may also have been a farmer, a home handicraft worker, a cocoon beater, a street vendor, and sometimes even a beggar. Some, as we have seen, were sold into prostitution. Most were at some time wives, daughters-in-law, and mothers.

These varied experiences suggest that there was for most no simple, clear-cut transition from peasant to proletarian. Although there was a working class in Shanghai throughout the decades following World War I, we find that the membership of that class was constantly shifting as women moved in and out of the mills, back and forth between the countryside and the city. Even in the city the line between peasant and proletarian was blurred, because a woman who worked in a cotton mill one year might spend the next year eking out a living by picking vegetables in the suburbs near the mills.

Dutiful Daughters

Whether she was born and raised in a rural village or in Shanghai, a woman who was eventually drawn into the cotton mills had been working for her family since she was a young girl. From the time she was five or six years old, a daughter was expected to help perform the tasks necessary for her family's survival, usually (at least at first) within the confines of her home. She rarely earned an independent wage, yet the fact that a daughter could do housework often made it possible for her parents to do work that did secure an income for the family.

The geographic and economic differences between Jiangnan and Subei are reflected in the kinds of work women from the two areas remember having done as young girls. "When I was young I would help my parents in the fields," Wang Luoying recalled of her childhood in Yancheng, in Subei. "Then there were lots of complicated things to do, working in the fields: we had to plant seeds, cut weeds, collect the crops. I would usually go pull weeds. We had to pull them; otherwise the rice or grain or beans could not grow. Also we would eat the wild plants I picked because the grain was not enough for us to eat."[1] Another woman, born in the Subei county of Xinghua, remembered working as a hired laborer along with her father and brother. At first she helped carry buckets of water to irrigate the fields; later, when she was about twelve, she guided the plough while her father and brother walked ahead in a harness and pulled it. She also helped her mother wash clothes and take care of her younger brothers and sisters.[2] Young girls in Subei commonly tended cows or helped their families collect salt. Some, when they were seven or eight, were considered old enough to help paddle the small wooden boats used to transport goods from one village to another.[3]

In Jiangnan villages handicrafts were more often a central part of the household economy than they were in Subei. Records of women workers who grew up in places such as Wuxi and Changzhou indicate that many learned to spin and weave cotton at home, as young girls. In Jiangyin, when hand weaving became widespread in the mid-1930's, young girls helped their mothers operate the looms in their homes. By taking turns they could weave continuously, for twenty-four hours each day. Other girls in Jiangyin, whose mothers knit socks for merchants under a putting-out system, helped by cutting out and attaching the trademark.[4]

Women who grew up in Shanghai had more varied early work experiences. Some, like those from Jiangnan villages, helped with spinning and weaving in their homes. Many were workers' daughters and from an early age they were expected to help with household chores so that their mothers could go out to work. The parents of some Shanghai-born girls did piecework for different kinds of shops, and by helping them young girls could increase the amount their parents earned. For example, a woman worker named Xu Hongmei grew up in the suburbs of Shanghai, in Baoshan where her parents owned some land. Her father farmed, her mother worked in a cotton mill, and she and her sisters helped her father with farm work. During the slack season her father would sew clothes in a shop owned by foreigners in the International Settlement. "My father would go there every day," she recalled. "He would have to leave at six in the morning, and he would not come back until the evening. He was paid according to how much he sewed every day, so if he brought some extra home for us to do he could earn more. Therefore during those times we worked in the fields during the day and at night we helped my father sew. I did this until I was twelve years old."[5]

The parents of some girls performed production tasks in their homes for factories. For certain operations in the matchmaking industry, for instance, middlemen distributed materials to women who did the jobs at home. The Shanghai Child Labor Commission found in 1924 that much of the work of making match boxes was actually done by five- to ten-year-old girls who worked alongside their mothers at home.[6]

Education was rarely part of the childhood experience of a woman who eventually worked in cotton mills.[7] More often a young girl was sent to work partly so that her brothers could go to school. Contemporary sociologists were impressed by the fact that girls became wage earners at a much earlier age than their brothers. While conducting her study of the budgets of 368 women workers in Shanghai, Cora Deng "often heard girls say that they were working in order to help with the family income while their brothers were learning a trade or attending school so as to be able to find employment at higher wages."[8] Herbert Lamson found that whereas girls became wage earners by the age of eleven or twelve, their brothers did not begin earning an income until they were twenty.[9]

BECOMING WAGE EARNERS

Most cotton mill workers began their factory careers as child workers, when they were nine or ten years old.[10] The decision as to when they would leave home to work was made by their parents and depended on both the availability of jobs and the family's financial situation. Some girls, like Song Ermei, entered the work force as their mothers withdrew. After working at a mill for many years, her mother became ill, and moreover she had an infant to care for. Song's mother quit working and Song worked instead."[11]

Once a girl began working as a wage earner, her contribution to the family income was often a critical one. In the twenty-one budgets of working families investigated by Lamson, the wages brought home by girls under the age of fifteen accounted for an average of 19.7 percent of a family's entire income. Lamson further calculated that with their daughters' contribution this group of working families had an average yearly surplus of $36.07, whereas without their contribution the families would have had an average deficit of $75.95 each year.[12] The importance of daughters' wages to the families was reflected in the attitudes of their parents, who began to regard daughters as valuable economic assets rather than the financial liability they had traditionally been perceived to be. Lamson's student investigators were struck by the changed attitude of parents toward their working daughters.

[One] woman stated to the investigator, "Yes, really today boys and girls are just the same. Girls can also support their parents. To me girls are better than boys, for my elder son is now seventeen years old, and since his graduation from primary school . . . he just stays at home with nothing to do."

In one family visited a mother was found preparing the evening meal in the late afternoon. The investigator noted and remarked on the fact that she was cooking some meat. The mother replied, "I myself do not eat this meat because it costs too much, 30 coppers for about two days' worth. It is for my daughter who is working in the factory and earning the money, so I have to treat her better."[13]

The fact that they now earned wages of their own made their first factory jobs different from their previous work. Many contemporary observers were struck by the increased sense of independence from their families displayed by young women who earned wages. Some, especially those who had just begun to work, turned their full wages over to their parents. But although most women continued to give a portion of the money they earned to their families until they married, as they grew older many began to keep some for themselves. Deng discovered that of the 368 women workers whose budgets she studied in 1937, 289 lived in their parents' homes, and of these, 127 (44 percent) gave their parents only part of their wages. "In talking with the girls on this point," Deng wrote, "they told the writer that in keeping part of their earnings they had more freedom about buying the clothes they wanted and also did not have to get permission from elders in the family. In a few cases, girls stated that in order to avoid turning over all of their earnings into the family purse, they simply did not report to the elders their total earnings."[14] They used the money they kept to purchase adornments that they otherwise would not have had the money, or the permission, to buy. Lamson was struck by the number of women who worked in the mills of Yangshupu who were buying such things as silk handkerchiefs, wristwatches, gold earrings, face powder or cream, and fashionable clothing.[15]

This phenomenon of fashionable young women workers often became newsworthy owing to the family conflicts it engendered. In one such case Xiao Feng, a nineteen-year-old from Yancheng, used the money she earned to buy a *qi pao*, to have her shoes embroidered, and to have her hair bobbed. When the aunt with whom she lived chastised and reprimanded her for this "inappropriate" behavior, Xiao Feng ran away from home and could not be found. It was suspected that she had gone to live with her boyfriend.[16]

An extreme statement of independence was made by those women who left their families' homes. Deng found a small group of women in the sample she studied who used their earnings to rent a room with several other women workers or to live in a YWCA hostel, despite the fact that their families all lived close to the factories where they worked. "These girls wanted to be independent and have more freedom than was possible if they lived with their families," Deng noted.[17]

For the vast majority of women, however, wage earning was not the harbinger of independence from the family that many observers believed it to be. In Deng's group, although 127 women kept part of their wages to spend as they pleased,

150 women gave all their earnings to their parents, who in return provided them with food, shelter, clothing, and sundries.[18] The majority of these women, then, did not have much say about how the money they earned was spent; it simply became part of the family treasury. This is the arrangement Yu Rong recalled: "As soon as I got my wages I gave the money to my mother, and then she would use it to buy things for the family."[19]

Whatever independence wage earning could have given women was probably counterbalanced by the important ways in which factory work strengthened ties with the family. A woman almost always went to her first job outside the home in the company of her mother or siblings. Yu Rong went to work in the same silk filature as her mother: her mother worked upstairs separating cocoons and she worked downstairs beating cocoons. Xu Hongmei's first job was in the silk filature where her two older sisters worked. A woman originally from Yancheng entered the Shen Xin Number Two Cotton Mill in 1925 with her older sister, and the two of them operated one reeling machine together. When the sister became ill and died, their mother took her place.[20] These stories are echoed by hundreds of others.

FROM BEATING COCOONS TO THREADING BOBBINS

Many women who later worked in cotton mills, whether they were from Subei, Jiangnan, or Shanghai proper, began their careers in silk filatures. The most important reason was that they could get work in the filatures at an earlier age: whereas silk filatures relied on eight- or nine-year-old girls to perform the painful task of beating silk cocoons in boiling water, cotton mills preferred to hire girls who were at least in their early teens.[21]

The conditions under which girls worked in the silk filatures were repeatedly deplored by Chinese social reformers and foreign visitors. According to the 1924 report of the Shanghai Child Labor Commission,

nearly all the young employees in the silk filatures are women and young girls. Generally speaking, one child is employed for every two adults. The children brush the cocoons and prepare them for the reelers by removing the waste and so exposing the silk thread. This operation is performed over basins containing nearly boiling water with which the fingers of the children frequently and necessarily come in contact, thereby becoming roughened and unsightly. . . . Owing to the presence of the hot water in the basins the temperature of the workroom is always considerably above the normal and the atmosphere is very humid. It was stated that fainting in hot weather is not uncommon. In the main the children present a pitiable sight. Their physical condition is poor, and their faces are devoid of any expression of happiness or well-being. They appear to be miserable, both physically and mentally. . . . The Commission is satisfied that the conditions under which these children are employed are indefensible.[22]

Beating cocoons, understandably, was considered one of the least desirable jobs available to women workers in Shanghai. "My work was beating the cocoons," Yu Rong recalled.

There were two big caldrons. They would be filled with boiling water, and . . . we would have to keep pushing the cocoons down under the water. The cocoons would have to be boiled until they were very soft before the thread could be pulled off.

When we worked in the silk filature our hands would swell up every night. So we would go to the medicine store and buy an ointment. We would put that on and then wrap up our hands. They would hurt and hurt at night.[23]

The pathos of work in the silk filatures was intensified by the way supervisors treated the young cocoon beaters. Forewomen did not always simply reprimand or beat girls who made mistakes but frequently punished the girls by hurling boiling water at them.[24] Most girls did not work in the filatures more than a year or two; they left as soon as they could find work elsewhere. "I could not stand working there," said a woman who had begun beating cocoons when she was nine years old.

So I told my mother that I wanted to quit. . . . Finally I met another girl who was my age. She worked in a cotton mill, and said it was probably a little better than silk filatures. At least they did not have boiling water. I asked her if she could get me a job in the mill. She said they were hiring then, and she could help. She was working night shift then, and told me to wait for her at the gate at 4:00 A.M., and then she would introduce me.[25]

Not all girls went directly from silk filatures to cotton mills. In between, some worked in wool or hemp mills, sock-knitting or safety-pin-making workshops, or candy-wrapping sheds. "From when I was nine until I was sixteen, I worked in five different factories," Shi Xiaomei recalled.[26] Once they had begun working as wage earners, they could scarcely afford to quit.

Getting a job in a cotton mill was considered a step up for most young girls. Besides the feeling that the working environment of a mill, despite the noise and dust, was undoubtedly preferable to that of a silk filature, the cotton industry was the only one that offered women year-round employment. Usually silk firms rented filatures for the number of months it would take to exhaust the cocoons they had purchased, and once the supply was processed the filatures were closed and the workers dismissed until the next year.[27] The work for women in wool-spinning and -weaving mills also was intermittent. "When they had wool they would look for workers," Shi Xiaomei recalled of the time she worked in a wool mill, "and when they didn't have wool, you would just go home."[28] Although the jobs in tobacco and egg plants were generally considered easier and were better-paying, these factories, too, hired women on a seasonal basis.[29]

Prospects for Millhands

Although babies and children accompanying their mothers were a common sight in Shanghai cotton mills, most girls did not begin working in the mills until they were in their early teens. As new hands they were classified as unskilled workers. It was usually several months before they took their first step up, graduating to the status of skilled worker. There were several ways to acquire a skill in the mill. The most common was to sneak into a workshop, learn a skill from a friend or relative on the sly, and then apply for a regular job when there was an opening. The other, less common, method of starting a career was to enter as a *yangchenggong*, or apprentice. After spending a year or two in a formal training program (during which time she was paid less than regular workers) an apprentice could take a test; if she passed, she was assigned a permanent position.[30]

Once she had achieved the status of skilled worker, a woman could move further up in the hierarchy of mill jobs in several other ways. Mobility for a woman most frequently meant being reclassified within her own workshop. For almost every job that a woman did in the mills, there was a series of ranks, each paid a slightly higher wage than the rank below. A woman progressed from one rank to a higher one because of seniority and because of the skill she had developed. We have a detailed description of how promotions worked in the Japanese-owned mills in 1925. An unskilled teenage worker entered as an apprentice and earned 0.15 *yuan* each day for two months while she studied a particular job. At the end of two months, if she passed a test, she became a tenth-grade worker. After three more months she might qualify to move up to the eighth grade; after six more months she could rise to the sixth grade. At the end of one year of steady work she would be somewhere between the first and fifth grades. There could be a difference of almost one half *yuan* per day in the wages paid for the lowest and the highest grades.[31]

In addition to differences in wages there were sometimes slight variations in the tasks assigned each rank. Although these differences might seem minor, they were significant to the workers, who were extremely conscious of their status in the mill hierarchy. This is evident in Chen Zhaodi's recollection of receiving treatment inappropriate to her rank:

When I entered the roving department at Nei Wai Thirteen I was a first-grade worker because my skill level was already high. If you were a first-grade worker, you did not have to carry the yarn back and forth yourself. Lower-grade workers did that. But the Japanese overseer wanted me to carry the yarn. I said I couldn't carry it, and anyway, I was a first-grade worker, so why should I do that? The overseer said, "Okay, then we will make you a second-grade worker!"[32]

Progressing from the lowest to the highest rank for a particular job was one kind of mobility available within a department. In addition, within each department there were several
types of jobs, some easier, some harder, each with different
remuneration. The wages paid to women working in the spinning department of the Tong Xing Mill in 1938 ranged from
0.50 *yuan* to 0.95 *yuan* a day, depending on whether the
woman was a piecer, a doffer, or a "group head," a machine
operative who assumed some supervisory responsibilities. In
other words, some women were earning about $14 a month,
and others were paid almost $27, nearly twice as much.[33]

The highest position women workers could aspire to was
that of forewoman, or Number One. (Anyone holding a
higher position did not come from the ranks of the workers.)
Only a very small percentage of women workers ever became
Number Ones, and most often the overseer selected those
with some education for promotion.[34] Those who succeeded
in being selected as Number Ones were clearly proud of the
superior status their rank conferred. The Number Ones "are
usually shrewd and business-like, with a full appreciation of
the dignity of their position," Mary Gamewell observed.

One recently entered the first class compartment of a tramcar. She
wore the loose blue gown, apron and head cloth of the working people and when the Chinese conductor came by he addressed her
gruffly. "Old woman, you belong in the third class. Get out of here!"
"Why should I get out?" she responded with spirit. "I have money
to pay for a seat in the first class." The conductor changed his tone
and manner at once, recognizing a dominant personality behind the
coarse clothes. "Pardon me, Madame," he said and meekly took the
proffered coppers.[35]

Most of the women who eventually became Number Ones
seem either to have been Shanghainese or to have come from
Wuxi or Changzhou,[36] probably because most of the technical
and managerial staff came from these cities in Jiangnan.

CHANGING WORKSHOPS

A second way for a woman to move up in the mills was to
move from one workshop to another, for there was often a
substantial difference in wages from department to depart-

TABLE 5   *Comparison of Wages for Spinning and Weaving,
Selected Years, 1928-1946*

	Average daily wage for women	
Year	Cotton spinning	Cotton weaving
1928(*a*)	0.44 *yuan*	0.35 (hand loom)
		0.60 (power loom)
1930(*b*)	0.421	0.583
1931	0.449	0.504
1932	0.448	0.581
1933	0.477	0.522
1934	0.470	0.588
1938(*c*)	0.60 (highest)	0.80 (highest)
	0.40 (lowest)	0.50 (lowest)
1946(*d*)	6,109.25	5,853.35

SOURCES: (*a*) Shanghai Bureau of Social Affairs, *The Index Numbers of Earnings of Factory Laborers in Greater Shanghai, July-December 1928* (Shanghai, 1928), pp. 7-13. (*b*) Shanghai Bureau of Social Affairs, *Wage Rates in Shanghai, 1935* (Shanghai, 1935). These figures represent the average of figures cited for time and piece rates for women workers. (*c*) Zhu Bangxing et al., *Shanghai chanye yu Shanghai zhigong* (Hong Kong, 1939), pp. 53-54. These are the wages for the Yi He Cotton Mill, the largest British enterprise. There are no figures for all of Shanghai for 1938. (*d*) Shanghai shehuiju, *Shanghai gongchang laogong tong ji* (Shanghai, 1946), pp. 49-52. These are the average of time and piece rates for women workers in devalued currency.

ment. The most obvious hierarchical division among women workers in the mills was that between spinners and weavers. Until the end of World War II weavers consistently earned approximately one and a half times as much as spinners (see Table 5).

We can only speculate as to why weavers earned more than spinners. First, weaving required more skill, and in general the women who worked in the weaving department were older than the women in the spinning department. In 1925 the average age of women in the spinning room of a large, Japanese-owned mill was sixteen; in the weaving department the average age of women was twenty-three.[37] Second, the difference in wages possibly reflected a difference in the sexual composition of the work force in the two departments: whereas the work force in the spinning departments of most mills had become overwhelmingly female by the mid-1930's, only about half the workers in the weaving departments were women.[38] Although a much more extensive study of how the entrance of women into each workshop affected wage levels would be necessary to substantiate this hypothesis, the hypothesis seems to account for the change that occurred after World War II, when women became the majority of the weaving work force. As Table 5 indicates, it was just at that time that their wages dropped below those paid to spinners.[39]

Although the difference between spinning and weaving wages seemed to be true of most mills, within each mill there were more particular hierarchies of jobs. In some mills rovers earned more than spinners, and in others reelers earned more than either. Although a job's desirability was usually determined by the money it paid, occasionally women preferred work that paid relatively low wages if it offered better conditions. Xu Hongmei, for example, worked in the stripping department at Tong Xing. "Actually stripping was better than spinning and weaving, even though the wages were low," she said. "In spinning the machines were high and we were too small to reach; in weaving the noise was so terrible."[40]

Although women had little say about where they began their careers—they entered whichever workshop the person introducing them worked in—they did devise strategies for moving from one workshop to another. Ultimately, job changes also depended on factors that were difficult to control, such as whether a given workshop was hiring and whether they could find an acquaintance to introduce them to the Number One in that workshop. In the meantime, however, many women acquired the skills that would make it possible for them to be hired as skilled workers in other departments, should the opportunity arise. "When I first came to Shanghai, I learned reeling," Wang Luoying recalled.

Reeling is simple, and easy to learn, but I wanted to be able to do spinning. If you could spin, then you never needed to worry about being unemployed. You could get work at any mill. So I started to learn spinning. I did it by studying secretly. After I worked on a day shift, then I would stay on during the night shift. I had a relative in the spinning department, so she taught me to spin. It did not even take me a full month to learn.[41]

Sometimes moving to a better job required switching mills. One woman started her career at the age of ten as a reeler in the Shen Xin Number Two Mill. When she was fourteen she left Shen Xin because she had heard that the Nei Wai Number Six Mill needed workers in the spinning workshop. Since as a spinner at Nei Wai she could earn more than she ever could as a reeler at Shen Xin, she paid a hoodlum five dollars to secure her an introduction for a trainee position at Nei Wai. After a two month apprenticeship she passed the test and was hired as a regular spinner.[42]

Women did not move from one mill to another only to switch workshops. In addition to hierarchies of jobs there were hierarchies of cotton mills, and it was considered preferable to work in certain mills and to avoid others.

THE COTTON MILL CIRCUIT

Although a woman worker may not always have been able to work in the mill of her choice, she did have preferences, based on work hours, wages, treatment by supervisors, and benefits.[43] Not surprisingly, wages were the most important consideration for women workers, and the recorded work histories of many women note "wages too low at ——— mill" or "wages higher at ——— mill" as reasons for switching from one mill to another.

The difference in what various mills paid for comparable jobs could be substantial (see Table 6). For instance, while a woman doffer in the spinning room of the Chinese-owned Yong An Number Three Mill earned 0.74 *yuan* per day in 1938, her counterpart at the Japanese-owned Nei Wai Number Nine Mill earned only 0.40 *yuan* a day.[44] Even mills that belonged to the same company, such as the fourteen different Nei Wai mills, often had significantly different wage scales.[45]

Other considerations too made certain mills more or less desirable than others. We have seen, for example, that many women from Subei preferred to work in Japanese-owned mills, where they were not subjected to the contempt and condescension of Chinese mill managers (see Chapter Three). Some workers appreciated the tea that many Japanese-owned mills offered during work hours. "After women worked in Japanese mills, they were not so willing to work in our Chinese mills," recalled an engineer employed during the 1930's by a

TABLE 6   *Comparison of Wages at Different Mills, 1925 and 1938*
(low/high; in *yuan*)

Mill	Roving	Spinning	Reeling	Weaving
1925				
Chen Tai (C)	.26/.36	.24/.36	.34/.39	—
Da Feng (C)	.29/.35	.23/.34	.33/.39	—
Feng Tian (J)	.30/.40	.33/.40	.33/.40	—
Gong Yi (C)	.36/.40	.25/.40	.35/.40	—
Nei Wai (J)	.30/.45	.31/.46	.30/.40	—
Shen Xin (C)	.31/.37	.20/.27	.37/.40	—
Tong Xing (J)	.37/—	.30/.40	.32/.40	—
Yong Yu (C)	.31/.35	.20/.25	.35/.39	—
1938				
Heng Zhang (C)	.48/.88	.28/.82	.48/.77	—
Shen Xin 9 (C)	.30/.95	.24/1.10	.41/.80	.60/
Tong Xing (J)	.50/.70	.50/.78	.48/.65	.45/.92
Yi He (B)	.35/.85	.40/.60	.40/.60	.50/.80

SOURCES: For 1925, Tang Hai, *Zhongguo laodong wenti* (Shanghai, 1926), pp. 150–52. For 1938, Zhu Bangxing et al., *Shanghai chanye yu Shanghai zhigong* (Hong Kong, 1939), pp. 50–58.
   NOTE: (B) denotes a British-owned mill, (C) a Chinese-owned mill, and (J) a Japanese-owned mill.

Chinese-owned mill in Shanghai. "The main reason was that work was harder in the Chinese mills. Take spinning, for example. In the Japanese mills threads did not break so often, but in Chinese mills women were really busy, because threads were always breaking."[46] Greater capitalization enabled Japanese mill owners to purchase superior raw cotton and to spend more money maintaining the machinery, so that their yarn was stronger and less likely to break than in Chinese mills.

If there was one mill in Shanghai that workers consistently sought to avoid, it was the large Shen Xin Number Nine Mill. Reputed to be the Chinese-owned mill whose supervisors most frequently beat and cursed workers, Shen Xin Nine also paid notoriously low wages.[47] In an article published in a workers' journal in 1938, a woman worker from Shen Xin Nine pleaded that

we want to make this so-called model mill a genuine model mill. The worker's life at Shen Xin Nine is considered the worst in all the mills of Shanghai. There are hundreds of supervisors all over the place. There are engineers, examiners, inspectors, overseers, assistant overseers, instructors, checkers, supervisors, etc., etc. From morning till night they come back and forth, and if they catch you resting for even a second they will hit you. Workers at the Japanese-owned mills say to us: "For us workers at Japanese mills, it is easy to rest during the day shift, and we can always sleep on the night shift. Why is it that the treatment you get at a Chinese mill is not even as good as ours at the Japanese mill?"

Among cotton mill workers in Shanghai, as soon as you mention the name Shen Nine, they will say, "Don't go there unless you are really desperate!" Anyone at Shen Nine, as soon as they have a chance, will leave and move to another mill.[48]

Workers went out of their way to condemn the treatment they received at Shen Xin Nine, but they were equally eager to praise the Yong An mills. In the same workers' journal a woman who worked at the Yong An Number Three Mill apologized for sounding like a publicity agent for the mill management: "I am not trying to help the capitalists boast," she wrote, "but the eating facilities at our mill are much better than elsewhere." Unlike other mills, she pointed out, Yong An provided equipment to steam workers' rice and vegetables. She also lauded the mill owner for providing work outfits, higher wages, and a health clinic.[49] Others were impressed by the consideration demonstrated by the Yong An management in allowing the workers to rest for a half hour each day during summer, and in giving them tea or boiled water to drink.[50] As mentioned in Chapter Six, Yong An also offered night workers a cup of coffee and two biscuits.[51]

Whether a woman worked at a popular mill or an unpopular one, she rarely stayed for very long. A survey of a Japanese mill in 1928 showed that the largest number of women had worked at that mill for one year or less, and fewer than half had stayed on for more than three years.[52] Most often a woman worked in at least three or four different cotton mills during the course of her career.[53] The rate of turnover among women workers was so high that many mills instituted a policy of withholding a new worker's first half month's wages as a deposit. This policy was intended to discourage women from jumping from one mill to another.[54]

The fact that women went from one mill to another with

such frequency did not mean that their geographic mobility in Shanghai increased. Moving from one mill to another rarely involved moving from one part of Shanghai to another; the cotton mill circuit for an individual woman usually consisted of the mills located in the district where she lived. Women often moved from one mill to another in the company of parents, siblings, relatives, or friends. Yu Rong's first job, for example, was at the Heng Feng Mill in Yangshupu. She worked there for three years, and then transferred to a Yong An mill. "I left Heng Feng because the two *shi-fu*'s [masters] who had taught me the work at Heng Feng had moved to Yong An, and so I just went with them."[55]

Cotton mill work was usually the highest rung a woman attained on the ladder of jobs available to women in Shanghai. Cotton mill workers rarely moved into the slightly more prestigious tobacco and perfume factories, which (as explained in Chapter Three) were the domain of Ningboese. No cases are known of women mill workers moving out of industrial work to take jobs as department store clerks, which were held by women with more education.

Although a woman worker's upward progress in the course of her career was clearly limited, no similar limits governed how far down she might drop. There were abundant cases of young women whose careers in the mills ended when they were sold to brothels, occasionally by their husbands but more frequently by kidnappers.[56] A number of women workers became kidnappers themselves. In extreme cases, these women, along with those who became opium addicts or robbers, ended their cotton mill careers in prison.[57]

Marriage, Motherhood, and Work

In addition to moving from workshop to workshop and from mill to mill, a woman usually alternated periods of working in a factory with periods of staying at home. The work record of a woman born in Shanghai in 1900 is illustrative. As a child she learned to hand-reel cotton, and at the age of twelve she entered the reeling department of Nei Wai Number Three. She worked there for six years, and then in 1918, following a neighbor who had worked with her, she transferred to Nei Wai Number Seven and worked there until 1925, when she married and began to have children. From then until 1928 she stayed at home, taking care of her children and doing housework. In late 1928, because of financial problems facing her family, she got a job as a piecer in the spinning room of the Tong Xing Mill. She worked there for seven years; then she got sick and returned home for two years. In 1937 she became a reeler at the Feng Tian Mill and worked until 1943, when because of a foot injury she once again returned home. From that time until the Japanese surrender in 1945 she wove at home. After the war she got a job as a reeler at the Tong Yi Cotton Mill, worked there for one year, and then moved to Guo Mian Number Two, where she worked continuously for nine years, until her retirement in 1955.[58]

Most women temporarily withdrew from the mill work force for similar reasons: marriage, childbirth, injury or illness, death of a family member, and dismissal.[59] For women who had begun working in their early teens, the first major break in their mill career was almost invariably due to marriage.

THE TIME HAS COME

Contemporary observers were frequently struck by the number of women workers already in their late twenties and still unmarried. At the Da Kang Mill, for example, people jokingly referred to the "three too many's" among women workers, one of which was "too many women who never married and have become old maids."[60] Lamson was surprised to hear of women in the villages he studied who had reached the age of 30 and were still single.[61] He and other observers assumed that these unmarried working women demonstrated increasing independence.

Upon closer examination, however, it seems that these women were noticed not because they were typical but rather because they were exceptional: women workers in Shanghai usually married between the ages of 18 and 24.[62] This seems to have been the case in the 1920's as well as in the 1940's, for there is no evidence that women married at a progressively higher age. But women who went to work in factories did marry much later than their rural counterparts, who normally were wed at the age of 15 or 16 and were considered old maids by the age of 20.[63] Apparently the opportunity for women to work in urban factories resulted in delaying marriage.[64]

This delay usually did not mean that they had greater power in making their own marriage arrangements; instead, the decision to postpone marriage was made by their parents on the basis of what was best for the family. It was financially in the interest of most parents to keep their daughters at home as long as possible, since the majority of single women turned a large part of their wages over to their parents. Once they married, this money would be given to the husband's family; and although the girl's own parents would be relieved of the burden of housing and feeding one member, they also would be deprived of a major source of income. A conversation Lamson had with a woman who lived in a village near Shanghai illustrates this point. Lamson asked the woman when her eighteen-year-old daughter, who worked in a cotton mill, was going to marry. The mother replied, "Oh, wait for another two years. Nowadays girls marry later than before. Some families still give their daughters away early, but most do not. Since they can earn money, we don't want them to get married very soon."[65]

The unusual cases of girls in their mid-twenties who had not yet married might likewise be explained by their families' circumstances and economic calculations. We do not know very much about these women as a group, but the little we know about some individuals suggests that they came from families that simply could not afford to "give away" an employed daughter. Yang Meizhen, a sociology student who conducted an investigation of women workers in Yangshupu in 1930, came across several unmarried women in their mid-twenties. When she attempted to find out why, she discovered that most did not have brothers. These women's sonless parents, dependent on their daughters' income and therefore especially loath to relinquish a daughter to a husband, were hoping to find a son-in-law who would come and live with them.[66] Unfortunately, Yang noted, most young men whose parents were still alive were not willing to accept this arrangement. Only orphans and hoodlums were interested.[67]

One other group of women delayed marriage even longer than was considered normal for working women in Shanghai: the mill workers of the 1940's who became active in the labor movement, the Chinese Communist Party, or both. Many women who joined the CCP, like Shi Xiaomei, did not marry until their late twenties. "I got married very late, when I was twenty-eight. That was after Liberation. At that time most workers got married around seventeen or eighteen. I did not get married until I was twenty-eight because I was a Party member, and I was too busy going to meetings and things. It was not until after Liberation that I had time to think about such things as marriage."[68]

In the late 1940's the postponement of marriage by female Party activists became so common that women workers who had not married by their mid-twenties were often suspected of being Party members. To protect female labor activists from persecution, the CCP instructed them to marry sooner. He Ningzhen, who worked for Shen Xin and joined the CCP in 1940, recalled that people in her factory began to suspect that she was a Party member.

The Party organization wanted to immediately introduce me to a prospective mate. [Laughs.] They wanted me to get married! Why? Because in old China, everyone knew that once a woman got married she wouldn't do anything. She would just go to work, and take care of the house, but she would not participate in any social activities. That way, if I got married, GMD people would not be so suspicious of me. So I did it. I didn't even know my husband before. The person they introduced me to was also a Party member. After I got married I still lived in the dormitory. I did not go stay at his house.[69]

Although He herself originally decided to postpone marriage (because she was too busy to get married), she nonetheless shared the fate of other women workers in marrying when and whom she was told to. In her case the Party, rather than her family, made these decisions for her.

MAKING A MATCH

Despite May Fourth Movement attacks on traditional, arranged marriages, most women workers (and indeed women of most other classes in Shanghai, save some intellectuals) had almost no voice in the selection of their mates. Contemporary sociologists such as Lamson and Yang encountered several remarkable mill workers who, presumably drawing on the leverage of their earning power, refused to marry the men chosen by their parents. Yet both sociologists found that the majority of women they interviewed balked at the idea of free marriage. Most women workers "think the idea of free marriages, of men and women engaging marriages by themselves, is disgraceful," Yang observed. Lamson's interviewees concurred that "it was shameful for a girl to choose her own husband."[70]

This reaction to free marriage was due only in part to the persistence of traditional values among women workers. It was most likely also a reaction to what free marriage meant in the context of urban working life, for to women workers the notion probably did not imply an "honorable" marriage between a man and woman who had freely chosen each other. Instead it probably connoted the "promiscuous and immoral" behavior displayed by some women workers, whose "scandalous" activities were often reported in the local news. For example, a pretty girl from Changzhou had come to Shanghai with two brothers. No sooner had she begun working in a cotton mill than she "rented a house and lived with a man from Hebei." Another young girl, a Shanghainese who worked in a cotton mill, was introduced to a dashing young man by the mistress of the foreman in her workshop. The couple rented a house together, where they lived for thirteen years.[71] Yet another woman mill worker was found cohabiting with a foreman from her mill, despite the fact that he was already married and had three children.[72] Some of these cases involved trickery by neighborhood hoodlums. "Many of these hoodlums look quite dashing," one contemporary observer wrote.

Some wear Western-style leather shoes, some wear silk clothes with a high collar. . . . There are some young women workers who are misled by their outward appearance and are deceived by their phony talk. They go off together to commit adultery (*zha pingtou*) and she becomes his wife. Inevitably all she earns is squandered by him buying clothing and jewelry. And in the end, often she is sold to a brothel by her hoodlum husband. This kind of thing often happens among women cotton mill workers.[73]

In this context marriages arranged in a traditional manner, if not always desirable, may have seemed safe; but as we shall see, this was not always true.

Some women's parents engaged them to a husband when they were only two or three years old. Others, at a like age, were sold as child-daughters-in-law (*tongyangxi*) and raised in the homes of their future husbands. Both these customs, common in Chinese villages for hundreds of years, were perpetuated by working-class families in Shanghai.[74]

The practice of selling daughters as child-daughters-in-law was most commonly resorted to by families who were relatively poor. In Shanghai Yang Meizhen found it to be most prevalent among Subei people.[75] From the perspective of parents who were in dire financial difficulties, selling a daughter both relieved them of a mouth to feed and gave them some ready cash. From the point of view of a young boy's parents, buying a child-daughter-in-law might save them money in the long run. Sometimes working-class parents, knowing that the alternative was to spend several hundred dollars to buy a bride for their son several years down the road, returned to their native village to buy a child-daughter-in-law. In the 1930's they might have had to spend only twenty or thirty dollars to purchase the daughter of a poor peasant family. They would bring her to Shanghai, raise her as a member of their household, and when she was twelve or thirteen, try to get her a job in a Shanghai mill.[76] The frequency of newspaper accounts reporting the tragedy of girls sold as *tongyangxi* who had initially been lured to Shanghai with the promise of a mill job, or who had been kidnapped after they started working, suggests that the trade in child-daughters-in-law was brisk.

Although almost all women's marriages were arranged by

their parents, many were not arranged until the girls were in their teens. Finding an appropriate mate was a task usually performed by the girl's parents, with the assistance of a matchmaker. Friends, neighbors, relatives, and co-workers were all potential matchmakers. Chen Zhaodi told of a matchmaker who assisted in arranging her marriage.

The matchmaker first goes to each family and boasts about how good the other is. She told my mother how rich the man's family was. My mother thought that was good, because then we could have a better life. She told the man's family that I was very beautiful and very honest. So, both sides agreed.

Then it turned out that the matchmaker had lied. She had said that the husband's father was a foreman. But actually he was just a worker who chopped rocks to make roads. For the matchmaker, the benefit of making a match is that she gets presents, like eighteen pork legs.[77]

Sometimes a matchmaker's fabrications were of a more serious order. Only after she married did one woman discover a major omission from the matchmaker's presentation of the prospective groom's virtues: he and both his parents were opium addicts.[78]

Often the Number Ones in the mill workshops acted as matchmakers for the young women who worked under their supervision.[79] And of course, because a woman worker's job security was in the Number One's hands, she rarely refused these arrangements.

When I was nineteen years old the Number One introduced me to a man. I thought I would rather die than get married to him, but I decided being miserable must be my fate. Eventually I married the man the Number One introduced me to. He had been married before, and had a child. His parents were very feudalistic. Since his previous wife's family had been rich they looked down on me, being so poor. His mother and I often argued and fought.[80]

Since many Number Ones had close relations with gang members, they often made matches with men who might otherwise have had difficulty finding a spouse.

There were ordinarily certain considerations in making a match. First, the prospective husband had to be from the same district as the bride-to-be.[81] Some families, after finding a candidate from the same native place, paid a fortune-teller to ascertain whether the young man's "celestial stems and terrestrial branches" were compatible with those of the bride-to-be. Finally, after a bride price was negotiated, the couple was considered engaged. The engagement agreement was tantamount to a contract, although it rarely involved a written document. Breaking this contract often required the sanction of the court, and even then, if a girl's parents did not approve, she was powerless to terminate the contract.

The case of a sixteen-year-old girl from Tongzhou who worked in a cotton mill in Shanghai, reported in the newspaper *Shen Bao*, illustrates the predicament of many women workers. When she was eleven her parents, assisted by a matchmaker from Tongzhou, had engaged her to a nineteen-year-old worker, also from Tongzhou. His family had paid the thirty-dollar bride price agreed on by the two families. (During the court hearing, the young man claimed he had actually paid the girl's family seventy dollars.) In the spring of 1930, when she was sixteen and still not formally married, the husband-to-be used the pretext of saving the girl from a bitter family argument to forcefully take her away to live with him (he had rounded up some thirty people to help him) and thereby fulfill the marriage agreement. The same day, she escaped and returned home. The girl subsequently found a lawyer to help her file a complaint with the district court, requesting that the marriage agreement be annulled. So long as the girl's parents were not willing to insist on dissolving the marriage agreement, the judge could not respect the girl's plea; he told her that as a sixteen-year-old she must accede to the wishes of her guardian.[82] Other cases reported in the newspaper suggest that most young mill workers caught in similar predicaments had very little success in escaping the obligation to marry.

Kidnapping the woman to whom a son was engaged was not always the criminal act it appears to be. Families that could not afford the expense of a formal wedding found "stealing the bride" a thrifty alternative: an ordinary wedding could cost the groom's family upward of one hundred dollars.[83]

Weddings were cause for great celebration in the lives of women workers. They were also occasions that vividly displayed economic differences among the workers. A family with means rented a first-class sedan chair to carry the bride, wearing a phoenix hat and the traditional red cloth over her face, to the groom's home. Others settled for second- or third-class sedan chairs, and those who were extremely poor made the move on foot. Relative affluence was similarly manifested in the length of time a woman took off from work for her wedding. "Most of us poorer workers got married on Sunday and then went to work on Monday," Chen Zhaodi recalled. "But workers who were better-off could take a few days of vacation."[84]

Many women whose families had migrated from rural villages to Shanghai returned to their hometowns for their wedding ceremonies. Although Yu Rong and her husband-to-be both lived in Shanghai, for example, they returned to Shaoxing where, on the day of the wedding, they met for the first time. Afterward her husband and parents returned to Shanghai, but Yu Rong stayed with her in-laws in the village until her first child was born. Then she went back to Shanghai and resumed her job in the mill.

Although a woman usually took time off for her wedding ceremony, her career seldom terminated with her marriage. Like Yu Rong, most women returned to the mills and continued to work, taking time off when they gave birth, but returning whenever possible to their jobs. Statistics on the marital status of women workers at the Shanghai Number One Mill in 1947 confirm that, despite management's preference for hiring single women, many married women were able to hold on to their jobs: some 73 percent of the total of 2,289 women workers at the mill were married.[85]

WORKING DAUGHTERS-IN-LAW

No matter where the bride and groom were from and no matter where the wedding took place, once they were married almost all working women moved to their husband's home and were subsequently considered part of their husband's family. For many young daughters-in-law the daily routine was much more demanding than it had been in their own parents' home. "After getting married I went and lived in his parents' house," Wang Fuying recalled. "When I lived with my parents I just worked in the mill, but I did not have to do housework too. Once I moved, I had to do both."[86]

In addition to helping with housework, a daughter-in-law was expected to give all her earnings to her husband's family. "If I wanted to buy things," one worker recalled, "then I would have to ask my parents-in-law."[87] After her parents-in-law died a woman handed over her wages to her husband. Some, like a woman who flared up when Yang Meizhen asked her whether she always gave her husband her wages, were less than satisfied with this arrangement. "I have to give my wages to my husband!" she complained. "If I don't, he will beat me. Since I am a woman I cannot succeed in beating him back. He always takes the eight dollars that I earn every month and uses it to gamble."[88] Furthermore, even if she wanted to, a young wife could not continue supporting her own parents. One woman remembered that she could still visit her parents, "and sometimes I could take them little things like peanuts."[89]

For a woman whose parents had sons this might not have seemed so tragic, but for someone like Chen Zhaodi, who had only a sister, it was an agonizing predicament. She remembered this as one of the most difficult situations in her life: "After I got married my mother had no income at all. Before I had given her my wages, so she did not have to go beg. But after that she went out begging every day and even still, she could not get enough to eat." Unbeknownst to her husband's family, Chen borrowed money and gave it to her mother. Shortly thereafter, the money was stolen.

I always feel bad about how I treated my mother at that time. I just blamed her for not being able to take care of money. "You who have so many years of experience, but you cannot even take care of money!" I said to her. I was just worried about the high interest rate on the money I had borrowed. My mother cried and cried, saying it was her fate to be poor, and that it was all her fault for never having provided me with a brother.

She got sick and died shortly after that. We just used boards from the bed she had been sleeping on to make a coffin.[90]

Although many women went back to work after they married, marriage usually meant continual childbearing. Most women started having children in the first year or two after they were married. "We had no way to control it, no education or contraception," Chen Zhaodi recalled. "If our period didn't come, then we knew we were pregnant. And if you got pregnant, then that was that."[91] Almost every time they gave birth they had to take time off work, even if only several days before and after delivery.

Until 1946, when as a result of a series of strikes women were guaranteed 56 days of maternity leave for each birth, pregnant women were often fired. Cotton mill managers supposedly propagated the "three don't wants": "We don't want old women, we don't want women with bound feet, and we don't want pregnant women." The last was the most serious, since most women who were still young and did not have bound feet were almost certain to become pregnant at some point, often well before they wanted or could afford to give up their wage-earning careers. Often a pregnant worker had an abortion, though at that time it was a dangerous procedure that resulted in the deaths of a sizable number of women.[92]

To protect their jobs, most pregnant women tried to conceal their pregnancy from the mill management and supervisors. Up to a certain point, wearing loose clothing was an adequate disguise. During the last months, however, women resorted to tying a cloth tightly around their abdomens. This practice, combined with the virtually complete absence of medical checks during pregnancy, contributed to the high incidence of miscarriages and stillbirths among mill workers.[93] A bathroom in a mill workshop was often the site of great commotion when a woman suffered a miscarriage during her working shift. Whenever this happened at the Da Kang Mill, groups of women gathered in the bathroom and burned tinfoil or paper money to scare away the evil spirits believed to inhabit stillborn babies.[94]

Because most pregnant women, even if they could anticipate their delivery date, continued to work until shortly before they were due, it was not uncommon for women to give birth while at work.[95] Tang Hai relates the following story of a woman who barely managed to finish her shift before delivering a child:

When I was working in the San Xin Cotton Mill there was a woman from Jiangbei who worked in the roving room. She was healthy and strong, and had already been pregnant for the full ten [lunar] months. But because she needed to make a living, she continued to work in the factory as before. One day she felt a pain in her abdomen and thought that the baby would soon be born. She thought of asking for time off to go home, but she also thought that it was already three o'clock. If she didn't finish the shift, there would be a deduction from her wages. So it would be better to finish the shift and go home when work let out. Therefore she continued working as before, until the quitting whistle blew, and went out holding her belly in both hands. But she hadn't even made it to the door when the baby was born, so in great difficulty she lay on the stone steps, and many men and women workers crowded around to see her![96]

Some more fortunate women were able to stop working several days before they expected to give birth. Yu Rong, for example, remarked that one reason that Yong An was considered preferable to other companies was that "if they knew you, and you were pregnant, then they would not fire you if you took some days off when you gave birth."[97] Most pregnant women who managed to take time off from work gave birth at home, usually with the assistance of a midwife. A 1950 report on the major problems facing women workers cited several extreme cases of women who died during childbirth as a result of the incompetence of midwives. "We have no idea exactly how many women have died in childbirth at the hands of these midwives," the author of the report lamented.[98] Some women gave birth without any assistance whatsoever. One of Lamson's students who interviewed women workers in a village near Yangshupu was aghast to discover that many women "give birth without any help, washing and dressing the child immediately, before anyone enters the room."[99]

Given the circumstances of women workers' pregnancies

and deliveries, it is not surprising that the infant mortality rate was high. Only a small percentage of their children survived: according to one estimate, 60–70 percent died.[100] A woman worker who had borne eight children commonly had only one or two survive their first year.[101]

How soon after giving birth a woman returned to work depended very much on her individual circumstances. For the first month a woman was considered a "red person," and ideally she avoided contact with other people. During this time she was to stay in bed at her in-laws' house. If the parents had been blessed with a baby boy, there was a party at the end of that month. "We would eat long-life noodles and hope that the son could grow up to be someone better than a worker."[102] No similar fanfare marked the end of a baby girl's first month.

But most women could not afford the luxury of staying home for one month. If she had someone to look after the baby, a woman returned to the mill within several days, to reduce the risk of losing her job. Otherwise, desperate to return to work immediately, she simply took her newborn baby with her (as we have seen in Chapter Five). Sometimes a woman who had none of these alternatives was forced to choose between giving her baby away and abandoning it, to protect her career.[103] Because of her family's desperate need for income, one woman had to give her first two babies to an orphanage:

When I got pregnant I was dismissed from the factory. After my baby was born my husband was unemployed, and our life was hard. So I had to put my child in an orphanage. I waited for three weeks after I gave birth, then spent five dollars to go to the foreman . . . to get a number to enter the factory. My husband went to peddle goods. But one time when he was selling rice he was seen by a Japanese person, who took it all from him and beat him up. At that time I had already given birth to a second child. We had no choice but to send the second child away too. . . . I sent a gift to the Number One I already knew in the factory, and went to the factory to register for a number. Then I resumed work.[104]

Often a woman did not return to work immediately after giving birth but instead stayed home to take care of the child.

During this time she might continue to earn some cash by working as a wet nurse. Although she may have intended to return to the mill, she could not control if and when she would be rehired. After Yu Rong had her first child, for example, her mother took care of it, and Yu Rong was able to return to work at Yong An almost immediately. But when her second child was born, in 1944, the factory was cutting back operations and reducing the number of workers. Unable to return to work, she stayed in her family's home village for several years, until she heard that the mills were hiring once again.[105] Chen Zhaodi stayed home for half a year after her first child was born, but when he was only six months old the child became seriously ill and died. Three days later Chen decided to return to work. It was wartime, however, and the mill where she had been working before she gave birth had closed. Fortunately, before long a woman with whom she had previously worked gave her an introduction to the roving department of the Nei Wai Number Thirteen Mill.[106]

It is more difficult to generalize about women's patterns of work after they married and began having children. Some, like Yu Rong and Chen Zhaodi, did not retire but rather kept on working except when childbearing forced them to stay home for a period of time. Others did not work during their child-bearing years, but then returned to steady employment in the mills when they were in their late thirties or early forties.[107] Unfortunately there are no systematic records of the ages at which women retired from the work force, and the only work histories that are available (the retirement cards of women workers from one mill) by their nature include only those women who did *not* terminate their careers when they began having children.

Nonetheless, since we know that women in their forties were never more than a small percentage of the work force, we must assume that the majority stopped working by the time they reached their late thirties. Many women probably never returned to the mills once they began having children. Some who had returned to their home villages when they married might never even have returned to Shanghai. A woman who continued to work after she began having children was likely to end her career when one of her children was old enough to enter the work force and contribute an income to the family.

Women Workers in War

The transience of the female work force—the patterns of movement into and out of the mills, and back and forth between city and countryside—was not simply the result of persisting traditional social relationships and customs among women workers in the city. During thirteen years of the three decades between World War I and Liberation, Shanghai was subjected to attack or occupation by the Japanese. To large numbers of women, particularly those who began mill work in the early 1930's, the war and the Japanese occupation were as important in shaping their careers as the dictates of marriage and motherhood were: the turning points in their careers coincide with these events. To understand the work histories of these women, and ultimately, as Chapter Eight will show, the development of a working-class consciousness among them, we must look at how they were affected by the events of the period from 1932 to 1945.

Claiming provocation by Chinese troops, Japanese armed forces attacked Shanghai at midnight on January 28, 1932, and moved to occupy the Chinese-owned parts of the city (see Chapter One). "Rifles and machine guns were brought into play, and for four hours the uninterrupted sound of these came to sleeping ears," wrote Eleanor Hinder, factory inspector for the Shanghai Municipal Council. "By four o'clock on that first awful night, a new horror appeared. Japanese planes were heard overhead. From my windows I could see blinding magnesium lights, followed by the dropping of bombs from these machines. This, within four hours of the commencement of firing, and over extremely densely populated areas. Horrors were then forecasted which have only too plainly been fulfilled."[108]

Zhabei, the factory district surrounding the northern train station, was the most severely damaged. Reuters reported: "The Chinese city of Chapei appeared to be one big bonfire, with flames leaping a hundred feet into the air, amid a roar audible at a great distance. Shanghai was brilliantly lit by this ghastly illumination. . . . Viewed from points of vantage in the International Settlement, Chapei seems to have become an inferno."[109]

Many women workers lived in Zhabei. In the wake of this attack they joined the swelling ranks of refugees, most of whom first fled to the International Settlement. Chen Zhaodi recalled the experience of her family at that time:

When I was nine years old, that is when the Japanese first invaded Shanghai and there was war. My family lived in Zhabei, on Taiyang Shan Road. We lived in a straw hut. When the war started our house burned down, and we fled to the south bank of Suzhou Creek. We lived along the side of the road. We slept on the street, at the entrance of the silk filature where I had been working. At that time there were a lot of people who had fled, and at night, when the factory closed, we would all sleep there at the gate. . . . The foreign police suspected that we were robbers, arrested us, and took us to the police station. We told them that we had fled home because it had been burned down. Then they sent us to a refugee camp. We were all locked up there and could not go out.[110]

Even women whose homes were not destroyed by the attack were affected, as many of the cotton mills temporarily ceased production. All the Japanese-owned mills closed, leaving approximately 50,000 workers unemployed, and all but two of the Chinese-owned mills were closed throughout the hostilities of spring 1932.[111] Most mills were closed for at least six weeks.[112]

Left without work and without any idea when the mills might reopen, the majority of female cotton mill workers who had originally migrated from the countryside returned once again to their home villages.[113] "The Japanese attack happened before I was married," Yu Rong remembered. "I was twenty-one at that time. We were scared, and we returned to our family's home in Zhejiang. . . . Actually it was cheaper living in the village. We could use the money we had earned in Shanghai, and there were not so many expenses, because we grew what we ate. I spent two months there at that time. There were lots of people going back and forth to Shanghai, and they told us when the situation there was safe."[114]

Like Yu Rong, most women who had fled to their home villages returned to Shanghai to work within a year. Soon afterward, in 1933, the cotton industry was hit by the depression, and for the next two years many women found themselves unemployed for months at a time (see Chapter One). The size of the cotton mill work force dropped from 149,000 in 1931 to 100,000 in 1935.[115] During this time many women who were unable to make ends meet in Shanghai returned again to their home villages.

By 1936 the cotton industry had begun to recover, and most women who had been out of work for several years were able to reclaim their jobs. But the outbreak of war in 1937 once again sent many women workers fleeing from their homes and jobs in Shanghai to their home villages.[116] Rural areas were also hard hit; by 1940 many parts of the surrounding countryside, particularly eastern Zhejiang, suffered acute food shortages. So although some women stayed in their villages until the end of the war, doing housework or working in the fields, many refugees returned to Shanghai, hoping at least to be able to purchase rice, and eventually to find work. One worker from the Shen Xin Number Six Mill recalled her experiences early in the war:

The night of the August 13th incident our factory stopped work. The people who lived in the area around the mill were all moving their household possessions and fleeing. Some of us workers stayed at the mill. On the fifteenth the Japanese troops had already begun firing near our factory, and on the morning of the nineteenth, a shell hit right above the spinning room. We all ran out.

First I returned to my home on Pingliang Road, and then, with my family, got on a small boat and crossed the river to Pudong. Then we went back to the French Concession. But because it was hard to travel along the roads, we did not get to the French Concession until eleven at night, and we had nowhere to live there. So we found a boat with some people, went back home to Gaoyou in Subei, and helped my parents-in-law in the fields.

After about a half year I returned to Shanghai and got a job working at the Xin Yu Cotton Mill.[117]

In fact the years between the initial blows of the war and the occupation in 1941 were a golden age for the Shanghai cotton industry, and it was possible for many workers to resume their former jobs.

Tens of thousands of workers who, like Chen Zhaodi, no longer had a home in the countryside swarmed into the International Settlement and were eventually housed in refugee camps. "I was fourteen when the war with Japan started," Chen Zhaodi recalled.

We lived on the streets for two months. At that time a lot of people went back to the countryside. But our family did not have anything in the village. We did not have any land, and we did not have any place to live, so we couldn't even be hired laborers. So we ran away and lived on the streets for two months. Then we were caught and put in a refugee camp again, this time at Xinzha Road. Two years later, when I was sixteen, my father died there. . . . The refugee camp was broken up in November, so we were all kicked out.[118]

Spending a year or two in one of the refugee shelters established in the International Settlement before the Japanese occupation in December 1941 was part of the experience of many women cotton mill workers. Theaters, guild offices, schools, banks, hotels, and restaurants were turned into refugee shelters.[119]

Life in a refugee camp was in some cases tantamount to imprisonment. A foreign observer who visited a refugee camp in Shanghai at this time described it as "a big empty house with improvised three-deckered wooden beds," providing shelter for two thousand people.

The house was so dark that the beds had to be lighted even at daytime by electric light, the power of which, however, was hardly more than that of a few fire-flies. In another one the condition was much worse. It was a mat-shed built on a piece of empty ground on an extra-Settlement road. Inside the shed one can hardly differentiate between the inmates lying about on the floor and the bundles of rags, baskets, etc. hanging down from the ceiling all over the shed. Adults complained they never got a hearty meal. . . . There was no running water in the camp, so the refugees had to dig a big hole outside the shed for water, which was muddy and with which they washed their clothes and even vegetables.[120]

Many internees died of cholera and other diseases that spread in epidemic proportions.[121] Those who survived were dispersed in December 1941, when the Pacific War began and the Japanese occupied the International Settlement. Workers whose homes had been destroyed congregated in straw shack settlements or, in some cases, obtained factory housing.[122]

Securing regular employment during the remaining years of the war was not easy, and a large number of skilled workers were always unemployed. But a minority of women were able to hang on to their jobs in the cotton mills, many of which had been taken over by the Japanese or else geared by their Japanese owners to better serve the war effort. One women remembered that at the time she began work at the Tong Xing Cotton Mill, just after the occupation began, the mill became the Tong Xing Army Clothes Factory. "When they changed production they didn't fire workers. Those who wanted to stay and work could stay on. When they changed production we had to learn the new operations, but as we were all very young we could learn them very quickly. Anyway, making uniforms was lighter work than spinning cotton, because there were sewing machines."[123]

Most women, however, had to look elsewhere for ways of contributing to the family income. Zhou Abao, for example, had moved to the International Settlement after her family's home in Zhabei was destroyed. Sometimes she was able to work at a small cotton-reeling workshop in the Settlement, and the rest of the time she and her friends went to the countryside to glean vegetable scraps, which they brought back to sell in Shanghai.

I would go pick vegetables with the other girls who lived near me. We were all from Subei. Every morning at eight we would go to the suburbs, beyond Zhabei. We could collect the vegetables that the peasants left on the ground. Since they didn't want them, they didn't care if we took them. We took wheat, potatoes, turnips, and even weeds. At lunchtime, when all the peasants went home to eat, we would just stay in the fields and eat whatever there was. In the summer we ate tomatoes, in the winter we ate carrots. We just wiped the dirt off with our clothes. At night we would carry whatever we had collected on our backs, back to our homes.

For those years, sometimes I had a real factory job, and whenever I didn't I would go pick vegetables.[124]

Many women became "rice runners," smuggling rice hidden in the seams of their clothes from the Shanghai suburbs into the concessions, where rice shortages caused frequent riots.

Whether or not they had regular work, eking out a living in wartime Shanghai was a challenge, and most women remember the war as one of the most difficult periods of their lives. "During the war our life was wretched," Wang Fuying's son recalled. "My mother would work, but her work was not enough to support our family. At that time what would we eat? We'd eat the garbage left by the Japanese. And we had to pay for it. We had to buy it. There were people who would collect it, and then sell it to people like us. We didn't have any clothes to wear. I, a little boy, had to wear girl's clothes."[125] Many women who had no jobs barely managed to survive by collecting garbage and selling it to families such as the Wangs. Others tried to survive by doing work, such as pulling carts, that had previously been done only by men. The more fortunate were able to get jobs as household servants.[126]

Women Workers and Peace

The year 1946 was another turning point in the careers of great numbers of mill workers. When the war ended, some mills reopened almost immediately, but many (particularly the Japanese-owned mills, which were taken over by the China Textile Reconstruction Corporation) were unable to resume operations for months (see Chapter One). Although the mill careers of many women came to an end during the war, to many others peace meant a resumption of their careers.

When the mills reopened, many managers hoped to use the opportunity to recruit a new work force. They publicized a list of eligibility requirements making it clear that women who had bound feet or were over twenty-five, illiterate, ugly, or fat were disqualified. Older workers organized in opposition, and eventually most mills consented to hire back some of those who had previously become skilled workers.[127]

A large number of younger women entered the mill work force for the first time in 1945-46. Those who began their careers during these years represented a new generation of mill workers, one whose past experiences differed significantly from those of its predecessors. Some members of this new generation were the daughters of workers, but many, unlike the prewar mill hands, appear to have come from families that had at one time been relatively prosperous. Unlike the women who had grown up in the 1920's, spending their childhoods doing farm work or handicraft work, many of these women had gone to school for several years before entering the mills. And unlike their predecessors who had begun work in the cotton mills in their early teens, if not sooner, many women in this new generation did not begin work until they were twenty years old.[128]

Finally, if World War II was the single most important event shaping the careers of the earlier generation of women mill workers, Liberation was the critical event in the careers of this later generation. After 1949 the work histories of these women were no longer marked by periodic migrations to and from the countryside. Maternity benefits and child care facilities made it a common practice for them to keep working throughout their childbearing years and well beyond: they were usually fifty years old before they retired.

The collective experience of this generation was forged in the atmosphere of social and economic change of the 1950's. How these changes affected the lives of female cotton mill workers, and how the workers' experience resembled or differed from that of their pre-Liberation predecessors, are questions that must await future research.

CHAPTER EIGHT   Visions of Change

The previous chapters have suggested many of the forces militating against the development of solidarity and of a working-class consciousness among women mill workers in Shanghai. We have seen, for example, that although the cotton mills employed several thousand women, they did not necessarily bring together people with different social and geographic origins. Instead, hiring practices and patterns of daily life tended to reinforce alliances between women from the same rural districts as well as antagonisms between those from different areas.

By returning to their home villages to celebrate family events such as weddings or to survive periods of unemployment, women reinforced ties based on identification with native place. War and the Japanese occupation increased the tendency of workers to return to their home villages, and also accentuated their tendency to move from one cotton mill to another and to alternate between mill work and employment as servants or vegetable peddlers. Finally, throughout the thirty-year period between World War I and Liberation, women continued to be tied to and absorbed in subordinate, traditional family roles. All of these elements strongly inhibited the development of ties between women based on their shared experience as mill workers—the development of working-class consciousness.

Beside this picture is a historical record that abounds with strikes involving thousands of women workers. Almost as soon as the first cotton mills opened in Shanghai, and continu-

ing through 1949, there were occasions when women workers
shut off their machines to demand higher wages, reduced
work hours, and welfare benefits. This record suggests that
women had, after all, transcended traditional divisions and had
developed a consciousness of themselves as workers, with interests very different from their employers'.

To reconcile these seemingly contradictory portraits of the
female work force we must realize that strike activity per se
cannot always be equated with the development of solidarity
and working-class consciousness. If we take a closer look at
the 1920's, we find that women were less likely to join explicitly working-class organizations, such as unions and the Chinese Communist Party, than to join traditional mutual-aid
organizations called sisterhoods (*jiemei hui*). Women of the
1940's still were more likely to join sisterhoods than other
organizations, but the sisterhoods of the 1940's were very
different from those of the 1920's. They had become political,
as well as social, protection organizations. The sisterhoods
were transformed at first through the YWCA's indirect influence and later through the CCP's more direct attempts to use
them to organize women workers.

Heroines of May Thirtieth: A Reassessment

If there was ever a time when the Shanghai proletariat commanded the center stage of Chinese history, it was the period
of the May Thirtieth Movement. From the founding of the
Chinese Communist Party in 1921 through the Guomindang
coup of 1927, the workers of Shanghai frequently engaged
in strikes. This strike activity reached its high point in the
aftermath of the May Thirtieth Movement: between 1925 and
1927 there were 171 strikes in the Shanghai cotton mills.
Workers demanded higher wages, shorter hours, recognition
for unions, rules forbidding corporal punishment, and equal
pay for men and women performing the same work. In March
1927 more than 800,000 armed workers of the Shanghai General Union spearheaded an insurrection that seized control of
Shanghai from the warlords (see Chapter Five).

This dramatic display of activity by Chinese workers during the 1920's has been the focus of most studies of the Chinese labor movement.[1] Jean Chesneaux's seminal study chronicles the politicization of the Shanghai proletariat during the period from the May Fourth Movement of 1919 to the coup of 1927. In Chesneaux's account Shanghai workers, led by the Chinese Communist Party, matured into class-conscious, anti-imperialist revolutionaries. Despite the importance he attaches to workers in the Shanghai cotton industry, and the lengthy descriptions he provides of women's living and working conditions, women workers are curiously absent from Chesneaux's discussion of the labor movement. One is left assuming that women workers were as class-conscious and revolutionary as their male comrades. This assumption is perhaps reinforced by the post–May Fourth feminist movement that developed alongside the workers' movement, as well as by the CCP's outspoken concern with the oppression of women.

It is not easy to identify the role played by female cotton mill workers in this labor movement. Statistics published by the Shanghai Bureau of Social Affairs indicate how many workers at each cotton mill were involved in these strikes, yet these records do not consistently specify the numbers of male, female, and child participants. When they do, it appears that large numbers of women mill workers frequently joined the strikes; in fact, women often made up the majority of striking workers. Moreover, since the majority of the work force in the largest and one of the most militant industries in Shanghai were women, it seems safe to assume that women accounted for a significant portion of the strikers.

If strike activity per se were a barometer of workers' organization and class consciousness, there would be little doubt that the record of women's participation in strikes in the 1920's manifested a high level of militancy and organization.[2] Yet strike activity, as we shall see, was a complex phenomenon. To infer anything meaningful about the nature of women workers' organizations and their consciousness, we must take a close look at their reasons for striking. Although information is insufficient for a systematic assessment of the 1920's, some of the available accounts suggest the kind of questions that must be raised: Did women strike for the same reasons as men? Did their reasons reflect class consciousness or traditional loyalties? Who were their leaders?

These accounts reveal that women did not always strike for the same reasons that their male comrades did. The strike that shut down many Japanese mills in west Shanghai in February 1925 began when forty male workers in the roving department of the Nei Wai Number Eight Mill were dismissed and replaced by women. The strike, which quickly spread to the other Nei Wai mills as well as to the Ri Hua, Feng Tian, and Da Kang mills, ultimately involved some 30,800 cotton mill workers. Although we do not know the exact number of women involved, it must have been a significant percentage, because there were fewer than 21,000 male workers in all the Japanese mills in Shanghai at that time.[3]

Zhang Guotao, who along with Deng Zhongxia headed the CCP's Trade Union Secretariat at that time, happened to visit Shanghai shortly after the strike ended unsuccessfully. In his autobiography Zhang recalls his discussion of the strike with Party members who had been involved in the organizing work. "The strikers," Zhang learned from his comrades, "under the slogan 'Oppose Japan,' had adopted the technique of preventing large numbers of women and child workers from going to their jobs."[4] In other words, although women did not go to work and therefore appeared to be "on strike," the reason was that male strikers physically prevented women from working. Even though women workers might have benefited had the strikers' demands been met, they were hardly acting voluntarily to assert their own demands.

Another strike during the same period suggests that this was not a unique case. On May 15, 1925, just after the worker activist Gu Zhenghong was killed by Japanese guards, some one thousand male workers swept through the workshops of the Nei Wai Number Five Mill, smashing machinery as they went. "Because the women workers were afraid of the male workers' rioting," the account reports, "they fled from the south to the exit, and then ran outside the mill."[5] Again, in the statistical record it appears that women workers were on strike.

These examples are not meant to suggest that in all, or even in the majority, of cases, women struck only because they were intimidated or coerced into doing so or physically were barred from their jobs. Nonetheless they can caution us against hastily concluding that the simple fact of strike participation implies organization, resistance, or working-class consciousness.

To be sure, many strikes during the 1920's were initiated and organized by women workers themselves. In May 1922, for example, women workers in the warping room of one of the Ri Hua mills went on strike when management turned down their request to be paid according to the piecework system.[6] Another strike began in May 1923 over a new kind of scissors introduced by management.

Although the extent to which women workers initiated strikes might indicate some level of organization, it does not necessarily imply the development of a working-class consciousness. For every case of women striking to demand wage increases or to protest beatings by foremen and Number Ones, there are cases of women striking to defend traditional loyalties. A particularly vivid example is the strike described in Chapter Four, which took place at a Japanese-owned Ri Hua mill in March 1926, when the Shanghai labor movement was near the zenith of its activity and militancy. The police had to be summoned to control a strike of 3,000 women workers protesting management's refusal to hire the woman introduced for a job by their Number One. Given what we know about the power the Number Ones had over the women in their workshops, this display of loyalty is not surprising. Once again, though, it reminds us that if the record of strikes is to tell us anything about the role of women in the labor movement, their organizations, and their class consciousness, we must know a great deal more than the number of women who allegedly went on strike.

That women of the 1920's did not always participate in strikes as revolutionary heroines might not be so surprising were these not the years when Shanghai was the cradle of a revolutionary movement, one with workers as its principal actors. Since the founding in 1921 of the Chinese Communist

Party, it had sought to instill a class-conscious, nationalistic fervor among Shanghai proletarians, and to organize male and female workers to participate in the revolution. Furthermore, as Elizabeth Croll has pointed out, the establishment of the CCP's Women's Bureau in 1923 "marked the first attempt by a political party in China to arouse and *organize* women as a separate social category."[7] Did these efforts have any impact on female cotton mill workers? Available records suggest that the impact during the 1920's was minimal.[8]

The CCP was by no means oblivious to the conditions of women workers in Shanghai. From their first issues, Party magazines such as *The Guide Weekly* published numerous articles that focused on women's work. The Party seems to have hoped that exposing the exploitation endured by women textile workers would contribute to the development of class consciousness among many sectors of the Shanghai working class, but since the overwhelming majority of women workers were illiterate, it is doubtful that these articles stirred them at all.

Most of the active Party-organizing efforts appear to have been aimed at male workers. One of the CCP's first attempts to develop contacts with workers in Shanghai was to establish workers' schools in several of Shanghai's factory districts. The scanty information available about enrollment in these schools indicates that of two hundred students at the workers' schools in 1921, only twenty were women.[9] This extraordinarily low percentage of women students was most likely not the result of an explicit Party policy to exclude women from the schools; instead it appears to have been by default that so few women attended. The CCP organizers made little effort to overcome traditional barriers to women's participation, which would have required running separate schools for men and women workers. During the 1920's it was socially acceptable for women to participate in activities only with other women, not with men. On some occasions male Party organizers exhibited little respect for this reality. One woman worker described her first meeting with Deng Zhongxia as follows: "I had come back from the night shift, so I was already in bed. Deng

Zhongxia sat on my bed, patted me and said, 'Young girl, did you work the night shift?' I was scared to death—no man had ever come in like that and talked to me. What was he doing sitting on my bed? At that time women were not supposed to talk to men!'"[10]

Female organizers may have been more sensitive to tradition. An intellectual from Hunan, Xiang Jingyu, wrote an essay in 1924 criticizing the "leftist error" of ignoring the traditional values prohibiting women's attendance at coeducational schools. "The result," she lamented, "is that workers' education becomes the monopoly of men."[11] Xiang's pleas for the establishment of separate schools for women workers appear to have fallen on deaf ears, for there is no evidence that her suggestion was adopted. It is not surprising that most leaders of the labor movement, the majority of whom had been educated in these schools, were male.

The recollections of a Party organizer reinforce this picture of an organizing strategy aimed at male workers. In 1924, he complained, the CCP still had almost no contact with women workers. "In general the number of workers with whom we had contact was more than before," he recalled. "However, the contact was not very solid. Furthermore it was limited entirely to male workers. As for the masses of women workers, we did not even have contact with one woman worker."[12] He went on to recall that when some of the Party members working at the West Shanghai Workers' Club had submitted a list of suggestions to the Party's Central Committee in 1924, all but one were accepted. That one was the request that a female comrade be sent to help in the organizing efforts. "They said that that would have to wait for future consideration," he recalled.[13] The Party's rationale for its seeming lack of interest in organizing women is unclear.

Although the CCP-sponsored workers' clubs had no women organizers, several female Party activists were devoted to the cause of organizing women textile workers in Shanghai during the mid-1920's. The best known were Xiang Jingyu, another intellectual from Hunan named Wang Yizhi, and Yang Zhihua. All three were enrolled at Shanghai University, where they attended lectures by Deng Zhongxia. Xiang was a prolific writer as well as an organizer, and she developed a reputation as a vigilant critic of what she perceived to be the bourgeois orientation of the Chinese women's movement. Her articles in women's magazines frequently chastised the movement's membership for being divorced from the masses of women workers.[14]

Although Xiang, Wang and Yang all had reputations as spokespersons for women workers and Xiang and Yang sometimes spoke before crowds of striking workers, it is not clear how much direct contact they had with female cotton mill workers. (One hindrance to developing contact was created by the Hunanese accent of Xiang and Wang.) And though it is possible to find references to other women who became leaders in the labor movement, they almost always turn out to be intellectuals like these. None of the active leaders at the time of the May Thirtieth Movement were women workers.[15]

For all these reasons the CCP failed to organize women workers effectively, as shown by their meager membership in labor unions. Union rosters are not available, but whereas we do not know the numbers of male and female union members in each industry, we do know that women, 52 percent of the Shanghai work force on the eve of the 1927 coup, made up only a scanty 15 percent of total union membership.[16]

Although they might not have joined labor unions or attended classes at CCP-sponsored schools, women mill workers of the 1920's did not experience work life as lonely individuals isolated from their fellow workers. Most joined the traditional mutual aid societies known as sisterhoods. To understand how mill work transformed women's social relationships and political awareness, we must look at these sisterhoods. The failure of outside organizers to mobilize women workers effectively during the 1920's can perhaps be partially explained by their ignorance of these existing organizations of women workers.

Burning Incense, Pledging Sisterhood

During the thirty years between the end of World War I and Liberation, women who worked in the cotton mills of Shanghai commonly formed sisterhood societies (*jiemei hui*). These sisterhoods developed out of the patterns of daily life, residence, and work, and reflected women's need for mutual aid and protection. As we saw in the account of the working day, from the moment women left their homes and set out for the mills, they depended on their fellow workers. To avoid injury or abuse by hoodlums they made arrangements to walk together to and from the mill; to survive a twelve-hour shift that allowed almost no time to eat, go to the toilet, or rest, they made work-sharing arrangements with women in the same workshop.

Developing a network of "sisters"—a group of other workers one could depend on for help—was part of the experience of growing up in the mills. "We younger workers would not help each other in the workshop," one woman recalled. "But when I was older, I had 'little sisters.' Then when I would eat one of them would tend my machine. It was we girls who worked in adjacent aisles who would help each other. This started when I was about fifteen."[17] These relationships, which began as part of the work routine, became social relationships as well. "After working a long time you'd start to have friends," the same woman continued. "And on Sundays, if you had time, you could go visit [them]. Maybe that started when I was seventeen or eighteen. All my friends then were cotton mill workers." It was with her co-workers from the mill that Chen Zhaodi, behind her mother-in-law's back, went to watch performances of local opera in the evenings.

These relationships often remained casual, but they were sometimes formalized as sisterhoods. One woman described this process as follows: "Originally we would go to work together and leave work together because it was not good to walk alone. After a while we would get to know each other. Then, if I thought that person was very decent, I would say to her, 'Why don't we pledge loyalty? Then if you have some problems I'll help you, and if I have some problems you can help me.'"[18] Pledging loyalty and thereby establishing sisterhood involved a ceremony, sometimes simply going to a restaurant, eating a meal together, and toasting loyalty to one

another with a cup of "one-heart wine." Because large numbers of women workers were Buddhists, those forming sisterhoods more often went together to a Buddhist temple and
burned incense before the statue of a deity. At the temple
"everyone would have to make a pledge," one woman explained. "We pledged to be loyal through life and death. And
if someone was halfhearted in her loyalty, then we prayed that
when she got on a boat, that boat would turn over."[19]

There were "sisterhoods of six," "sisterhoods of eight,"
"sisterhoods of ten," and so on. Once they had pledged loyalty
the members of the sisterhood called each other by kinship
terms based on age; for example, the oldest was Big Sister, the
next oldest, Second Sister. In some groups members wore
identical long blue cotton gowns when they went out together,
to express their unity.

Sisterhoods fulfilled vital needs for their members both inside and outside the mills. In addition to spelling each other at
work and getting together at a member's house to chat after
work or on Sundays, sisters protected each other from harassment by male workers and overseers on the shop floor and by
hoodlums on the street. "There would be hoodlums waiting
at the factory gate, watching us young girls," Song Ermei recalled. "So we pledged sisters would leave the factory together, and when these guys made trouble we would try to
fight them together."

Members of a sisterhood also helped each other financially.
To meet the expenses of extraordinary events such as weddings
and funerals, to pay the costs incurred when a family member
was ill, or even to buy a "luxury item" such as a dress or coat,
a worker usually needed more money than she could save from
her wages, and more even than her family's combined resources could furnish. Sisterhoods of women workers provided an alternative to stamp money lenders.[20] To prevent
members' having to borrow from these usurers at exorbitant
interest rates, women often paid a "sisterhood fee," each
member contributing a small amount of her salary each month
to this fund. If a sister needed to borrow money, she could
draw on this fund and repay the amount borrowed later, with

interest of five to ten percent.[21] One worker described the way her sisters pooled their resources:

Maybe four of us girls got together. Each month, when we got our wages, we would each donate a certain amount to the kitty. Then we would determine who needed money the most that time. For example, it was very hard for us to buy a *qi pao* in those days, a good blue one. So sometimes we would use the money to make a *qi pao* for whichever person needed it. Or maybe someone would use [the money] to make a coat. If one of the members had family problems, like someone needed to see a doctor, or someone had died, they would use the money for that.[22]

A woman who pledged sisterhood was formalizing relationships with people outside her family as she began to perceive a bond with the women she worked with in the factory. This does not mean, however, that she perceived all other women mill workers, or even all other women who worked in the same mill, as potential sisters. Patterns of migration to and settlement in Shanghai, and hiring practices that usually resulted in concentrations of people from the same district in particular workshops, usually also resulted in sisterhoods composed of women from the same native place. These women shared a common dialect, style of dress, and eating habits. A woman from Wuxi, when asked whether she had ever joined a sisterhood, replied, "There was no one else in my workshop from Wuxi, so who could I pledge sisterhood with?"[23] Women who pledged sisterhood were both confirming bonds between those from the same native place and emphasizing the separateness of those from different native places.

Although it seems that, as the name implies, sisterhoods were usually made up of women, there is some evidence that the members of sisterhoods were not exclusively female. In describing the sisterhoods, one woman explained, "when ten of us women workers pledged sisterhood, we usually included one male worker and two or three tough women workers. Otherwise our group would not have power for defense."[24] A similar practice among prostitutes in Shanghai suggests that this was not completely atypical. "Wild chickens," the lowest class of prostitutes and the only ones who went out onto the streets to attract customers, also formed sisterhood societies. Their sisterhoods often consisted of nine prostitutes plus one man, usually a hoodlum who had connections with the local police, included to help protect the women if anyone tried to abuse them while they were out at night.[25]

Unfortunately we do not know whether the practice of including men in sisterhoods of women mill workers was widespread, nor do we know what role the men played. Perhaps men provided physical protection when necessary but did not participate in the other functions of the sisterhood, such as work sharing, economic mutual aid, and socializing. Male mill workers had brotherhoods (*xiongdi hui*), which would have performed those functions. Like the women, eight to ten men pledged loyalty to each other by burning incense, and like the women, members of brotherhoods called each other by kinship terms—Oldest Brother, Second Brother, and so forth.

Membership in sisterhoods was not restricted to workers of the same status. In some cases a sisterhood included a woman who worked as a Number One in the mill or a woman who was influential in the neighborhood, usually because of gang affiliation. Some women might have chosen to simultaneously pledge sisterhood and pledge loyalty to a godmother (in the way described in Chapter Four). The woman who described the sisterhoods as including one male and two or three tough women implied such a merging of the two forms. "Tough" in Shanghai parlance at that time implied gang affiliation. Moreover, during the War of Resistance, when the Chinese Communist Party attempted to adapt organizational forms familiar to women workers by establishing sisterhoods, some were heterogeneous groups. One account told of a sisterhood that included several ordinary mill workers, a woman who was a Number One, and an older woman who was married to a gang leader.[26] In these sisterhoods we find women of different status in the mill and of different ages bonded together. They were apparently not always the egalitarian organizations that the term sisterhood implies.

Even if the sisterhoods sometimes included men and Number Ones, and even if women in the mills did not perceive themselves as sisters to all of their fellow women workers, the fact remains that women workers bonded together in formal organizations with some of their co-workers. They could have simply continued to help each other at work, walk together to and from the mill, and socialize together without bothering to go to Buddhist temples, burn incense, and pledge sisterhood. Why was it necessary for them to create an organization?

In forming sisterhood societies women workers in Shanghai were adopting and transforming what appears to have been a traditional form of organization among Chinese women. Traditional women's organizations are a subject about which very little research has been done. The two examples of sisterhood societies that have been studied—those formed by peasant women of Shunde, near Guangzhou, in the late nineteenth century and those formed by women in Chuansha prefecture (near Shanghai) in the early twentieth century—share several features. Women who joined sisterhoods, both in Shunde and in Chuansha, were in some sense deviants from the traditional family system. The sisterhoods at Shunde were formed by women who lived together in Buddhist vegetarian halls and vowed never to marry, and at Chuansha young widows who refused to remarry were the core of the sisterhoods. In both cases the members of sisterhoods could live together apart from their families because they earned an independent cash income: in Shunde the women's income came from the silk industry, and in Chuansha from cotton spinning and weaving. Their affiliation with lay Buddhist sects, their independent income, and their desire to live outside the traditional family system were the essence of both kinds of sisterhoods.[27]

How were these two groups related to the sisterhoods formed by women cotton mill workers in Shanghai, where the members did not live together or demonstrate any desire to challenge traditional social relationships? Was this organizational form transmitted from rural areas to the city, and if so, how? Was a tradition of folk Buddhism among some women workers crucial to the initial formation of sisterhoods in Shanghai? The answers to these questions require much

more extensive research about the history of sisterhoods, research that might uncover a close relationship between regions with Buddhist sects and the origins of sisterhoods. An
equally possible finding, though, is that sisterhoods were
formed by women in villages throughout China and, furthermore, that there were many different kinds of sisterhoods,
the only common element being the ceremony of pledging
loyalty to one another. One final possibility is that the sisterhoods were not so much geographically as historically specific. Conceivably the formation of sisterhood societies was
a product of the breakdown of kinship networks attendant
on social and economic change in the late nineteenth and early
twentieth centuries.

Explaining the formation of sisterhoods among women
mill workers requires that we examine not only traditions of
immigrants but those of other sectors of Shanghai society as
well, for pledging sisterhood appears to have been a widespread practice in the city. How common sisterhoods were,
and which groups of women formed them are difficult questions. Unlike unions or native place associations, whose existence can be confirmed by the written records they produced, sisterhoods in Shanghai left only scattered, incidental
references. But in addition to the sisterhoods among prostitutes referred to above, there is evidence of sisterhoods among
concubines and among dance hostesses, among silk workers,
and among women in the Shanghai police department.[20] Sisterhoods were by no means unique to women cotton mill
workers.

Although our understanding of the history of sisterhoods
in Chinese society is far from complete, we can infer from the
information assembled above that the sisterhoods of women
mill workers were not entirely the product of the specific conditions under which women lived and worked in Shanghai.
Women workers, who depended on one another to survive,
did not create new organizational forms, nor did they often
adopt those imposed by outside organizers. The sisterhoods
can perhaps best be understood as a transitional adaptation of
a traditional practice to meet the new needs of women workers

in an urban, industrial environment. Women drew on traditional ties with those from the same native place when they formed sisterhoods, yet the sisterhoods involved something more than these traditional relationships. New workers, even those with many co-workers from the same native place, did not have a group of sisters to depend on. To some degree the relationships between sisters developed while women worked in the mills, and in that sense they were indeed a product of factory life.

Although the sisterhoods were not self-consciously political, they often took actions that had political implications. Sometimes groups of sisters, banding together to protect one member, opposed or even physically attacked their employers. "One time a girl worker was being harassed by an overseer," one woman remembered. "She told us sisters, and we all attacked that overseer and beat him up."[29] Sometimes the cause of mutual protection put them in situations resembling strikes: if a Number One threatened to fire a woman who belonged to a sisterhood, her sisters would refuse to work until the Number One revoked her threat.

These were common, spontaneous incidents, but it does not require much stretching of the imagination to visualize the use of these loyalties in an organized labor movement. If one member of a sisterhood shut off the motor of her spinning frame or loom, her sisters could be expected to shut off their machines too, if for no other reason than loyalty. Women's participation in the labor movement, then, might depend on individual women in the sisterhoods who had visions of change. Where might these women come from? Communist organizers of the 1920's certainly had a vision of change, but they did not work through the sisterhoods. The separation of men and women, regional affiliations, and ties with godmothers and gangs—all of these undermined class solidarity and might have made the CCP wary of using the sisterhoods for organizing.

In the late 1920's the first outside organization kindled political awareness in a group of women workers, who in turn gradually began to transform the sisterhoods they belonged to. This organization was not one that hoped to mobilize

women to participate in a revolutionary movement but, ironically, was a foreign missionary organization, the Young
Women's Christian Association.

The YWCA and Women Workers

The YWCA was the first outside organization that a significant number of women workers joined. It provided one of
the few forums in Shanghai where women workers of dispa-
rate origins, who worked in different cotton mills and often in
different industries, met together. Although the number of
women who participated in YWCA programs was never more
than a small fraction of the female work force, an overwhelming majority of women workers who became active in the labor movement and in the CCP after 1937 attribute their initial
"political awakening" to the night schools run by the YWCA
for women workers.

The YWCA had existed in China since 1890. From early on
it had had a less religious orientation than most missionary
groups, and by the end of World War I, though spreading
Christianity remained one of its avowed goals, converting
workers was clearly secondary to social welfare work.[30] This
was especially true of the industrial department staff, who
seemed even less tolerant of religious gospel than their counterparts in other departments. Agatha Harrison, a British ex-
pert on industrial affairs, was hired as the first secretary of the
industrial department of the Shanghai branch in 1920. She had
been "very frank in saying that she is not a member of any
church . . . and when she was asked point-blank whether she
approved of the taking of Christianity to non-Christian countries . . . she replied that she was not sure, but that probably
she would become sure on seeing the need for it on the spot."[31]
Nothing in the record of her work in China indicates that she
ever discovered such a need.

After Agatha Harrison arrived the YWCA began to develop
an industrial program,[32] focusing initially on informing the
public rather than on educating workers themselves. The foreign staff based in Shanghai after World War I, appalled by
what they saw of the working conditions of women and chil-

dren in Shanghai's factories, made the Child Labor Campaign its first major industrial project (see Chapter One). During the mid-twenties, the YWCA undertook a small, experimental program of popular education for women workers, including a settlement house in the Zhabei silk district, a noontime literacy class at an egg-packing factory, and a class for forewomen at the Nanyang Brothers Tobacco Company. These programs involved only a small number of women, both ordinary workers and their supervisors.[33]

The development of a large-scale and far-reaching industrial program was partly the result of the increasingly militant labor movement and the Nationalist revolution of the late 1920's. The foreign secretaries who witnessed these events urged the YWCA to commit itself to serving the masses of ordinary women workers. The justification for devoting itself to workers' education, one of the American secretaries wrote, "exists in the fact that the labor movement is the big factor in the future making of our economic society and that it makes all the difference in the world what that labor movement thinks. If we wish to help to create that thinking we will need to do it where the workers are."[34] Hoping to train women to become leaders in the labor movement, the YWCA began a full-fledged program for women workers in 1928.

Almost paradoxically, this program emerged in the wake of the White Terror of 1927. Most members of the CCP who survived the arrests and executions fled Shanghai, and until the war with Japan started in 1937, they devoted themselves to organizing a rural revolution. The Shanghai General Union was disbanded, and the GMD enacted a series of laws severely restricting labor organizing and strike activity. During the Nanjing decade unions continued to exist, but they either were controlled by the GMD or were "yellow unions," with strong ties to management.[35] The YWCA was therefore one of the few organizations during the 1930's that tried, quietly and modestly, to instill in women a radical understanding of their position as women and as workers.

The YWCA's industrial program during the 1930's was inspired primarily by Cora Deng, who became the organization's national industrial secretary in 1930. Deng, a native of

Hunan, had joined the student department of the YWCA there at the time of the May Fourth Movement in 1919 and had worked with Maud Russell, an American YWCA secretary active in Changsha. From Russell, Deng had her first introduction to revolutionary ideas. "Maud helped me to study English," Cora Deng recalled. "And she also taught me to read something about revolution. She asked me to study with her a book called *Dialectical Materialism*. I had very poor English at that time, and those big words in that book—I had to use a dictionary all the time to find out what the real meaning was. Whatever little knowledge I had about socialist thinking was started through my contact with Maud."[36] Deng visited rickshaw drivers and factory workers with Russell and gradually became interested in developing a program for working women. After studying sociology at Jinling College in Nanjing, Deng was given a YWCA scholarship to spend a year studying at the London School of Economics. Returning to China and assuming the leadership of the YWCA's industrial program, she hoped to help women understand their function in the Chinese economic system.

Between 1928 and 1930 the YWCA established schools in all the major factory districts of Shanghai: there were two schools in Xiaoshadu and one each in Caojiadu, Yangshupu, Pudong, and Zhabei. Establishing schools was only the first step, however. Attracting students came next. The YWCA staff quickly realized that "such publicity facilities as newspaper advertisements, handbills, posters, etc., are of no use because the women cannot read them."[37] Instead they relied on word of mouth. When the YWCA planned to open a new school, the secretaries would tell several enthusiastic students, who would in turn tell all their friends. Another method was to offer entertainment programs in working-class districts. "Such meetings always appeal to Chinese," one secretary wrote, "especially to those of the working class who do not have much chance of seeing moving pictures, plays, etc. Then, before the great crowd, the importance of education is explained, followed by the announcement of the plans of the school. At the end of the program many eager faces will look up saying that they want to come to the school."[38] By first catering to the social interests of women workers, rather than by creating its own agenda and assuming that women would be interested, the YWCA gradually developed a following among women workers. As one worker very candidly put it: "I went to the school because it looked like fun, not because I really wanted to learn to read. They would sing and perform plays, so I thought it would be more fun than staying at home."[39]

The YWCA schools offered a three-year program of study, with classes five days a week for an hour and a half each session. Women on the night shift went to classes held in the morning, and those who worked the day shift went in the evening, often to their parents' chagrin. "My mother kept saying I shouldn't go," Gu Lianying recalled.

"Your work is hard enough. You don't need to go to school on top of that," she would tell me. She said I would not have enough time to sleep and if I did not sleep I would not be able to work, and if I did not work then we could not live. But I insisted that I wanted to go. I went every day. When we did the night shift we would get off work at 6:00 A.M. I'd go home, eat breakfast, and then go to school. Among my "little sisters" in the mill there were three or four others who went to the school.[40]

Absenteeism due to illness, family obligations, exhaustion, and bad weather was a major problem at the schools. When a student failed to appear for several days, a teacher visited her at home, and if a woman was seriously ill, the teachers arranged for her to be seen by a doctor on the YWCA staff. Funds helped pay for hospitalization when necessary. Teachers frequently tutored convalescing students at home. The teachers' persistence was crucial in keeping women workers involved in the YWCA's program over several years.[41]

The YWCA's innocuous descriptions of the three-year program of study are probably what led the Guomindang to tolerate the schools' existence. But the GMD might have found the actual content of some courses to be more objectionable. For the first two years women took classes in writing, arithmetic, geography, history, current events, singing, and recreation. In their third year students could choose elective courses such as those about industrial problems, trade unionism, and labor legislation.[42] The textbooks that were used are no longer available, but Zhang Shuyi, the head of the Labor Bureau of the Shanghai YWCA during the 1930's, remembered two of the texts that beginning students used. "One was the one required by the GMD, with the Three People's Principles. Aside from that we also put together a simple text for them, teaching them what imperialism was, how to be patriotic, why workers were oppressed, and why workers' lives are so inferior to those of the capitalists."[43] A course in letter writing supplemented the lessons of these texts. Students used a booklet called "Xiu Ying's Letters," a compilation of letters written by a woman working in Shanghai to her family in a village and her family's letters to her. The letters described the conditions that forced women to leave the countryside and work in cities, as well as the poverty of urban industrial life.[44] Following the pattern of this text, students wrote letters relating their own families' experiences.

Zhong Shaoqin (Helen Zhong), who taught intermediate classes, used the pretext of teaching letter writing to encourage women to become activists. She had students read and discuss the factory law of the Shanghai Municipal Council and then required them to make lists of conditions at their respective factories that failed to conform to its safety provisions. Their main project for the class was to write letters to the Municipal Council, reporting these illegal conditions. "Of course the letters would not be effective," Zhong commented, "but this was a way of teaching. From this they could realize that if you wanted to be liberated, you had to rely on yourself."[45]

Once a week, instead of the regular class session, all students participated in club activities such as singing, story-telling, and acting, cultivating skills that would enable them to become leaders in the labor movement. "We would have debates," one woman recalled of the club meetings she had attended. "One side would argue that it was our fate to be poor; the other side would argue that it was because of the social structure that we were so poor."[46] Sometimes the clubs organized programs to be performed for a larger audience of women workers who lived in their districts. At one Labor Day celebration in 1931, for instance, one of the women in the clubs delivered a speech about the standards of work desired by women workers. The speech was followed by a short play, written and performed by other club members, entitled "The Gifts and the Givers." It depicted

a student, on her birthday, receiving many gifts from her family and friends. In a dream the workers who have made the various articles which she has received as gifts come to her and tell her of the contribution which they have made to her happiness, or the conditions under which they have worked to make them, and asking her to remember not only her friends who have given her the gifts but also the women and girls who have worked so hard to produce them. The play ended with the entrance of the Spirit of Labor Day and a worker. With them the student rises and sings a labor song.[47]

Aside from the obvious purpose of attempting to reach and educate more women, the YWCA's staff hoped that planning these programs would give women experience in conceptualizing and organizing a project together, "all of which are very essential to a labor movement."[48]

Given what women workers learned at the YWCA schools, it is not surprising that many YWCA students became activists in the labor movement. One woman recalled her first confrontation at the age of fifteen, with a Number One who was beating other women workers in the mill. "Other people would not talk back to the Number Ones," she remembered, "but I would. It was because I was not satisfied." When asked why she was not satisfied, she replied, "It was because I was going to a night school—a YWCA night school!"[49]

Although the teachers at the YWCA schools did not actively instigate strikes, they played an important role once strikes developed. At school women from one mill could discuss their strike efforts with women at other mills and obtain their support. In this way they often catalyzed the spread of strikes from one mill to another. Gu Lianying explained how this happened during a strike that started at the Japanese-owned Tong Xing Mill in 1936:

At our school there were some women who worked at Tong Xing, so they told us about their strike. We all went to have a look, and we went to where workers lived, to try to persuade them not to go to work. All of us from the school went together, in the evening when we had free time.

The Japanese finally conceded, and raised their wages. When we saw that they got a five-*fen* [one half *jiao*] raise, we all said, "We have to think of a way to demand this too." We at Yong An ended up striking as well.[50]

The roles of YWCA students as activists and the night schools as meeting centers became even more pronounced in the period between the end of World War II and Liberation. Before turning to that period, however, we must look at the war itself, for it was in the context of the Japanese assault on Shanghai that the program developed by the YWCA was extended beyond the confines of the night schools and involved numbers of women far greater than the number who studied literacy at the schools.

From the time the National Salvation Movement began in 1936, the YWCA had included patriotism, nationalism, and anti-imperialism on its agenda for workers' education. People familiar with conditions in the occupied Northeast were invited to speak to women workers at the night schools about Japanese aggression in China. When there were large anti-Japanese demonstrations, women workers from the night schools attended, along with their teachers.

After the outbreak of war in August 1937, the YWCA's night schools were temporarily shut down. Many former students devoted themselves to patriotic work, and some of the most dedicated joined the Working Women's Battlefront Service Unit. "Clad in army uniforms," teams of thirty women workers went to "work with the army and the country people at the very front. . . . They talked to groups and went to call from home to home to tell them about this war of resistance and to persuade them to cooperate with the army."[51] The teams also took care of wounded soldiers and helped with chores around the army camps.[52]

Large numbers of YWCA students, unemployed because of factory shutdowns at the beginning of the war, drew on the education they had received at the YWCA and engaged in mass education work throughout Shanghai. Some helped with a citywide plan to set up informal schools in neighborhood alleyways. "The girls themselves are writing wall newspapers, opening classes, directing singing, giving talks and conducting discussions on the national emergency," one report announced.[53] Others went to teach at the refugee camps set up by the YWCA for unemployed women. "It is run like a big old Chinese family," one observer said of such a camp. The camp operated as a cooperative: based on their interests and skills, women divided up responsibility for daily chores such as cooking, cleaning, gatekeeping, and nursing. During the day they could learn how to sew clothes, make paper flowers and toys, embroider, and knit. They sold the items they produced, and used the proceeds to purchase food and supplies for the co-op. The women could also attend literacy classes; most women in the camps had had no previous opportunity to study. Like the classes at the night schools, the literacy programs at the refugee camps were blended with politics—particularly anti-Japanese propaganda, as well as history and social analysis. As opportunities arose, the YWCA staff made arrangements for women in the camps to secure regular jobs.[54]

The YWCA was not the only organization represented in the refugee camps. The CCP had become legal in 1937 with the establishment of the anti-Japanese united front with the GMD. Although the Party's organizing network remained based in the countryside as it had been since the Party was driven from the cities in 1927, some Party cadres returned to organize in the cities. They saw in Shanghai's refugee camps an opportunity to conduct mass education. Several Party members who were sent to teach and organize activities later referred to the refugee camps as the "liberated zones of Shanghai."[55]

The Chinese Communist Party and Women Workers

In the context of the occupation of Shanghai by the Japanese, the CCP once again sought to organize the city's women workers. During this time it developed an organizing strategy very different from the one it had used during the 1920's. The two cornerstones of the revised strategy were the YWCA schools and the sisterhoods.

AGAINST THE JAPANESE

Tactics used by the CCP during the 1920's (such as making speeches, distributing leaflets, and establishing workers' clubs) were not viable at a time when the Japanese arrested blatant political activists. Under these circumstances the Party began trying to adapt organizational forms already existing among women workers, such as the sisterhoods and YWCA schools, to attract members. Instead of trying to persuade workers to take steps that would depart from their normal daily routine, Party organizers tried to understand and become a part of that routine.

Although the CCP's previous lack of success among Shanghai's women workers demanded the development of this new strategy, the Party's new sensitivity in recruiting women might have been partially the result of organizing tactics developed during its exile in the countryside. By the early 1940's, large numbers of Party members had experience in mass work that demanded the closest possible attention to the circumstances of those they hoped to organize.

It is not clear when this strategy was first implemented in Shanghai. The first important evidence is a report written by Ma Chunji in 1941. Very little is known about Ma's background, except that he had been a Party organizer responsible for workers' education in Shanghai since the late 1930's. Ma's paper is significant because it is the only known report that deals exclusively and extensively with the obstacles to organizing women workers in Shanghai. Moreover, it is the first report indicating that Party members had made an effort to understand the specific problems and motivations of women workers.[56]

One of Ma's major points in this report was that Party members should unite with women in their everyday organizations. "Because of subjective and objective circumstances of women's lives, they must often help each other," Ma wrote. "In order to prevent people from flirting with them, or to prevent hoodlums from trying to steal their wages, they often walk together to and from work. On their time off, when they go to buy things, they also usually go in groups of seven or eight. In all of these groups one or two are at the center. If we can attract them, then it is easy to attract others in their group."[57] In addition to urging them to reach ordinary women through the sisterhoods, Ma encouraged organizers to pay attention to the women who held positions of power in the mills. The way to do this, he argued, was by adopting the same methods customarily used by women workers themselves to obtain the protection of those with power, that is, pledging godmothers. Party members, he said, should become goddaughters to the Number Ones in the mills. He also encouraged them to pledge older women who guarded and supervised the workers' dormitories as godmothers. "Then, under the cover of these godmothers, it is possible to organize all the women who live in that dormitory."[58]

The organizers who implemented these strategies most likely did not need to be instructed on the nature of women workers' internal organizations. Unlike their predecessors of the 1920's most organizers at this time were workers themselves, often women who had been students at the YWCA night schools and had joined the CCP after the war began. Some Party members already belonged to a sisterhood and could simply seek to influence their sisters. Gui Jianying recalled that she had been a member of a sisterhood long before becoming a Party member in the early 1940's, but that after she joined the Party her sisterhood became "a form of public organization for the Party."[59] More frequently, activists encouraged women to pledge sisterhood with other workers. Even these sisterhoods formed under the auspices of the Party adhered to the original form. Party members accompanied their sisters to Buddhist temples, burned incense with them, bowed to the statue of Guan Yin, and pledged to be loyal to their sisters through life and death. Like the traditional sisterhoods, those organized by the Party sometimes included Number Ones and women married to gang members who wielded local influence.[60]

If these new sisterhoods differed from the traditional ones, the differences were manifested only in small, almost imperceptible ways. After a group of women pledged sisterhood at the Da Kang Mill, for instance, they each contributed a small sum of money to buy a piece of white cloth. They cut the cloth into squares, sewed handkerchiefs, and on each one embroidered the words "working together with one heart."[61] Although members of traditional sisterhoods occasionally made identical gowns or identical handkerchiefs to symbolize their relationship as sworn sisters, they were not likely to have expressed their common interests as workers with such a motto.

Likewise, members of sisterhoods commonly got together on Sundays to go window-shopping or to go to a park. Party members encouraged and participated in these activities, gradually introducing new dimensions. When they went to parks, for example, Party members spent part of the time telling their sisters about the progress made by women through the Russian Revolution, and about the work of the CCP in Yanan.[62] Party organizers encouraged women who were sympathetic to these ideas to attend YWCA schools.[63] Some eventually joined the CCP themselves.[64]

During the war the Party did not seek to mobilize its recruits to participate in a revolutionary movement. Instead it tried to organize women to resist the Japanese, who controlled most of the mills that continued to operate in Shanghai during the war (see Chapter One). Because dramatic strikes or demonstrations would have resulted in Japanese retaliation against activists, Party members in the mills tried to organize women workers to subvert production in as many inconspicuous ways as possible.

A common form of resistance was stealing. "Under the Japanese we would steal lots of things," remembered a woman who worked in a mill during the war.

This was organized by the Communist Party. In the factory there was lots of stray cotton cloth and thread. We would take it out with us, and then we would sell it and make some money. To get it out of the factory, past the guards who would search us, sometimes we used our rice boxes. Sometimes they would find it when they searched us. But the people who did the searching were Chinese, so sometimes they would just let us go. They were with us. Also, some of us women workers, we would put the things in our bras, and then they would not find them. And sometimes everyone in a workshop would make a plan to steal a lot of yarn or cloth. All at once, together, we would just rush through the gate. That way they couldn't stop us.[65]

Stealing was not restricted to the cotton cloth and yarn the workers helped manufacture. During this period of acute food shortages, even the vegetables grown by the Japanese on the mill premises were fair game. "When the Japanese were asleep we would go to the garden and steal the vegetables they were growing," Chen Zhaodi recalled. "We used the cotton bags from the spinning department to put the vegetables in."[66]

Another subversion tactic organized by Party activists was to decrease the quantities of yarn and cloth produced in the workshops. Women set the machines at slower speeds and often stopped work altogether whenever the Japanese overseers were absent from the workshop. Sometimes they used a riskier scheme, turning their machines off until the overseer approached, and then switching them back on until he had passed. They hoped that the overseer would never realize that the majority of machines were off or, if he did, that he would be stymied in his attempts to find someone to blame.

Women in each department devised tactics to reduce the profits the Japanese made from textile production. In the spinning rooms, women piecers purposely wasted yarn by cutting extra-long pieces whenever they had to retie broken threads. When the Japanese caught on, they instituted a system of weighing the waste yarn of each worker at the end of her shift and imposing a fine if it exceeded a prescribed weight. The women were not deterred. They retaliated by periodically taking heaps of waste yarn they had generated to the bathroom and disposing of it there. Weavers purposely made mistakes, producing bad cloth that sorters then knowingly packed along with the good cloth to be shipped to buyers.[67]

Whether or not the Japanese ever suffered significant losses from this subversion is not as important in the present study as the nature of organization that was required to implement the resistance. In some cases groups of women organized these

schemes under the guise of sisterhoods. According to one account, ten women workers in a Shanghai cotton mill formed
a sisterhood "to arouse support for underground resistance
against the Japanese."[68] There might not have been newsworthy strikes or dramatic displays of workers' militancy during
the Japanese occupation, but theft, slowdowns, and attempts
to produce inferior goods all required coordination, suggesting a degree of solidarity among women workers that had not
previously existed.

These activities also attest to the extent to which an outside
organization, the CCP, gradually transformed women's relationships and consciousness by using traditional forms of organization as a starting point. One result was that the Party
developed a base among women workers that played an important role in gaining women's participation in the postwar
labor movement.

Of course, the wartime conditions under which the Party
organized women workers were highly atypical. First, the
work force was only a small fraction of its size before and after
the war. Second, women's need for organization was perhaps
greater under wartime conditions. For basic needs ranging
from obtaining rice to protecting themselves from rape by Japanese soldiers, women needed one another's help even more
than before. Finally, the nature of the enemy was very different
from what it had previously been. It had not always been easy
persuading women to perceive capitalists as the enemy and to
struggle against that enemy. But when the capitalists were the
Japanese, whose armies had invaded China and occupied
Shanghai, women were more inclined to resist.

Despite this uniqueness, there were important continuities
between wartime and postwar organizing techniques. Women
who had become accustomed to sabotaging the Japanese mills
drew on this experience after the war. Many women workers
who joined the Party during the war continued to work after
the Japanese surrendered, and played a major role in mobilizing women workers to participate in the labor movement. Finally, the organizing strategy developed by the CCP during
the war was carried over into the postwar period.

TOWARD LIBERATION

By the end of 1945, when the formerly Japanese-owned mills still had not resumed operations at full capacity, workers in Shanghai organized demonstrations with some 50,000 participants to demand that they be rehired or be given severance pay. Those who went back to work in the mills organized to demand shorter hours, welfare benefits, and wage increases based on the wildly fluctuating cost-of-living index. For the first time since the 1920's a CCP-led urban labor movement became a major political force, and women were prominent in that movement.

A history of the post–World War II labor movement in Shanghai, a movement that was intertwined with other mass movements responding to civil war and severe economic dislocation, is beyond the scope of this study. But several important themes of this movement are relevant to a discussion of women workers' organizations and consciousness: the CCP's mobilization of, and its increasing popularity with, women workers, the sisterhoods as a foundation for political organizing, the emergence of women workers as leaders of the labor movement, and the increasing importance of issues specifically pertinent to women, such as maternity leave and nurseries, as items on the agenda of the labor movement.

Under Guomindang rule the CCP was again driven underground, and organizing once again became a clandestine activity. Although many of the underground Party members were women who had joined the Party during the war, the augmented postwar work force was composed mostly of women who had not been in the mills during the war. The first task of Party members was therefore to establish credibility among these workers. Like CCP organizers during the occupation, they accomplished this not by holding meetings or espousing political principles, but rather by interacting in ways that were customary among women workers, earning their respect and trust.

Acts such as securing medical assistance for women who encountered life-threatening complications when giving birth at work helped Party members win the gratitude of the women in their workshops. Fan Xiaofeng, a woman worker who was also a Party activist and a leader in the labor movement, explained that even the ability to cut hair could be used to earn support for the Party among the workers:

First we just tried to develop friendships with women, and later we could talk about workers' conditions. At that time I knew how to cut hair. Every week I would cut hair for many people. I could go to their homes on Sunday. They welcomed me because barbers were expensive. And I could cut hair really fast—in just a few minutes! I would do anything to help out in their houses, so they liked me to visit. Then I could talk to the young women in their homes. Otherwise, to go talk to a young girl, they would not like that at all. Mothers-in-law would be really upset. You cannot imagine how fierce Chinese mothers-in-law are. So, first I would go and take care of their housework, and I would be very polite, calling the mother-in-law *nai nai* [lit., "grandmother"; loosely, a term showing respect], etc. Then they would think I was a very proper person. After that I could talk to the daughter or daughter-in-law. Chinese folk really like people who are hard-working and diligent and polite. If you go to someone's house as if you are something great, then no one will pay any attention to you.[69]

Party members continued to use the tradition of pledging sisterhood as a way of organizing women who worked together in a particular mill. Although many women may have continued to pledge sisterhood in a traditional sense, those associations initiated by the Party moved further and further from the relative spontaneity of the traditional sisterhoods. They no longer represented simply the affirmation of casual work-sharing relationships among eight to ten women who worked together in a workshop or who walked together to and from the mill.

Pledging sisterhood during the postwar period became a much more calculated, deliberate act. At the Heng Feng Mill, for instance, the Party branch was reported to have conducted pledging-sisterhood ceremonies on three specific occasions: in a ceremony at the end of 1946 women in the blowing and stripping departments swore sisterhood; a ceremony held during the summer of 1947 initiated women in the weaving, preparation, and spinning departments; and at the end of 1947, some inspectors, accountants, and Number Ones from the spinning room joined. To avoid arousing the suspicion of GMD spies, older workers with influence, as well as wives of neighborhood hoodlums, were included in each sisterhood so that it would bear resemblance to the traditional form.[70] In other mills some Party-inspired sisterhoods included up to two hundred women.

As members of sisterhoods, women often engaged in activities that indicated an even greater departure from the past. On March 8, 1946, members of the Party branch at the Zhong Fang Number Twelve Mill (formerly the Japanese-owned Da Kang Mill) organized an International Women's Day celebration, inviting groups of sisters from nearby mills in Yangshupu. Some 1,500 women attended a meeting held at one of the factory-owned dormitories and heard He Ziying, representing the Shanghai Women's Association, talk about her visit to the Soviet Union and about feminist ideas such as equal pay for women's and men's work. They also learned to sing the March Eighth Song.[71] On the same day, Party activists at mills in western Shanghai mobilized 30,000 sisters to attend a Women's Day demonstration at Jessfield Park, and some joined a march across town to the Da Guang Ming auditorium, where the Women's Day celebration sponsored by the mayor's wife was being held. "We arrived just when their meeting was breaking up, so all the high-class women with their high heels were leaving," Tang Guifen wrote. "The women in our demonstration yelled, 'We want freedom, we want liberation!' "[72]

In mobilizing sisterhoods to participate in these activities—and, more frequently, in strikes—Party members gradually identified women who were activists and invited them to join the Party. No available statistics indicate the number of women workers who became bona fide Party members, but the number undoubtedly was only a small fraction of the total female work force. More significant is the degree of influence the Party was able to exercise among women workers by developing branches in most mill workshops.

For those women who did join the Party, membership in a branch might not have seemed entirely dissimilar to membership in a sisterhood. Although joining the Party did not involve a ceremony of burning incense and pledging loyalty, Party branches were organized by workshop and by sex: an individual branch might have been called the Party Branch of Women Workers of the Weaving Department at the Tong Yi Cotton Mill. Like a sisterhood, it was made up of a small number of women who worked in the same department of the same mill and hence were most likely from the same native place.[73]

Moreover, members of a Party branch met to discuss strategy under the guise of sisterhood gatherings. "Sometimes my sisters would come to my house to chat on Sunday—just like they always had—but no one knew that what we were actually doing was holding a meeting," Sun Zhaodi recalled. "Nobody in my family knew I was in the Communist Party or leading activities."[74] When Party members from different branches needed to meet to coordinate their plans, they assembled at the YWCA night schools. The importance of the YWCA schools to the Party's postwar organizing and strike-planning strategies is suggested by the claim, made by the Party thirty years later, that the YWCA night schools were in fact "run by the Party underground." It is impossible either to confirm or to refute this assertion completely, but it does appear that between the war's end and Liberation an increasing proportion of teachers at the night schools were Party members. During this period of underground organizing, the YWCA schools continued to provide both leadership training and a setting for establishing contact between the Party and potential leaders in the labor movement. The most important female Party organizers of the postwar period (women such as Tang Guifen, He Ningzhen, Gu Lianying, Fan Xiaofeng, and Gui Jianying) all began their political careers as students at the night schools.

Although the organizations women joined during the postwar period were nominally the same as before, that is, sisterhoods, the YWCA, and the CCP, each of these organizations had undergone a major change in orientation. After the war if a woman worker joined any organization, it was most likely a sisterhood as before and not an explicitly political, working-class organization. The sisterhoods of the forties, however, were very different from those of the twenties and thirties. In many cases they had become aggressive political groups rather than defensive organizations representing women's need for mutual aid and protection. Some women workers joined the YWCA by going to the night schools, but the YWCA of the late 1940's too was a far cry from the foreign-run missionary organization of the 1920's. It might not have preached revolution, but it did give women the education, social analysis skills, and organizational ability they needed to become active participants in and leaders of a revolutionary movement. Finally, from the vantage point of Shanghai's women mill workers, the Chinese Communist Party was no longer an alien organization, composed of outsiders and intellectuals who spoke unintelligible dialects. Most of the Party activists responsible for organizing women workers were the co-workers, neighbors, friends, or pledged sisters of the women they sought to organize.

On Strike

The transformation of women workers' organizations during the postwar period might lead one to expect that women's participation in the labor movement during this period was very different from what it had been in the 1920's. If the YWCA had in fact cultivated a group of women workers with the vision and the skills to lead a labor movement, if the nature of the sisterhoods had been changed by women from the YWCA schools and from the Party, and if the CCP had developed a base among women workers, there should be evidence of women playing a much more aggressive role in strikes and giving voice to demands specific to their condition as women.

In early 1948 at the Shen Xin Number Nine Mill, 6,000 women workers struck, demanding among other things distribution of rice and coal rations and enforcement of provisions for paid maternity leave. They occupied the mill for four days, and it took several hundred policemen equipped with three army tanks to force the workers out of the mill. So violent was this strike that it came to be known as the February Second Bloodbath at Shen Xin Nine. An account of this strike suggests some of the ways the changes described above were reflected in the postwar labor movement.[75]

In some important ways the conditions of women workers at Shen Xin Nine in 1948 were much better than they had been in previous decades. As a result of citywide strikes in 1946, women at almost all Shanghai's cotton mills, including Shen Xin Nine, had won a reduction in the workday from twelve to ten hours, monthly wage adjustments according to the cost-of-living index, eight weeks of paid maternity leave, and child care facilities provided by the company. That mill owners had acceded to these demands, however, did not mean that they were consistently carried out. Disputes between workers and management over the implementation of reforms had become an underlying theme of the postwar labor movement.

At Shen Xin Nine, one of the mills where these disputes were most frequent, very few women had been able to take advantage of their right to eight weeks of maternity leave. The procedures for obtaining permission to take the leave were so cumbersome that they deterred most women from applying. Of greater concern to most women was the threat that any woman who stayed away from work a single day beyond the eight weeks granted would be automatically fired. The child care facilities that were supposed to be available were almost nonexistent. The nursery set up at the mill after 1946 "was very pretty," recalled one woman who had worked there at the time. "But it never had even one child in it. It was just for the owner to [show] to foreign guests who came to visit the factory."[76]

Management's failure to provide maternity leave and child care facilities vexed the workers, but they had survived in the mills for many years with neither of these benefits. The precipitating issue in 1948 was the calculation of wages. The sky-rocketing inflation of this period is part of the oft-told story of the economic upheaval during the final years of Guomin-dang rule. Most workers vividly recall that the moment they were issued their wages they rushed to the mill gate, where their relatives would be waiting to take the money and purchase goods as fast as possible. A five-minute delay could mean a substantially higher price for the goods. This rise in the price of goods was accompanied by a dramatic decline in the real value of workers' wages, a decline that was most dramatic in 1947 and 1948. In 1947 the value of wages at Shen Xin Nine was 98 percent of what it had been in 1946; by 1948 it had plummeted to 35 percent of its 1946 value.[77]

Even when workers had sufficient funds, there were severe shortages of basic commodities during this period, making it difficult, and often impossible, for workers to purchase rice, coal, and oil. By late 1947 most mills in Shanghai had agreed to distribute these goods to workers as rations. The owners of Shen Xin promised to provide rations but had failed to deliver them. "The coal is still in the mines at Nanjing," the mill owners replied to workers' demands for rations. "Wait until the mines have been opened and the roads built, and then we can have the coal transported here. The rice is in Wuxi, and the peasants have not even finished growing it."[78] All these issues came to a head in early 1948. As the Spring Festival approached, workers became increasingly restless, realizing that it would be impossible to buy goods for the holiday celebrations. Furthermore, they had been promised a traditional New Year bonus but had never received it. Under these circumstances workers started organizing to strike.

Whether or not the CCP officially sanctioned a strike at this time, Party members at the mill played a major role in its planning.[79] Shortly before the strike started, Party members had arranged through the YWCA night schools for women to see a Russian film that portrayed women strikers fighting the Russian troops sent to force them to surrender. "That film really gave us some ideas of how to struggle," one of the strike leaders recalled.[80] He Ningzhen, a Party activist at Shen Xin Nine who had been away from work for several weeks taking care of a newborn infant, returned to work at the mill with her baby on her back just days before the strike started and worked with the other thirty-odd Party members in the mill to coordinate plans for the strike. They agreed that on January 30, at 9:00 A.M., workers throughout the mill would shut off their machines. At that time there were 6,000 women and 1,000 male workers employed at Shen Xin Nine.[81]

Apparently workers were not the only ones who knew the

time the strike was scheduled to begin. At 8:30 A.M., as everyone was watching the clock and anxiously waiting for the moment to arrive, the machines suddenly stopped and there was silence. It was a power failure. Party members, assuming that management was hoping to thwart them, came up with a new plan: at 12:30, while most of the staff would be more engrossed in eating lunch than in attending to their supervisory duties, workers would shut down the machines.

The electricity came back on shortly, and everyone returned to work. The mill staff nervously waited to see what would happen at nine. Nine o'clock came and went, and nothing happened. The strike had been averted, or so it seemed. As noon approached, workers began to take turns eating lunch while foremen, inspectors, and most Number Ones went to the staff cafeteria to eat. At 12:30 sharp, just as planned, a worker ran out of the coppersmith workshop yelling, "The coppersmiths have shut down!" The weavers immediately turned off their machines, then the rovers and spinners, and within five minutes not a machine in the entire mill was running. The strike was on.

In each department workers gathered to select representatives and to discuss the demands that would be presented to management. In the spinning room a woman worker named Qi Huaixiong, a student at a YWCA night school, climbed onto a table, spoke about the benefits workers should be entitled to, and then led a discussion. Similar sessions took place in workshops throughout the mill. The workers agreed to demand rations, the right to extend maternity leave if necessary, a Spring Festival bonus, and a monthly adjustment of wages according to changes in the cost of living. With the demands prepared, several hundred representatives went to call on the mill owners, but the owners refused even to meet with them.

Meanwhile, the workers settled in for a protracted stay at the mill. In the spinning room women sat on top of the bobbin bins, in the weaving room they made themselves comfortable on bolts of cloth, and in the roving room they collected bundles of roving and made them into pillows. Groups of women in each workshop sat, eating dried melon seeds, and chatted. Eventually Party members organized teams to go to each workshop and make sure that workers cleaned up and that no damage was done to the machines. When the strike started, some overly zealous workers had gotten carried away and had run up and down the rows of machines, breaking threads and smashing bobbins.

As the afternoon wore on, management began to worry about what would happen when the night shift workers arrived. Guards were dispatched to block the doors of the factory dormitories and prevent workers from leaving. These efforts were to no avail, however: the night shift workers, determined to join the strike, broke the dormitory windows, climbed out, and ran toward the mill gate. They forced the gate open and flocked into the workshops, where they were warmly greeted by their friends. By early evening all 7,000 workers were on the mill premises.

At midnight management finally agreed to negotiate with the workers. To the workers' demand for maternity leave extensions, management replied, "If we were to operate maternity leave in accordance with the workers' demands, then this factory would become a convalescent home and we would have to shut down." They were no more amenable to the other demands, and negotiations ended in a deadlock.

For the next three days the workers refused to give in. Most of the time they stayed in their workshops. "During strikes we would sit in the workshop and gossip, or go to other workshops and get news," Chen Zhaodi recalled. "We younger workers sometimes played games. We got to know each other better."[82] Students from the YWCA schools, putting their education to use, went from workshop to workshop teaching workers songs and performing skits to dramatize strike issues. They also organized groups to make flags out of hemp sacks (one of the products of the Shen Xin Nine Mill) for use during a demonstration planned for the second day of the strike. Women used their work tools to cut the sacks, and stray yarn to embroider the words "workers unite" on each flag. When the demonstration began, women waving these handmade flags led the ranks of workers emerging from each department and marching toward the area where a rally was to take place.

During the first three days of the strike, women camping in their workshops were not completely isolated from the world outside. Family members gathered at the mill gates, shouting to them to stop the strike so as not to jeopardize their wages. At night thugs hired by the mill owners made strange noises outside the mill, trying to trick superstitious workers into believing that ghosts and demons had come to punish them for their delinquent behavior.

People also came to support them. At the YWCA night schools women from other mills learned about the strike at Shen Xin Nine and immediately organized support activities. Women from neighboring mills arrived with supplies of bread and vegetables for the striking workers. Among those who came to express their support were representatives of the Shanghai dance hostesses' organization. Unbeknownst to the women at Shen Xin Nine, on January 31 (the second day of the strike) some 6,000 dance hostesses, demanding that the government lift its ban on commercial dance halls, marched to the offices of the Shanghai Bureau of Social Affairs. A riot broke out when the dance hall hostesses entered the building and ran from office to office smashing furniture, breaking windows, and destroying official documents.[83] News of that struggle made the women at Shen Xin Nine even more determined to persist with their strike.

Workers had occupied the mill for three days and nights when the situation finally reached a turning point on February 2. Negotiations had failed, and the workers showed no sign of giving in. The mill owners, becoming desperate, called upon the GMD police to force the workers to return to their jobs. As dawn broke on February 2 more than five hundred policemen, some on horseback, surrounded the mill. This was the beginning of the daylong pandemonium that resulted in the February Second Bloodbath.

Qi Huaixiong led a group of women up the back stairs to the roof of the factory building. They each carried a pile of leaflets that had been run off on a borrowed mimeograph machine during the preceding days. When they reached the roof they began to throw down the leaflets to the crowds of workers on the street below who were on their way to work at neighboring factories. Within an hour workers from the nearby Tong Yi Cotton Mill and Fu Xin Flour Mill emerged on the roofs of their factories to announce that they too had shut down their machines, to demonstrate their solidarity with the workers at Shen Xin Nine.

By this time, on the street below, a standoff had developed between the workers and the police. The police chief pressed the workers to stop the strike. "Our country is facing hard times," he yelled. "I hope you will lighten up a little. In a few days it will be New Year, and you must consider the situation from all sides." To which the workers responded, "We have already thoroughly considered the situation. We want to eat! We demand that the factory give us rice!" Finally the police chief ordered the workers to return to the workshops and start their machines. "If you don't start your machines," he yelled, "we are going to open fire." Not a single worker moved.

When several police armed with bayonets charged toward the main gate of the mill and tried to force their way in, hundreds of workers rushed to stop them. The police were only temporarily deterred; the chief gave orders for the tanks to start rolling. They moved toward the mill gate, firing as they went, thereby forcing their way into the mill compound.

All along, a group of women workers had been arming for a fight. They used the bobbin- and yarn-transporting carts to move supplies to the third floor and then onto the roof. Led by He Ningzhen the women had stockpiled bricks, machine parts, 5,000 metal food bowls, and ten oil drums filled with rocks. As a tank forged ahead into the mill yard, the women on the roof hurled their ammunition down onto the tank. Other women joined them on the roof, replenishing the supplies. One fifty-year-old woman, grasping an iron rod she had found in the spinning room, yelled at the others, "I'm an old woman, and in all my years here I have never seen anything as outrageous as this. I am going to fight them!" And with that she hurled the iron rod down toward the tank. With their improvised ammunition, the women destroyed the engine of the tank, but a second tank moved toward the gate to replace the first. When the women on the roof had exhausted their supply of missiles, those below took over. Hundreds of them stood in the tank's path, trying to prevent it from moving forward. Several male workers commandeered a Dodge truck parked on the mill premises and drove it at full speed toward the tank. They crashed into it, destroying both vehicles. As the troops directed a third tank to enter the mill, workers shook a guardhouse loose from its foundations and pushed it down to block the path of the tank. Other workers aimed water hoses at the police.

The police retaliated with tear gas and vomit gas, and raised their guns and began firing at workers who refused to disperse. Caught in the pressing crowds, several pregnant women miscarried. At one point during the skirmish a woman wearing red to signify her recent marriage sneaked up behind one of the policemen and seized his gun. No one knew who she was. The police remembered only her red clothes and later arrested all women dressed in red.

The fighting reached its climax with a showdown between the police and He Ningzhen, the only person left on the roof of the mill. "It was five o'clock, and since it was winter, it had already started to get dark. They had started throwing tear gas bombs, and my eyes were so watery that I couldn't see. I was so surprised when suddenly some police came up from behind me on the roof and grabbed me." He Ningzhen tried to fight them but they shot her, wounding her leg, and carried her down to the cafeteria on the third floor. Determined to escape, she ran toward the window and—without even stopping to look—jumped out. Workers below watched with horror as she fell. She was saved by a laundry rack, draped with clothes, that happened to be hanging out of the second-floor window. Caught on the poles, she gave herself a push and continued her leap down to the ground, suffering serious injuries. She was taken to a police hospital.

By the end of the day three women were dead and five hundred injured. Police arrested 132 men and 104 women, of whom thirty were suspected of being the girl dressed in red. News of the February Second Bloodbath quickly spread

throughout the cotton mill world of Shanghai. Almost immediately a meeting was held at a YWCA school, where representatives from other cotton mills learned what had happened at Shen Xin Nine. They organized a support committee
(headed by Tang Guifen, a YWCA student, Party member, and
head of the union at the Tong Yi Cotton Mill), which decided
that on February 22, at 2:22 P.M., workers and students
throughout Shanghai would don black armbands to commemorate the three women who had been killed on February
2. In mills throughout the city groups of women began making the armbands. At the Zhong Fang Number Twelve Mill,
several activists found a sewing machine and for several days
turned their dormitory into an armband-producing workshop. Fourteen workers at Zhong Fang Twelve, arrested for
engaging in strike support activities, joined the Shen Xin Nine
workers in the city jail.[84]

Ultimately the mill owners conceded to at least some of the
workers' demands: all workers received coal and rice rations.
The imprisoned workers were released and returned to work.
Whatever disputes might have erupted after the strike settlement were forestalled by larger political events. Communist
victory was imminent by mid-1948, and the Party was beginning to prepare for the final showdown in the cities. Although
the victory of workers at Shen Xin Nine was cheered at the
Sixth All-China Labor Congress, held in Harbin in August
1948, the main message of the meeting was that the Party
underground in Shanghai and in other urban centers should
refrain from instigating violent confrontations between workers and capitalists. Henceforth they should organize workers
into "factory protection teams," to prevent destruction of
machinery and raw materials before and during the Communist takeover.[85]

The strike was not completely forgotten, though. The
women who participated in the strike were celebrated as revolutionary heroines in one of the first feature films made by
the Shanghai Film Studio after Liberation, "United for Tomorrow." The women who had played an active role in leading the strike, He Ningzhen, Tang Guifen, and Fan Xiaofeng,
were rewarded with positions as officials in two newly formed

groups, the Federation of Labor and the Women's Federation. Many of the women who worked at Shen Xin Nine in 1948 have since retired or died. Those who continued to work there enjoyed the benefits they had fought for in 1948, as well as many others: a paid lunch break, a cafeteria, guaranteed maternity leave and child care facilities, health care, and sick leave.

Conclusion

The story of the Shen Xin
Nine strike attests to the important changes that had taken
place in the organization and consciousness of women mill
workers since the strikes of the 1920's. Women strikers of the
1920's showed little evidence of class consciousness or revolutionary commitment. Most struck because they wished to
defend traditional loyalties, or sometimes because they were
physically forced to strike. Few women joined working-class
organizations such as labor unions, and no woman worker
emerged as a leader in the labor movement.

The 1948 strike, by contrast, was led primarily by women.
Women strikers not only enlisted the support of male workers
to demand benefits like maternity leave, but made speeches,
organized singing and dramatic performances, and formed
teams to collect ammunition for battles against the police.
Women workers from neighboring mills expressed solidarity
by bringing food to the strikers, by shutting down their machines, and later by sewing armbands to commemorate the
women killed during the strike; and even women not involved
in mill work, notably the dance hostesses, openly supported
the strike. These developments represent a transcendence of
the parochialism that had inhibited women's political activities
in the past.

What accounts for these changes? Clearly there is no simple
equation between the development of industry, the formation
of the working class, working-class consciousness, and revolutionary activity. In particular, the experience of working in
the cotton mills did not of itself cause women workers to de-

velop a working-class consciousness. Those aspects of factory work that might theoretically have brought women together were overshadowed by forces keeping them apart, most of which remained powerful through the 1930's and 1940's.

The work force of the 1940's, as it had been in previous decades, was in many ways a transient one. Most mill workers were the daughters of peasants who had migrated to Shanghai but retained close ties to the countryside. For occasions such as marriage and childbirth, on holidays, or at times when they could find no work, women returned to their home villages— sometimes permanently, but more often temporarily. For most of their working lives they moved back and forth between city and countryside. Japanese attacks on Shanghai in the 1930's and the ensuing war meant that women migrated even more frequently.

In the 1940's, as in the 1920's, women were no more tied to the cotton industry than to the city. Although many women continued to work after marriage, and in many cases after childbirth, most did not remain in a particular cotton mill for very long. Women not only moved frequently from one mill to another, but often interspersed cotton mill work with employment in other factories or with work as vegetable peddlers, wet nurses, or maids. These patterns hampered the development of a consciousness of themselves as members of an industrial proletariat. Likewise, they made it difficult for women to develop relationships with other women based on a shared experience of working in the cotton mills.

Women, did, to be sure, develop new social relationships in Shanghai, but typically as an extension of older, more familiar native place networks. As we have seen, differences in local dialects, as well as job and residential segregation, kept women of different geographic origins separated from, and sometimes antagonistic toward, one another. Even membership in sisterhoods, though occasioned in the first instance by the particular difficulties women faced as urban factory workers, was based primarily on shared geographic origins rather than on a shared identity as workers. Indeed, the new relationships sometimes defied class solidarity, as when women pledged loyalty to become the goddaughter of a gang member or a Number One in the cotton mill.

Two other aspects of working-class life help explain why women were not disposed to become active participants in the labor movement. First, most women workers regarded gangs and local hoodlums as a problem far bigger than that of mill owners and managers. The Green Gang's power over women workers increased during the 1930's, and through the 1940's large numbers of women workers were under the direct charge of labor bosses in the contract labor system. Second, many cotton mills were owned by foreign capitalists, particularly by the Japanese; and insofar as workers in these mills felt antagonistic toward their owners, it was to a considerable extent as foreigners rather than as capitalists. Moreover, as we have seen, foreign ownership   particularly after the Japanese attack on Shanghai in 1932—served to further intensify divisions and antagonisms between women from Jiangnan and those from Subei.

Yet changes did occur, and in certain ways the female cotton mill work force of the 1940's was different from that of the 1920's. More women workers in the 1940's had some, albeit not very much, education, more came from middle-class backgrounds, and after the war more were recruited through the *yangchenggong* system, which housed them in dormitories and provided them with formal training. Also after the war the cotton mills previously owned by Japanese capitalists (the majority of cotton mills in Shanghai) were nationalized and taken over by the China Textile Reconstruction Corporation.

Important as these changes may have been, however, they do not account for women's increased participation in the labor movement. Women who became active as labor leaders were as likely to be illiterate as literate (with the exception of those who attended the YWCA schools), no more likely than not to be *yangchenggong*, and less likely than not to have a middle-class background. Nor does the nationalization of the previously Japanese-owned mills relate in any clear way to patterns of labor protest. Strikes in the postwar years were as

likely to occur at mills owned by Chinese capitalists, such as
Shen Xin, as in those now owned by the China Textile Reconstruction Corporation. If we are to understand the type of consciousness and organization displayed by women workers in
the Shen Xin Nine strike of 1948, we must look to other
factors.

First we must recall that Shanghai's women workers had
never been passive victims of industrial poverty or capitalist
exploitation. They constantly forged relationships with other
women workers to exercise some degree of control over their
lives, even if it was only minimal. Though the sisterhoods
were initially defensive in nature, it is important that such organizations were in place when the political context changed.

It was not by confronting capitalists but by resisting the Japanese that large numbers of women workers acquired their
first political experience. Yet the consciousness manifested in
the 1948 strike extended far beyond the politics of resistance
developed during the war. The difference lay in political education, which led to the emergence of women workers with a
vision of change. The first organization to provide an effective
political education for women workers was not the Chinese
Communist Party but the YWCA. Beginning in the 1930's the
YWCA night schools taught women workers how to read,
how to speak in public, and how to analyze the social structure
of which, as women and as workers, they were a part. The
YWCA schools were the first to arrange social activities with
women from various mills and industries. In due course some
graduates of the YWCA schools became political activists. By
the 1940's many of those women had joined the CCP; even
more interesting, many women Party members had joined the
YWCA.

As we have seen, the Chinese Communist Party was inef-
fective in its attempts to organize women workers in the
1920's. Among the reasons were that it had only a score of
organizers attempting to mobilize thousands of workers, that
women workers were given lower priority than men, and that
most organizers were male intellectuals. But perhaps the most
important reason was the CCP's mistaken assumption that
Shanghai women workers would perceive themselves as hav-

ing interests in common with other workers—both male and female, both within their own factories and outside.

In the 1940's the Party's methods were very different. Instead of making speeches, distributing leaflets, and attempting to persuade women to join unions, Party organizers went to visit women workers at their homes, helped them with daily chores such as laundry and shopping, and accompanied them when they went with friends to parks or to hear local operas on their day off. Instead of attempting to impose new organizational forms on women, Party organizers joined and adapted pre-existing social and political forms: the sisterhoods and the YWCA. These changes in organizing style were made possible partly because the number of organizers had vastly increased and partly because more were female, were from the same regions as women workers, and were themselves (or had been) workers. Yet we must also recognize that the Party had radically altered its understanding of the nature of working-class consciousness. By the time of the 1948 strike at Shen Xin Nine, the Party acknowledged the reality that for women workers class consciousness would not transcend, but would at most coexist with, other loyalties.

Superficially the story of the Shen Xin strike suggests that women workers had emerged as class-conscious revolutionary heroines. And in a sense they had. The more profound significance of the strike, however, is its demonstration of the complexity of class and revolutionary consciousness. Patterns of localism and traditional hierarchical loyalties are perhaps not as antithetical to working-class consciousness as many pre-Liberation Party organizers and contemporary students of working-class history have assumed. Working-class consciousness, if it has any meaning, must be able to embrace multiple loyalties. Even at their most class-conscious, female cotton mill workers in Shanghai did not see themselves exclusively, or even primarily, as members of a working class.

Reference Matter

Notes

The following abbreviations are used in the Notes. Complete authors' names, titles, and publication data are given in the Bibliography, pp. 279–89.

RSCLC "Report of the Shanghai Child Labor Commission"
SGYLW Shanghai gongren yundong lishi weiyuanhui
SSKJY Shanghai shehui kexueyuan, jingji yanjiusuo
SSKLY Shanghai shehui kexueyuan, lishi yanjiusuo
SWZX *Shanghai wenshi ziliao xuanji*

INTRODUCTION

1. Thompson, pp. 191–92.
2. Ibid.
3. Chesneaux, *Chinese Labor*.
4. See, for example, Young; Davin; and Wolf and Witke.
5. The only treatments of this period are that by Pepper and a brief discussion by Selden, pp. 58–120.
6. Shaffer, "Modern Chinese Labor History," p. 35.

CHAPTER I

1. Fortune, pp. 110–12. For a more extensive discussion of Shanghai's advantages as a center for the tea and silk trades, see Murphey.
2. Murphey, p. 111. By 1855, 58 percent of China's tea exports and over 60 percent of its silk exports were shipped from Shanghai.
3. Ibid., p. 112.
4. Sun Yutang, vol. 1, p. 1231. From 1865 until 1937, Shanghai was unrivaled as China's major port for both foreign and domestic trade. See Murphey, 116–17. Also see Huang Wei.
5. Fortune, p. 114.
6. Hauser, pp. 60–70; Pott, p. 19.
7. Xu and Wang; see also Kelley.

8. Gamewell, p. 43. For a discussion of the movement of trading companies from Guangzhou to Shanghai, see Fairbank, *Trade and Diplomacy*.

9. *All About Shanghai*, p. 53.

10. Jones, pp. 73-96.

11. Feuerwerker, pp. 31-32.

12. Sun Yutang, vol. 1, pp. 1175, 1195. Also see Shih, p. 51.

13. Li Hongzhang, assisted by Sheng Xuanhuai, then inspector general of the Maritime Customs in Tianjin, invested in a new mill, the Hua Shen Cotton Mill, which was established in 1894. This mill was subsequently reorganized several times, changing names to You Xin, Ji Cheng, Yong Ji, and San Xin, and finally in 1930 it was bought by the Rong brothers and became the Shen Xin No. 9 Mill. Fong, *Cotton Industry*, pp. 3-4.

14. This mill later became Fu Tai, and then Heng Feng. Sun Yutang, vol. 1, p. 1197.

15. The three mills were Da Shun, Yu Yuan, and San Tai. Fong, *Cotton Industry*, p. 4.

16. The next largest center was Hankou, with about 13,000 factory workers, and then Guangzhou with some 10,000 workers. Sun Yutang, vol. 1, p. 1202.

17. Bourne, pp. 230-31.

18. Rui Ji was bought by the British firm Arnhold Brothers and Co. in 1913 and became the Oriental Cotton Spinning and Weaving Co.; in 1929 it was sold to the Rong brothers and became Shen Xin No. 7. Yan, pp. 345-46.

19. The Japanese purchased Da Shun and San Tai, which became the Shanghai No. 1 and No. 2 mills.

20. Since Nei Wai 1 and 2 were in Japan, the mill built in 1911 was called Nei Wai 3; Nei Wai 4 was built in Shanghai in 1913, and Nei Wai 5 in 1914, and Nei Wai 6 in Qingdao in 1916. In 1918 the company bought the Chinese-owned Yu Yuan, which became Nei Wai 9; the same year they constructed Nei Wai 7, and in 1919, Nei Wai 8, both in Shanghai. Nei Wai 10 and 11 were built in Qingdao in 1919. Nei Wai 12 and 13 were built in Shanghai in 1931, 14 and 15 in 1923. Yan, p. 351.

21. SSKJY, *Hengfeng*, pp. 1-13.

22. Bush, pp. 53-55.

23. Extract from letter from Grace L. Coppock, Dec. 1, 1914 (World YWCA Archives, Geneva).

24. Bush, p. 58; SSKJY, *Rongjia*, vol. 1; Huang Yifeng. The Rong family in the early 20th century also operated several silk cocoon firms in Wuxi.

25. Bush, pp. 61-62; SSKJY, *Yongan*; SSKJY, *Shanghai Yongan*.

26. Hauser, pp. 112, 121.

27. Gamewell, p. 46.

28. Fairbank, *Chinabound*, p. 64. The house described belonged to Ken Cheang, whose family members were some of the chief managers of the Nanyang Brothers Tobacco Co.

29. Ju, p. 7.

30. Cited in Pan, p. 93.

31. Ju, p. 8.

32. Gamewell, p. 48.

33. Ibid., p. 9.

34. Chung and Bagwell.

35. Ibid., pp. 8-11. At this time 62 percent of the cotton spindles in China were concentrated in Shanghai.

36. SSKJY, *Shanghai penghuqude*, pp. 4-9; Lamson, "Housing," p. 147.

37. See, for example, Deng Zhongxia; Ba; Xiang.

38. Anderson, pp. 131-62; Chesneaux, *Chinese Labor*, p. 229.

39. Chesneaux, *Chinese Labor*, pp. 262-89; Wusa yundong bianxiezu.

40. Chesneaux, *Chinese Labor*, pp. 345-71; Huang and Zhou; Isaacs, *Tragedy*.

41. Chao, p. 119.

42. Shanghaishi mianfangzhi. There were in Shanghai 11 Nei Wai, 4 Ri Hua, 3 Shanghai, 3 Dong Hua, 2 Xi He, 2 Da Kang, 2 Feng Tian, and 2 Tong Xing mills. In contrast, the only Chinese companies that owned more than one mill at this time were Shen Xin, which had 3, and Pu Yi and Yong An, which had two each. Furthermore, the Japanese mills were much more heavily capitalized than the Chinese mills: whereas there was an average capital investment of 81.08 *yuan* per spindle and 1,157.35 *yuan* per loom in Japanese-owned mills in China in 1930, only 50.49 *yuan* was invested per spindle and 630.50 *yuan* per loom in the Chinese-owned mills. Chao, p. 142.

43. Pott, p. 240.

44. Hauser, p. 193.

45. "Unemployment in Shanghai," ILO China correspondent, Monthly Report, Feb. 1932 (ILO Archives, Geneva).

46. Hauser, p. 202.

47. Chao, p. 167.

48. Japanese mill owners had reduced the price per bale of 20-count yarn from 187 *taels* in June 1931 to 133 *taels* in October 1932. During the same period, the price per bale of yarn produced in Chinese-owned mills dropped from 189 *taels* to 156 *taels*. Chao, p. 167.

49. Coble, pp. 150-51.

50. Ibid., p. 156. Also see Lillian Li.

51. Hauser, p. 307.

52. Barnett, pp. 76-77.

53. Hauser, pp. 310-15.

54. For a detailed description of Shanghai during this period, see Tao.

55. Altogether there were 16 mills taken over by the Japanese, including Heng Feng, Shen Xin 5, 6, and 7; Yong An 1, 2, and 4; Cheng Tai; and Da Feng.

56. Chao, p. 131.

57. Deng Fa, pp. 18-27.

58. Letter to YWCA, Apr. 22, 1938 (World YWCA Archives, Geneva).

59. Davidson-Houston.

60. Letter from Lydia Johnson, Feb. 4, 1942 (World YWCA Archives, Geneva).

61. SSKJY, *Hengfeng*, p. 67.

62. Shanghaishi mianfangzhi.

63. Charles Ferguson, "Present Status of Shanghai's Cotton Industry Compared with 1936," Dec. 24, 1945, Boise Cascade Corporation Archives, Boise, Idaho. Courtesy of Warren Tozer.

64. Pepper, p. 22.   65. Ibid., p. 23.

66. Ibid., p. 20.   67. Ibid., p. 67.

68. "Report of the China Textile Industries, Inc., 1946," ILO China correspondent, Monthly Report, Apr. 1947 (ILO Archives, Geneva).

69. "Shanghai Labor as a Newspaper Man Sees It," ILO China correspondent, Monthly Report, June 1946, p. 47 (ILO Archives, Geneva).

70. Davidson-Houston, p. 189.

71. SGYLW, *Shanghai gongren*, vol. 4, p. 32.

72. "Shanghai jeifang sanshi zhounian zhuanji" (A Special Collection Commemorating the Thirtieth Anniversary of the Liberation of Shanghai), *SWZX*, 1979.

73. Margaret Garvie, letter, July 7, 1950 (World YWCA Archives, Geneva).

CHAPTER 2

1. The following account, except as otherwise noted, has been reconstructed from the following sources: Guo and Zhong, pp. 31-32; *Manual of Job Descriptions*; Peake; Shanghai fangzhiju; Shanghaishi fangzhi gongyeju (The Shanghai Textile Industry Bureau), *An English-Chinese Textile Dictionary* (Shanghai, 1979).

2. Bush, p. 60.

3. Interview with Shi Wenran, Shanghai, Sept. 16, 1980.

4. Interview with Yan Ke, Shanghai, Jan. 22, 1981. These students were admitted to the program by dint of personal introductions, followed by a test of Chinese, foreign languages, and general knowledge. In the mill management hierarchy, they were above the foremen and Number Ones, most of whom were selected from the ranks of workers.

5. Moser, p. 69.

6. Ibid. Although Moser does not name the mill, his description suggests that the mill he visited was almost certainly one of the Shen Xin mills.

7. Chao, p. 159. This figure is for 14-count yarn.

8. Moser, p. 69.

9. Peake, pp. 85-86.

10. SSKJY, *Rongjia*, vol. 1, p. 132.

11. *Zhongguo jingji*, p. 107.

12. Interview with Fang Xianchao, Shanghai, Dec. 15, 1980.

13. *Xin qingnian*, 7 (1920), no. 6: 4-9.

14. Interview with He Zhiguang, Shanghai, June 26, 1980.

15. Materials provided by the Institute for Historical Research, Shanghai Academy of Social Sciences.

16. Interview with retired mill managers at Putuo District Federation of Industry and Commerce, Shanghai, Nov. 5, 1980.

17. Interview with He Zhiguang. Despite legislation that, after 1929,

made it illegal to hire workers under the age of 10, many mills circumvented the law by lying about the workers' ages. As one observer put it in 1930, "These rules forbidding child labor are honored more in the breach than in their observation." Moser, p. 68.

18. Interview with He Zhiguang.

19. "Woman Worker Describes Cotton Mill Conditions," *China Forum*, 3 (1933), no. 1: 15.

20. SSKJY, *Rongjia*, vol. 1, p. 639, and *Yongan*, p. 231. It could be argued that the distinction was based on skill levels, but even if we look at the wages paid to men who did the least skilled jobs, the decrease during this period was still much less than that for women. At Shen Xin, wages in the blowing department decreased by only 1.2 percent, while those paid in the spinning department decreased by 24.3 percent.

21. Interview with Wu Zanting, Shanghai, Jan. 22, 1981.

22. "Fangzhi jiangongyu shiye wenti" (The Problem of Reductions in the Work Force and Unemployment), *Fangzhi zhoukan*, 4 (1934), no. 24: 615.

23. Zhongguo fangzhi, *Diliu chang gaikuang*; "Shanghai dishier fangzhichang laogong fulishe gaikuang" (The General Situation of Welfare Facilities for Workers at the Shanghai Number Twelve Textile Mill), *Fangzhiran gongcheng*, 8 (1946), no. 2: 47-48; "Jieshao shanghai fangjian dier fangzhichang" (Introducing the Shanghai Textile Reconstruction Corporation Number Two Mill), *Fang jian*, 1 (1948), no. 7: 23-24; "Yongan gechang gaikuang" (The General Condition at Each of the Yong An Mills), *Fangzhi zhoukan*, 9 (1948), no. 4: 51-56.

CHAPTER 3

1. Clarissa Spenser, "Shanghai YWCA: The Chinese Mill Woman," 1907 (World YWCA Archives, Geneva).

2. Udaka, p. 329; Minami manshū, pp. 2-3.

3. Gamewell, pp. 14-15.

4. Lamson, "Industrialization," p. 1060.

5. Ibid., p. 1032.

6. Zhongguo kexueyuan, vol. 2, p. 421.

7. Lamson, "Industrialization," p. 1034.

8. Gamewell, p. 43.

9. Lamson, "Housing," p. 149.

10. Cora Deng, "Economic Status," p. 88.

11. Woodhead, 1924, p. 656.

12. In the mills for which there are statistics, the percentage of women workers from Shanghai never exceeded 15 percent and was usually lower. See Udaka, p. 329; Minami manshū, pp. 2-3; Zhongguo fangzhi, *Shanghai diersan* and *Diliu chang gaikuang*.

13. Zhang Fangzuo, "Shachang guanbu gaige yu jubuzhenglizhi wojian" (What I Have Seen of Reforming the Management Section of Cotton Mills), *Huashang shachang lianhehui jikan*, 7 (1926), no. 3.

14. Geelen and Twitchett, p. 41; Cressey, pp. 295-300.

15. Yu Fanggan and Wang Maosui, "Yixingzhi nongmin qingkuang (The Condition of Peasants in Yixing), *Dong fang zazhi* (The Eastern Miscellany), 24 (1927), no. 16: 77. Also see Chiao, Thompson, and Chen.

16. Interview with Fan Xiaofeng, Beijing, Dec. 6, 1980.

17. Unless otherwise specified, the following discussion of Gaixiangong is based on Fei, pp. 12-16.

18. Ibid., pp. 170-71.

19. He based this calculation on the assumptions that under normal conditions they could produce six bushels of rice on one *mu* of land each year and that each bushel of rice would be sold for $2.50. This calculation is for land-owning peasants. Tenants who had to deliver 20 bushels of rice to their landlord as rent payment were in an even more difficult situation. Ibid., pp. 202-3.

20. The highest price of native silk was over $1 per *liang*, and an average household could produce 280 *liang*. Thus they could earn almost $300. Subtracting $50 for the cost of production, they were left with a surplus of $250.

21. Ibid., p. 202.

22. For a discussion of the impact of this and the world depression on China's silk trade, see Liu Ta-chun, *Silk Reeling*.

23. Fei, pp. 170-71.

24. Ibid., p. 97.

25. *North-China Herald*, Nov. 3, 1928.

26. The data about the origins of the workers are not very precise in specifying where women came from. Workers who were listed as coming from Wuxi might have come from any number of small villages in the Wuxi district, or they might have come from the city of Wuxi itself. Nor do the data indicate the prior occupations of the workers. Thus a worker from Wuxi might have worked as a silk reeler in the village, a maid in the town, or even a worker in one of Wuxi's mills. Understanding the reasons for and patterns of migration of women from Jiangnan cities to Shanghai requires a more extensive study of industrial, as well as rural, labor in this area.

27. SSKJY, *Rongjia*, vol. 1, p. 119.

28. Zhongguo fangzhi, *Shanghai diyi chang*, pp. 124-28.

29. Geelen and Twitchett.

30. Interview with Chen Zhaodi, Shanghai, Apr. 11, 1981.

31. Cao Hui, "Jiangbei funü shenghuo gaikuang" (General Conditions of Women's Life in Jiangbei), *Nüsheng*, 2 (1934), no. 10: 10-11.

32. Ibid.; also see Wang Nanbi, pp. 614-15.

33. *Shen Bao*, Jan. 4, 1930.

34. "Flood Damage in China During 1931," *Chinese Economic Journal*, 10 (1932), no. 4: 344. For an extensive discussion of natural disasters in Jiangsu during the Republican period, see Stross.

35. Ibid.

36. *Maritime Customs Decennial Report, 1912-21*, vol. 1, p. 386. Cited in Zhongguo kexueyuan, vol. 2, p. 639.

37. Stross, p. 43.
38. Muramatsu found that in the rent books, these tenants who had migrated from the Subei were often called immigrants.
39. *North-China Herald*, Oct. 4, 1865. Quoted in Perry, p. 53.
40. Zhu Bangxing et al., p. 596.
41. Interview with Chen Zhaodi.
42. *Xin qingnian*, 7 (1920), no. 6; Tang Hai, p. 123.
43. Jin Yuan, "Jiangbeiren zai Shanghai" (Jiangbei People in Shanghai), *Nüsheng*, 2 (1934), no. 12: 10-11.
44. Du, pt. 3, pp. 76-77; also see Jue.
45. SSKJY, *Nanyang*, p. 74.
46. Deng Yuzhi, pp. 9-12.
47. *Xin qingnian*, 7 (1920), no. 6: 9.
48. Retirement cards, Cotton Mill A (hereafter cited as "retirement cards"). These retirement cards are filled out when a worker retires, and only began to be used after 1949. Therefore, there are not cards for every worker who worked in the mill in the years before Liberation, but rather only for those who worked until after 1949. A worker's work history is recorded on this card.
49. Interview with He Zhiguang.
50. Zhongguo fangzhi, *Shanghai dishisi*, pp. 63-65.
51. Retirement cards.
52. Lamson, "Housing," p. 147.
53. Zhu Bangxing et al., pp. 81-82.
54. Interview with Xu Shumei, Shanghai, Oct. 18, 1982.
55. *Shen Bao*, May 6, 1924.
56. Interview with Xu Shumei.
57. Chesneaux, *Chinese Labor*, p. 123. Also see Leung.
58. See Dublin; also Hareven.   59. Wada, pp. 24-25.
60. Interview with He Zhiguang.   61. Zhong.
62. Differences in conditions in Japanese-owned and Chinese-owned mills will be discussed more extensively in Chapter Seven.
63. Yuzhi, "Guanyu Shanghaide shiye gongren" (Concerning the Unemployed Workers in Shanghai), *Nü qingnian yuekan*, 11 (1932), no. 4: 45. The name Yuzhi is probably a pseudonym for Cora Deng (Deng Yuzhi).
64. Ibid.
65. Ibid.

CHAPTER 4

1. Tang Hai, p. 97. Also see Great Britain Foreign Office, pp. 20-21.
2. Tang Hai, p. 98.
3. Udaka, pp. 98-99.
4. *North-China Herald*, Mar. 6, 1926.
5. Ibid.
6. Interview with Xu Hongmei, Shanghai, Apr. 23, 1981.

7. Interview with Gu Lianying, Shanghai, Apr. 24, 1980.

8. Interview with He Ningzhen, Shanghai, May 6, 1981.

9. Interview with Gu Lianying. The YWCA schools were one of the few institutions that brought together women from different places. In the schools, Jiangnan, Shanghai, and Subei women not only attended class but also participated together in discussions, outings, meetings, singing, and drama.

10. Interview with retired mill workers, Shanghai No. 2 Textile Mill, Oct. 25, 1980.

11. *North-China Herald*, Nov. 3, 1928.

12. *Shen Bao*, Jan. 4, 1930.

13. Interview with Gu Lianying.

14. Ibid.

15. Interviews with Xu Shumei; Zhu Fanü, Shanghai, Oct. 11, 1982; and Xi Peiyu, Shanghai, Sept. 20, 1982.

16. SSKJY, *Rongjia*, vol. 1, p. 139.

17. Interview with Zhu Fanü.

18. Morris, pp. 135-36.

19. For a description of earlier attempts to implement this system, see SSKJY, *Rongjia*, vol. 1, p. 336, and *Yongan*, p. 91.

20. Zhongguo fangzhi, *Diliu chang lukan*, p. 253.

21. Interview with retired mill managers at Putuo District Federation of Industry and Commerce.

22. For example, at the Shanghai No. 1 Mill, of the 102 apprentices recruited in the first group, 12 percent were from Shanghai, 28 percent from Yancheng, 12 percent from Wuxi, and 12 percent from Wujin. See Zhongguo fangzhi, *Shanghai diyi chang*, p. 91.

23. Interview with Xu Hongmei.

24. "Women zai gongchang" (We Are in the Factory), *Funu*, 3 (1947), no. 10: 17.

25. Ibid.

26. Zhongguo fangzhi, *Diliu chang gaikuang*.

27. Interview with Li Youying, Shanghai, Nov. 20, 1980.

28. Ibid.

29. Zhongguo fangzhi, *Diliu chang lukan*.

30. Ibid.

31. "Women zai gongchang" (We Are in the Factory), *Funü*, 3 (1947), no. 10: 17.

32. Interview with Li Youying.

33. Zhongguo fangzhi, *Diliu chang lukan*, p. 263.

34. Ibid.

35. Interview with Yan Ke.

CHAPTER 5

1. Xia, pp. 42-48.

2. Cora Deng, "Contract Labour Dormitory," p. 1.

3. Chen Hansheng.

4. Xue, pp. 172-74. Xue notes that the business of marketing young boys was referred to as "moving stones."

5. See, for example, Shan, pp. 22-23.

6. *North-China Herald*, Mar. 20, 1935.

7. SSKJY, *Yongan*, p. 87.

8. Cora Deng, "Contract Labour Dormitory," p. 3.

9. Xia, pp. 30-32. Also see SSKJY, *Rongjia*, vol. 1, p. 578; SSKJY, *Yongan*, pp. 88-89; *Shen Bao*, May 12 and 22, 1930.

10. Xu and Wang; Cole.

11. Of the 27 contracted girls whose cases were investigated by the Shanghai Municipal Council in 1937, "the majority—22—were in age between 15 and 19 years when they commenced work; two were between 10 and 14 years, and there were three above 19 years." Shanghai Municipal Council, *1938*, p. 41. This distribution is corroborated by Xia and by the oral histories in *Baoshengongde xueleichou*. Also see *Baoshengongde chouhen*.

12. Interview with Zhang Xiaomei, Shanghai, Feb. 25, 1981.

13. *Baoshengongde xueleichou*, pp. 44-45.

14. Zhu and Mei, pt. 2, p. 118.

15. Xia, pp. 44-45; *Baoshengongde xueleichou*.

16. Gronewold, p. 37.

17. Xu Xingzhi, "Baohuoxiade baoshengong" (Contract Labor Under Fire), *Zhanshi helian xunkan* (1937), no. 4: 140.

18. SSKJY, *Rongjia*, vol. 1, p. 581. A similar contract is reproduced in Simine Wang, p. 18.

19. *Baoshengongde chouhen*, p. 39.

20. SSKJY, *Yongan*, p. 88. Of the 27 girls investigated by the Shanghai Municipal Council in its 1937 study, 24 had contracts of two years, and 3 had contracts of three years. Payments ranged from $25 to $45. Shanghai Municipal Council, *1938*, p. 41.

21. SSKJY, *Rongjia*, vol. 1, p. 243.

22. Shanghai Municipal Council, *1938*, p. 41; Sun Baoshan, p. 431.

23. Interview with Zhang Xiaomei.

24. *Baoshengongde chouhen*, p. 39.

25. Interview with Zhang Xiaomei.

26. *Baoshengongde xueleichou*, p. 44.

27. *Baoshengongde chouhen*, pp. 12-13, 40.

28. *Baoshengongde xueleichou*, p. 44.

29. Jiu Zhongguode, p. 171.

30. *Shen Bao*, Apr. 28, 1930.

31. Shan, pp. 22-23.

32. SSKJY, *Rongjia*, vol. 1, p. 577; *Pengyou*, 1 (1938), no. 6: 2; "Shachang gongrenzhongde baoshenzhi" (Contract Labor Among Cotton Mill Workers), *Fangzhi zhoukan*, 2 (1932), no. 19: 472-73. Although it has often been asserted that contract workers were paid as much as 40 percent less than other workers, there is no evidence that this was the case.

33. *Baoshengongde xueleichou*, p. 51.

34. SSKJY, *Rongjia*, vol. 1, p. 597.
35. *Baoshengongde xueleichou*, p. 47.
36. Zhong, p. 45.
37. Xia, pp. 2-5.
38. Cora Deng, "Contract Labour Dormitory," p. 3.
39. Sun Baoshan, p. 469; Cora Deng, "Contract Labour Dormitory," p. 2; SSKJY, *Rongjia*, vol. 1, p. 578.
40. Xia, p. 50; Sun Baoshan, p. 431; Shanghai Municipal Council, *1938*, pp. 41-42. At the Shen Xin No. 9 Textile Mill, the management required after 1937 that contract workers eat lunch at the mill cafeteria for *yangchenggong*. It cost $4 per person per month. See Zhu Bangxing et al., p. 79.
41. *Pengyou*, 1 (1938), no. 6: 2.
42. *Shen Bao*, July 15, 1934. In this case the contractor was taken to court by the girl's uncle and charged with having violated Section 240 of the legal code, which made the use of force to destroy the virginity of a girl who had not yet completed puberty a crime.
43. *Shen Bao*, Aug. 26, 1930.
44. SSKJY, *Rongjia*, vol. 1, p. 577-78.
45. Shanghai Municipal Council, *1939*, p. 58.
46. Sun Baoshan, p. 469.
47. Shanghai Municipal Council, *1938*, pp. 41-42.
48. *Baoshengongde xueleichou*, p. 59.
49. "Wode baofan shenghuo" (My Life as a Contract Worker), *Nü qingnian yuekan*, 15 (1934), no. 4: 23-24.
50. "Chinese Labor and the Contract System," *People's Tribune*, 5 (1933), no. 8: 410. Also see Sun Baoshan, p. 469.
51. Interview with Zhang Xiaomei.
52. Xia, pp. 33-34.
53. Shanghai Municipal Council, *1939*, p. 58. Unfortunately the details of this study are not available.
54. Interview with He Zhiguang; Cora Deng, "Contract Labour Dormitory," p. 1; Sun Baoshan, p. 470.
55. Luo Chuanhua, p. 271.
56. SSKJY, *Rongjia*, vol. 1, pp. 576, 579-80; *Jiu Zhongguode*, p. 171.
57. Cora Deng, "Contract Labour Dormitory," p. 4.
58. Shindo, p. 42.   59. Shunzo, p. 498.
60. Ibid.   61. Ibid., p. 491.
62. Torgasheff; also see Wright.
63. "Contract System for Chinese Dockers," ILO China correspondent, Monthly Report, Nov. 1932 (ILO Archives, Geneva).
64. Odell, pp. 163-64. When, after World War I, ICMC was bought by the British firm Arnhold Brothers Co. and became the Oriental Cotton Spinning and Weaving Co., a similar system of contract work was employed. "In the Oriental Cotton Mill we use a labor contractor," the director of the mill wrote to the British consul in 1925. "This contractor employs a number of Number One women, who have charge of a number of frames

and who engage the necessary labor." See H. Arnhold to Consul Brenan, Aug. 4, 1925, in Great Britain Foreign Office, pp. 20-21.

65. SSKJY, *Hengfeng*, p. 7.

66. *Xin qingnian*, 7 (1920), no. 6: 1-41.

67. This system did not become widespread until after World War II, when almost all cotton mills in Shanghai set up worker training bureaus for young women workers (see Chapter Four). In the mid-1920's several such bureaus were established. These fledgling institutions resembled neither the training bureaus of a later date nor the contract labor system, although all three are often perceived, erroneously, as one phenomenon.

68. SSKJY, *Yongan*, p. 91; materials provided by the Institute for Historical Research, Shanghai Academy of Social Sciences.

69. Tang Hai; Udaka; Chen Da; RSCLC; and Ma Zhaojun.

70. Isaacs, *Five Years*, p. 93.   71. Y. C. Wang, pp. 433-35.

72. Ibid.   73. Interview with He Zhiguang.

74. *North-China Herald*, Feb. 16, 1929.

75. Interview with Chen Shulu, Shanghai, Nov. 19, 1980.

76. Coble.

77. "Shachang gongrenzhong zhi baoshenzhi" (The Contract Labor System Among Cotton Mill Workers), *Fangzhi zhoukan*, 2 (1932), no. 19: 472.

78. Ibid., pp. 472-73.

79. *North-China Herald*, Apr. 12, 1932. At this point these mills were only employing 3,000 out of the normal 25,000 hands.

80. Xia, p. 21.

81. Sun Baoshan, p. 472. The authors of *Jiu Zhongguode* estimate that at the time of the Japanese attack in 1932, half the 48,000 workers in Japanese-owned mills were contract workers. That would amount to 24,000 workers in the Japanese mills alone (over twice the estimate made by Sun for all the mills). No source is given for this figure.

82. "Baoshenzhixia zhi Shanghai ri shachang nügong" (Women Workers Under the Contract Labor System in the Japanese Cotton Mills in Shanghai), *Guoji laogong tongxun*, 4 (1937), no. 7: 54-55.

83. "Shourongsuolide baoshengong" (Contract Workers in the Refugee Houses), *Zhanshi funü* (1937), no. 2: 2.

84. Shanghai Municipal Council, *1938*, p. 40.

85. Wang Ruyi, "Zai wei baoshengong hujiu" (A Further Appeal for Contract Workers), *Zhanshi funü* (1937), no. 7: 2-3.

86. *North-China Herald*, Nov. 10, 1937.

87. Ibid.

88. Hinder, p. 30.

89. Shanghai Municipal Council, *1939*, p. 54.

90. Tu, pt. 3, p. 75.

CHAPTER 6

1. The description of this exhibit is based on a personal visit and on the exhibit's display labels, reprinted in SSKLY, *Wusa yundong*, pp. 212-31.

2. See, for example, *Zui ede jiu shehui*; *Jiu Zhongguode*.

3. A vivid fictional portrayal of early-morning market activities is given in Zhou Erfu, p. 56.

4. Interviews with Gao Jun, Shanghai, May 11, 1981 and Sept. 27, 1982.

5. Interview with Chen Zhaodi.

6. According to a survey made in 1929-30, an average of 2.33 adults lived in each room, measuring 3¼ meters square. Shanghai Bureau of Social Affairs, *Standard of Living*, pp. 140-42.

7. Lamson, "Housing," pp. 144-45.

8. Shanghai Bureau of Social Affairs, *Standard of Living*, p. 143.

9. Interview with Wang Luoying, Shanghai, Feb. 25, 1981.

10. Shanghai Bureau of Social Affairs, *Standard of Living*, p. 143.

11. Interview with Wang Luoying; Shanghai Bureau of Social Affairs, *Standard of Living*, p. 155; Zhou Erfu, p. 88.

12. Zhong, p. 44.

13. Xue, p. 171. Also see Lamson, "Housing," pp. 144-45. The absence of flush toilets was not peculiar to working-class districts. Most of the Shanghai population had to use chamber pots. John Powell, editor of the *China Weekly Review*, complained that "the International Settlement possessed no sewage disposal system or modern plumbing, except in one or two new buildings located on the Bund. Modern flush toilets were regarded, along with screens and electric fans, as 'unhealthy.' Bathrooms were equipped with round earthenware tubs in which one sat upright to take a bath, and with sanitary devices known as 'commodes' which consisted of a square wooden box with a hole in the top and an earthenware chamber pot. The house boys collected the pots in the mornings and derived a considerable income by selling the contents to the farmers for use as fertilizer." Powell, pp. 25-26.

14. Interview with Wang Luoying; Zhong, p. 44; Zhu Bangxing et al., p. 78.

15. Not all women had to perform all these tasks in the morning. What a woman did depended largely on the composition of her household, and her position in it. One worker remembered that when she was still young and had just started working, "my mother did the cooking. And in the morning she would take care of getting us up and making breakfast. My poor mother—she had to get up at three or four in the morning." A YWCA worker observed that women who grew up in their own parents' homes were much more fortunate than those who grew up in the homes of future in-laws, where they were expected to get up early and prepare breakfast for themselves and other family members before going to work. See Bai, "Shachangli," pp. 66-67.

16. Interview with Xu Shumei.

17. Interview with Gao Jun.

18. Gamewell, p. 223.

19. Interview with Wang Fuying and her son, Shanghai, July 2, 1981.

20. Interview with Chen Zhaodi.

21. "Yeli du Suzhouhe nannügongde beiju" (The Tragedy of Male and Female Workers Crossing Suzhou Creek at Night), *Laodong jie*, 23 (Jan. 1921): 8.

22. Gamewell, p. 92.

23. Interview with Xu Hongmei; Zhu Bangxing et al., pp. 80-81.

24. Yang Meizhen, "Yangshupu yishizhu," p. 7.

25. "Shanghai Yongan shachang gaige nügong exi" (The Yong An Cotton Mill in Shanghai Reforms Bad Habits of Women Workers), *Guoji laogong tongxun*, 6 (1939), no. 2: 74.

26. Zhong, p. 43.

27. Xia, p. 53.

28. Bai, "Shanghai," p. 60; "Yi ye nügong de riji" (A Page of a Woman Worker's Diary), *Nü qingnian yuekan*, 15 (1936), no. 4: 21.

29. Zhu Bangxing et al., p. 34. Several mills required workers to arrive a half hour early. Interviews with Gao Jun; Shi Xiaomei, Shanghai, Mar. 11, 1980.

30. SSKJY, *Rongjia*, vol. 1, p. 177. There were identical fines at the Yong An mills. See SSKJY, *Yongan*, p. 85.

31. SSKJY, *Rongjia*, vol. 1, p. 177.

32. Fong, *Cotton Industry*, vol. 1, pp. 134-35; interview with Gao Jun.

33. Zhu Bangxing et al., pp. 80-81; Bai, "Shanghai," pp. 52-53. Some mills issued "grease shoes" in addition to "grease clothes."

34. Moser, p. 69.   35. Gamewell, p. 222.

36. Xia, pp. 15-16.   37. Ibid., p. 16.

38. British Economic Mission, *Report*, p. 54.

39. Bai, "Shanghai," p. 53.

40. Zhou Erfu.

41. Bai, "Shanghai," p. 56.

42. Zhongguo fangzhi, *Shanghai diersan*, p. 31.

43. British Economic Mission, *Report*, p. 54.

44. Shu Yi, "Shanghai shachang nügongde shenghuo xiankuang" (The Present Condition of Women Workers in Shanghai Cotton Mills), *Nüsheng*, 2 (1933), no. 6: 7.

45. Interview with Wang Luoying.

46. *Shen Bao*, May 2, 1924.

47. Zhu Bangxing et al., p. 37. One of the gains of the strikes in 1925 was two 15-minute rests a day: one at nine and one at three. After the Japanese attack on Shanghai in 1932, however, these breaks were eliminated in the Japanese mills, and soon afterward the Chinese mills followed suit. The only exception was the Chinese-owned Hong Zhang Mill, but it was only a group of male workers who enjoyed this privilege.

48. Interview with Wang Luoying; SSKLY, *Wusa yundong*, vol. 1, pp. 214-15.

49. SSKJY, *Rongjia*, vol. 1, p. 131.

50. Ibid., p. 180. Also see SSKJY, *Yongan*, p. 84.

51. Bai Ying, "Zuogongde touyitian" (My First Day of Work), *Nü qingnian yuekan*, 5 (1936), no. 6: 29.

52. Zhu Bangxing et al., p. 37.

53. Gamewell, pp. 224-25.

54. Bai, "Shanghai," p. 53; Zhu Bangxing et al., p. 37.

55. Zhu Bangxing et al., pp. 78-79.

56. Bulle, p. 11.

57. RSCLC, p. 548.

58. Fang, *Chinese Labour*, p. 38.

59. Interview with Yu Rong, Shanghai, Mar. 30, 1980.

60. Bai, "Shanghai," p. 57. Workers complained that in 1931, when the Rong family bought the San Xin Mill and established Shen Xin 9, one of the things management did was to enforce stricter rules about nursing infants. In the past workers could freely come and go, and children could be brought into the workshops for nursing. But the managers at Shen Xin 9 decided that workers could not come and go at whim, and children could not be brought into the mill. They had to be left at home; when it was time for nursing, someone could bring them to the factory gate and they could nurse there. See SSKJY, *Rongjia*, vol. 1, p. 590. Women who could afford to hire a wet nurse did not have to worry about having someone bring the infant to the mill. Lamson interviewed one woman worker who paid a wet nurse $72 for one year. She herself earned $220 a year. See Lamson, "Industrialization," pp. 1057-58.

61. Before 1945 virtually every mill had 12-hour shifts, and in almost all cases they ran from six to six. The only exception is the Shen Xin No. 1 Mill, which before 1925 started the shift at 4:30 and ended at 5:00. Counting a half hour off for lunch, this was a 12-hour shift. Guo and Zhong, p. 35. The other exception was weaving: weaving departments did not always operate at night. Instead a day shift lasted 12 to 16 hours. See SSKJY, *Hengfeng*, p. 51.

62. Bai, "Shanghai," pp. 52-53.

63. Moser, p. 70; SSKJY, *Yongan*, p. 85.

64. Moser, p. 70.

65. SSKJY, *Yongan*, p. 85.

66. Harrison.

67. *Evening News*, July 25, 1935, cited by Liu Ta-chun, *Growth and Industrialization*, p. 169.

68. SSKJY, *Shanghai penghuqude*, p. 24.

69. Interview with Zhu Fanü.

70. *Shen Bao*, May 26, 1930.

71. Interview with Xi Peiyu; SSKLY, *Wusa yundong*, vol. 1, pp. 217-19.

72. Interviews with Xi Peiyu and Zhu Fanu. Also see SSKLY, *Wusa yundong*, vol. 1, pp. 216-17.

73. Ibid.

74. Interview with Han Jinmei, Shanghai, Oct. 11, 1982.

75. Interview with Wang Gaokun, Shanghai, Oct. 6, 1982. Also see SSKJY, *Shanghai penghuqude*, p. 25.

76. Interview with Yang Meiying, Shanghai, May 10, 1981.

77. Interviews with Xi Peiyu and Zhu Fanü.

78. Gamewell, p. 210. Also see *Shanghai heimo*, pp. 1-31.

79. *Qinghongbang kaoyi*, pp. 124-28; Chesneaux, *Secret Societies*, p. 50.

80. Interview with Zhu Fanu.

81. Interview with Gu Lianying.

82. Ibid.

83. Only recently have well-off families been able to purchase refrigerators. Even today, the number of households with refrigerators represents a tiny minority.

84. Shanghai Bureau of Social Affairs, *Standard of Living*, pp. 110-15.

85. Bai, "Shachangli," pp. 66-67.

86. Interview with retired mill workers, Fangualong, Apr. 22, 1980; interview with Shi Xiaomei.

87. Zhong, p. 44. Of the 305 working class families' budgets studied by the Shanghai Bureau of Social Affairs in 1930, 75 had boarders in their homes. See Shanghai Bureau of Social Affairs, *Standard of Living*, p. 91.

88. Tu, pt. 3, p. 10.

89. Interview with Shi Xiaomei. In fact most working-class homes were not equipped with electricity. For light, people depended on lamps that burned kerosene or native oil. Shanghai Bureau of Social Affairs, *Standard of Living*, p. 155. Of the 305 families studied, 274 (89.8 percent) used kerosene lamps.

90. Zhu Bangxing et al., p. 35.

91. Harrison.

92. Zhu Bangxing et al., p. 35; interview with Wang Luoying.

93. Interview with Yu Rong.

94. Kyong, "Industrial Women," pp. 3-4.

95. Interview with Gui Jianying, Shanghai, May 13, 1980.

96. Yang Meizhen, "Yangshupu nügong."

97. S. C. Wu, secretary general of the National Anti-Tuberculosis Association, "Minutes of the First Conference on Mass Chest Survey for Industrial Groups," in ILO China correspondent, Monthly Report, July 1948 (ILO Archives, Geneva).

98. Chang Chu-fang, "Chinese Cotton Mills in Shanghai," *Chinese Economic Journal*, 3 (1928), no. 5: 909. Chang notes that some mills rotated shifts every 10 days.

99. Zhu Bangxing et al., p. 34.

100. Ibid.

101. Ibid.

102. ILO China correspondent, Monthly Report, July 1935 (ILO Archives, Geneva).

103. Li Xin, "Cong yiqiange yexiao xuesheng kan Shanghai nügong" (Looking at Women Workers Through One Thousand Students at the Night Schools), *Shenghuo zhishi* (1946), no. 36: 7.

104. "Shanghai nügong shenghuo jianying" (A Glimpse of the Life of Women Workers in Shanghai), *Guoji laogong tongxun*, 6 (1939), no. 8: 75-76.

105. Tang Hai, p. 140.

106. SSKJY, *Yongan*, p. 83.

107. Bai, "Shanghai," p. 56.

108. Huang Miding, a graduate student at Shanghai University who conducted a survey of workers in Yangshupu in 1947, found that most women workers in cotton mills were Buddhists. See Huang Miding. Yang Meizhen

made a similar observation (see "Yangshupu nügong"). The history of the Da Kang Mill noted that among women workers there were "three too many's" (see p. 182). One of these was that too many women were vegetarian and believed in Buddhism. Materials provided by the Institute for Historical Research, Shanghai Academy of Social Sciences.

109. Interview with He Ningzhen.

110. Tu, pt. 3, p. 90.

111. "Shenxin jiuchang nügongyou sushe fangwenji" (A Record of a Visit to the Women Workers' Dormitory at the Shen Xin Number Nine Mill), *Fangzhiran gongcheng*, 2 (1948), no. 4: 13.

112. Materials provided by the Institute for Historical Research, Shanghai Academy of Social Sciences.

113. Cora Deng, "Economic Status," p. 72. Shanghai Bureau of Social Affairs, *Standard of Living*, p. 106.

114. *Shen Bao*, Aug. 22, 1923.

115. Lamson, "Housing," p. 145.

116. Interview with Chen Zhaodi.

117. SSKJY, *Rongjia*, vol. 1, p. 138.

118. Interview with Gu Lianying.

119. Interview with Chen Zhaodi.

120. Zhu Bangxing et al., pp. 95-96.

121. Interview with Gu Lianying.

122. Interview with Wang Fuying.

123. Wagner, p. 43.

124. Shanghai Bureau of Social Affairs, *Standard of Living*, pp. 111, 159.

125. Interview with Xu Shumei.   126. Ibid.

127. Ibid.   128. Interview with Gao Jun.

129. Ibid.

CHAPTER 7

1. Interview with Wang Luoying.

2. Interview with retired mill workers, Shanghai No. 2 Textile Mill.

3. This discussion of the work experiences of young girls is based on the retirement cards of Cotton Mill A.

4. Institute of Pacific Relations, pp. 238-41.

5. Interview with Xu Hongmei.

6. RSCLC, p. 550.

7. Retirement cards. In one mill the women who did have a year or two of schooling as young girls were almost invariably from Wuxi. There is some indication that this changed over time. Although it was never the case that the majority of cotton mill workers were literate, those who were born in the late 1920's and entered the mills in the late 1940's were more likely than their predecessors to have had some education. Furthermore, for that group, those who were educated were not only from Wuxi but from other cities as well, including Shanghai, Ningbo, Shaoxing, Yancheng, and Dongtai. This

finding probably suggests not that education was more common for women, but that women from families of an economic status higher than their predecessors' began entering the mills after World War II.

8. Cora Deng, "Economic Status," p. 72.

9. Lamson, "Factory Workers," pp. 1244-45.

10. Retirement cards.

11. Interview with Song Ermei, Shanghai, Nov. 11, 1980.

12. Lamson, "Factory Workers," pp. 1246-47. Lamson's finding is corroborated by Yang Ximeng's study of family budgets of 230 cotton mill workers, conducted in 1930. He found that daughters contributed an average of 19.1 percent of the family income. See Yang Ximeng, p. 34.

13. Lamson, "Industrialization," pp. 1074-75.

14. Cora Deng, "Economic Status," pp. 46-47. Deng herself noted that although the women included in her study were typical insofar as they represented the major industries employing women, as well as the different industrial districts, there were several ways in which these women may have been somewhat atypical. She observed that their participation in YWCA classes meant that they were probably a little younger and slightly more "independent" than most workers, and were probably from families whose economic conditions were better than average, since they could afford to pay, even if only a small amount, for education and recreation. Ibid., p. 10.

15. Lamson, "Industrialization," pp. 1074-75.

16. *Shen Bao*, June 13, 1930.

17. Cora Deng, "Economic Status," p. 36.

18. Ibid., p. 46.

19. Interview with Yu Rong. Lydia Kung also concluded, on the basis of a study of women factory workers in Taiwan in the 1970's, that although earning a wage outside the home enhanced the value of daughters, wage earning did not result in increased independence or power for women within their families. See Kung.

20. Interviews with Yu Rong; Xu Hongmei; and retired workers, Shanghai No. 2 Textile Mill.

21. Deng Yuzhi.

22. RSCLC, p. 549.

23. Interview with Yu Rong.

24. Ibid.; interview with Sun Jianmei, Shanghai, Mar. 11, 1980. Also see *Zui ede jiu shehui*, vol. 2, pp. 22-27.

25. Interview with retired mill workers at Fangualong.

26. Interview with Shi Xiaomei. Also see Retirement cards.

27. Liu Ta-chun, *Silk Industry*, p. 92.

28. Interview with Shi Xiaomei. According to the records of the Zhang Hua and the Da Hua wool mills (where half the workers were female), whereas 60 percent of the male workers were permanent, virtually all the women workers—except the forewomen—were temporary. See Shanghai-shi, p. 155.

29. Chung and Bagwell, p. 14.

30. See Chapters Four and Five for a discussion of the *yangchenggong* system.

31. Tang Hai, p. 156.

32. Interview with Chen Zhaodi.

33. Zhu Bangxing et al., p. 56.

34. For example, at the Shen Xin No. 9 Mill in 1948 there were only 100 Number Ones, of whom 79 were female. This figure represented less than 1.5 percent of the total work force. See Shenjiuchang feichu namawen zhidu gongzuo zongjie (A Summary of the Work of Eliminating the Number One System at the Shen Xin Nine Mill). (Materials provided by the Institute for Historical Research, Shanghai Academy of Social Sciences.)

35. Gamewell, p. 226.

36. Retirement cards.

37. Wang Qingbin et al., pp. 376-78.

38. Fong, *Cotton Industry*.

39. One possible explanation is that whereas until the war weaving was the purview of Jiangnan women, after the war Subei immigrants began to enter the weaving workshops, thereby lowering the wages. There is no evidence for this explanation, however.

40. Interview with Xu Hongmei.

41. Interview with Wang Luoying.

42. Interview with retired mill workers, Shanghai No. 2 Textile Mill.

43. It seems to be only Party activists or other people with some political consciousness who perceived the mills as uniformly brutal places in which to work. Fan Xiaofeng, for instance, said in an interview: "I worked at almost every factory. I'd work at one and discover that they exploited workers, then I'd go to another and discover that they exploited workers. They were all the same—either they'd beat you, or they'd have low wages. There was no ideal factory. From this I understood one thing: none of the factories operated by capitalists and imperialists was good to workers. They all oppressed and exploited us. So, later, because of this education, I participated in the revolution."

44. Zhu Bangxing et al., p. 56.

45. Ibid., pp. 54-58.

46. Interview with Shi Wenran.

47. Zhu Bangxing et al., pp. 58, 70-71.

48. Jin Xiang, "Women yao ba 'mofan' bianwei zhenzheng de mofanchang" (We Want to Make the So-Called Model Factory into a Genuine Model Factory), *Pengyou*, 1 (1938), no. 6: 26-29.

49. He Ziqing, "Yongan sanchang tongxun" (Bulletin from Yong An Number Three Mill), *Pengyou*, 1 (1938), no. 6: 29-30.

50. Zhu Bangxing et al., p. 37.

51. Interview with Yu Rong.

52. Fong, *Cotton Industry*, vol. 1, p. 126. The retirement cards of Cotton Mill A corroborate this observation, and also indicate that it remained true until 1949.

53. Retirement cards.

54. Zhu Bangxing et al., p. 60; interview with He Zhiguang.
55. Interview with Yu Rong; also see retirement cards. "Sister transferred" or "mother transferred" appears frequently on retirement cards among the reasons for women moving from one mill to another.
56. See, for example, *Shen Bao*, June 21, 1930; Nov. 20, 1930; Aug. 21, 1930; Apr. 28, 1930; May 26, 1930.
57. Xu and Liu. This study, based on interviews with 359 women criminals in three women's prisons in Shanghai, found that one-third of these women were originally factory workers. The authors also found that the largest single group, i.e., 33 percent, were women from Subei.
58. Retirement cards.
59. Ibid. Fong cites a study of the reasons listed for workers leaving one mill in Shanghai. Out of 2,150 workers who left, 608 (28.3 percent) left for a "long absence"; 385 (17.9 percent) left—presumably were fired—for "loafing, laziness, and bad work"; 244 (11.3 percent) left because of sickness or injury; 168 (7.8 percent) left because of "domestic affairs"; 259 (12.0 percent) left to return to their native place; and 129 (6.0 percent) left for marriage or birth. The rest were dismissed for reasons such as insufficient height, stealing, disobedience, fighting, strike participation, and picketing. Fong, *Cotton Industry*, vol. 1, p. 122.
60. Materials provided by the Institute for Historical Research, Shanghai Academy of Social Sciences.
61. Lamson, "Industrialization," p. 1073.
62. See Retirement cards. Also see Yang Meizhen, "Yangshupu hunyin," p. 8. The author, a student at Shanghai College, was able to obtain the following statistics for the Hou Sheng Cotton Mill when she conducted her survey in 1931. Of 187 women workers, 109 were married between the ages of 15 and 20; 43 married between 20 and 25; and 19 married after they were 25. The remaining 16 either were married or were child-daughters-in-law before they were 15. See below for discussion. Fang Fu-an's survey shows that most women workers married at age 22. See Fang, "Shanghai Labor."
63. Cora Deng, "Economic Status," p. 22.
64. Some studies of the role of women in industrialization have found a steadily increasing marriage age. In her study of working women in contemporary Hong Kong, for example, Salaff found that whereas in 1964 less than half the women workers who were 20-24 years old were unmarried, by 1974 68 percent were still unmarried. See Salaff, p. 29.
65. Lamson, "Industrialization," p. 1073.
66. Yang Meizhen, "Yangshupu hunyin," p. 8.
67. Ibid.; Margery Wolf, in her study of women in Taiwan, also found that parents who had a daughter but no son tried to find a prospective son-in-law who was willing to enter their household. She found that, as in Shanghai, men who were willing to agree to this arrangement either were of dubious character or were treated with mistrust derived from the conventional wisdom that "there is nothing more abominable . . . than an unfilial son, a man who abandons his parents and leaves his ancestors to suffer unknown deprivations in the afterlife." See Wolf, pp. 191-204.

68. Interview with Shi Xiaomei.
69. Interview with He Ningzhen.
70. Yang Meizhen, "Yangshupu hunyin," p. 6; Lamson, "Industrialization," p. 1075.
71. The woman then became sick, at which point the man disappeared. She eventually went to court to sue her husband for having used her earnings, and to request a divorce. The judge informed her that since they had never been formally married but had only lived together, she was free to separate from him whenever she so desired. The news report does not indicate how the suit was resolved. *Shen Bao*, July 13, 1930.
72. Liu Ta-chun, p. 168.
73. Zhu Bangxing et al., p. 92.
74. For an analysis of the practice of *tongyangxi*, or "minor marriages," see Wolf and Huang.
75. Yang Meizhen estimated that some 80-90 percent of the brides of working-class couples in Yangshupu had been child-daughters-in-law. See "Yangshupu hunyin," p. 7.
76. Zhu Bangxing et al., p. 90.   77. Interview with Chen Zhaodi.
78. Interview with Xu Shumei.   79. Zhu Bangxing et al., p. 92.
80. Materials provided by the Institute for Historical Research, Shanghai Academy of Social Sciences.
81. Bai, "Shanghai," p. 58. Virtually all the oral history interviews I conducted corroborate this point.
82. *Shen Bao*, Apr. 21, 1930.
83. In the 230 families whose budgets were studied by Yang Ximeng in 1930, the amount spent for weddings ranged from a low of $7.59 to a high of $250. The average in his group was $100.25. See Yang Ximeng, p. 75.
84. Interview with Chen Zhaodi.
85. Zhongguo fangzhi, *Shanghai diyi chang*, p. 105. There are no comparable statistics for earlier periods, and it is thus difficult to determine whether this percentage represents a departure from conditions before World War II. Statistics about the ages of women workers in a cotton mill in 1925 suggest that it might have been slightly less common before the war for women to continue working after marriage. Of the 1,340 women working in the mill, there were 234 (17.5 percent) who were 21 to 25 years old; 116 (8.7 percent) who were 26 to 30; and only about 50 women (less than 4 percent) over the age of 30. If we assume that most married by the time they were 21, roughly one-third of the women worked after marriage. See Udaka, p. 330.
86. Interview with Wang Fuying.
87. Interview with retired mill workers, Shanghai No. 2 Textile Mill.
88. Yang Meizhen, "Yangshupu hunyin," p. 7.
89. Interview with retired mill workers, Shanghai No. 2 Textile Mill.
90. Interview with Chen Zhaodi.
91. Ibid.
92. Zhong, p. 48.
93. Miscarriages were so common that when cotton mills finally began

to grant women maternity leave in 1946, the lack of provisions for leave for women who had miscarried was considered a major flaw. See "Huxi shida shachang laogong fulibanli qingxing" (The Condition of Providing Benefits for Workers at the Ten Large Cotton Mills in Western Shanghai), *Zhongguo gongren zhoukan* (Chinese Workers' Weekly) (1946), no. 10: 2.

94. Materials provided by the Institute for Historical Research, Shanghai Academy of Social Sciences.

95. Lamson, "Industrialization," p. 1069.

96. Tang Hai, p. 261.

97. Interview with Yu Rong.

98. Wu Yunzhi, "Fuying weisheng wenti" (The Problem of Women's Maternity Health), in Shanghai zonggonghui nügongbu, p. 92.

99. Lamson, "Industrialization," p. 1096.

100. Zhong, p. 48.

101. Wu Yunzhi, "Fuying weisheng wenti," p. 92.

102. Interviews with Chen Zhaodi and Xu Shumei.

103. Zhong, p. 48.

104. Materials provided by the Institute for Historical Research, Shanghai Academy of Social Sciences. Also see Li Shaoyang, "Nügong yu yuyingtang" (Women Workers and Orphanages), *Laodong jie* (1920), no. 4: 3.

105. Interview with Yu Rong.

106. Interview with Chen Zhaodi.

107. Retirement cards.

108. Eleanor Hinder, letter to World YWCA, Feb. 9, 1932 (World YWCA Archives, Geneva).

109. "War in Shanghai: Flight to the Settlement and Chapei on Fire," *The Illustrated London News*, Mar. 5, 1932 (World YWCA Archives, Geneva).

110. Interview with Chen Zhaodi.

111. Yu Zhi, "Zhong Ri zhanzheng duiyu Shanghai gongyejie de yingxiang" (The Effect of the War Between China and Japan on the Industrial World of Shanghai), *Nü qingnian yuekan*, 11 (1932), no. 6: 17.

112. Bush, p. 203.

113. Retirement cards.

114. Interview with Yu Rong.

115. Chinese-owned mills were particularly hard hit. The number of workers in the Japanese-owned mills dropped only from 51,000 to 44,000 during these years; the number in Chinese-owned mills dropped from 85,000 to 45,000. Shanghaishi mianfangzhi, pp. 42-58.

116. Retirement cards. According to one estimate, 84,255 women worked in industry in the International Settlement before the outbreak of hostilities in 1937; in May 1938, there were 56,158 women factory workers. ILO China correspondent, Monthly Report, June 1938 (ILO Archives, Geneva). For a discussion of the cotton industry during World War II, see Chapter One.

117. SSKJY, *Rongjia*, vol. 2, p. 326. For a variety of personal accounts of the first days of the war, see Zhu and Mei.

118. Interview with Chen Zhaodi.

119. Zhao Pochu, "Kangzhan chuqi Shanghaide nanmin gongzuo" (Refugee Work in Shanghai in the Beginning of the War of Resistance), *SWZX* (1981), no. 4: 37. Within a day after the war began, 26 camps were set up in the Settlement, housing 30,000 refugees. By the end of 1937 there were 190 camps, housing about 95,000 refugees. Throughout 1938 the number of camps decreased, and by 1939 only 29 camps were operating, housing approximately 31,000 refugees. On the eve of the Japanese occupation of the Settlement, there were still 16,000 refugees in 13 camps. See Barnett, pp. 44-45.

120. Letter to YWCA, Apr. 22, 1938 (World YWCA Archives, Geneva).

121. Wales, p. 87.

122. The straw shack settlements expanded most dramatically during the war. See SSKJY, *Shanghai penghuqude.*

123. Interview with Xu Hongmei.

124. Interview with Zhou Abao, Shanghai, Sept. 28, 1982.

125. Interview with Wang Fuying and her son. For a description of the problems of food supplies, rice riots, fuel shortages, and the declining value of workers' wages, see Barnett, p. 46. He summarized the harsh conditions imposed by war by citing the numbers of corpses disposed of in the streets. In 1935, before the war, there were 5,590 corpses collected in the streets of Shanghai. In 1937 the number rose to 20,746, and in 1938 it soared to 101,047. Also see Hinder.

126. Retirement cards.

127. SGYLW, *Shanghai gongren,* vol. 4, p. 56.

128. Retirement cards.

CHAPTER 8

1. See Chesneaux, *Chinese Labor;* Chan; and Shaffer, *Mao and the Workers.*

2. Some writers, such as Bobby Siu, have found in this record evidence of a "women's labor movement," which during this period "moved from sporadic skirmishes to cohesive strikes and organizations." See Siu.

3. See Sato, p. 26. For an account of this strike see Deng Zhongxia.

4. Chang Kuo-t'ao, vol. 1, p. 414. Zhang also learned that this strategy had been adopted from the Anyuan Miners Union strikes.

5. SSKLY, *Wusa yundong,* vol. 1, p. 599.

6. Deng Zhongxia, p. 36.

7. Croll, pp. 119-20.

8. Most of the records relevant to Party history, including its programs for organizing women workers, remain inaccessible to foreign scholars, and therefore this discussion of the CCP is meant to be suggestive, not conclusive.

9. SGYLW, *Shanghai gongren,* vol. 1.

10. Interview with Liu Guibao, Shanghai, Nov. 11, 1980.

11. Xiang, pp. 145-47.

12. SSKLY, *Wusa yundong*, vol. 1, p. 286.

13. Ibid, p. 287.

14. Xiang. Gipoulon points out that despite her reputation as an organizer of women workers, Xiang's concerns were not restricted to working-class issues.

15. An account of the Feb. 1925 strike is typical. It reports a crowd of striking workers, "which appeared to be led by a female student waving a white flag." Woodhead, 1926, pp. 915-16.

16. Mao Chi-chun, "The Unemployment Problem in the Municipality of Shanghai," *Chinese Economic Journal*, 3 (1928), no. 5: 219.

17. Interview with Gu Lianying.

18. Interview with Gui Jianying.

19. Interview with Song Ermei.

20. The authors of *The Standard of Living of Shanghai Laborers* noted that "stories were told by the working people themselves as well as in newspapers as to how such illegal usury had ruined many a family. . . . Instances are not lacking, telling how when hard pressed by the excessive demand of the money lenders, some of the victims went so far as to commit suicide, others had to sell their children to meet the obligation, and in some cases they were driven desperate and turned into criminals or outcasts of the community." See Shanghai Bureau of Social Affairs, *Standard of Living*, p. 109.

21. Cora Deng, "Economic Status," p. 73. Of the 368 women workers studied by Cora Deng, 114 participated in this kind of economic mutual aid group.

22. Interview with He Ningzhen.

23. Interview with Xi Peiyu.

24. Interview with Han Jinmei.

25. Materials provided by the Institute for Historical Research, Shanghai Academy of Social Sciences. This source does not explain the relationship of the male to the sisterhoods of prostitutes. Since the men who acted as pimps are discussed in a separate section of the article, it seems safe to assume that these men were not pimps.

26. Ma Chunji, "Shanghai nügong."

27. Topley, pp. 67-88; Prazniak; and Sankar.

28. See Mao Tun, p. 111; Pai, pp. 60-61; Wu, p. 33.

29. Interview with Han Jinmei.

30. For a discussion of the early development of the YWCA in China, see Drucker.

31. Letter to Grace Coppock, Dec. 8, 1920 (World YWCA Archives, Geneva).

32. Efforts to conduct industrial work before 1920 were sporadic. For an account of these projects, see Bagwell.

33. See Bagwell; also see Porter.

34. Lily Haass to Mary Dingman, Jan. 5, 1928 (World YWCA Archives, Geneva).

35. The CCP had not entirely abandoned the urban labor movement dur-

ing the early 1930's, but it appears that no attempts were made to organize in the cotton industry. For a discussion of organizing and the labor movement during this period, see Hammond.

36. Interview with Cora Deng, Shanghai, Apr. 15, 1980.

37. Kyong, "Education," p. 15.   38. Ibid, p. 16.

39. Interview with Gao Jun.   40. Interview with Gu Lianying.

41. Interview with Zhong Shaoqin, Beijing, May 17, 1980; also with Li Mingjian, Shanghai, Oct. 28, 1980.

42. "Report of the Third Conference of Industrial Secretaries," January 1933 (World YWCA Archives, Geneva).

43. Interview with Zhang Shuyi, Beijing, May 16, 1980.

44. "Huiyi Shanghai nüqingnianhuide nügong yexiao" (Recalling the YWCA Night Schools for Women Workers in Shanghai), *SWZX* (1979), no. 5: 85.

45. Interview with Zhong Shaoqin.

46. Interview with Gu Lianying.

47. "Women Workers Hold Joint Labor Day Celebrations," May 3, 1931 (YWCA National Board Archives, New York).

48. Kyong, "Education," p. 16.

49. Interview with Gu Lianying.

50. Ibid.

51. Liu Yu-hsia and Chang Shu-yi, "Mass Education Work in the YWCA of China," in "Report to the National Committee, YWCA of China," Apr. 1940 (World YWCA Archives, Geneva).

52. Analogous groups were formed throughout China during the war, e.g., the Yunnan Women's Battlefield Service Unit and the Guangxi Women's Battalion. See Croll, pp. 176-77.

53. "Examples of Special Wartime Projects," 1937 (World YWCA Archives, Geneva).

54. "A Brief Summary of the YWCA Industrial Camp for Refugee Women and Children, 1938-39" (World YWCA Archives, Geneva).

55. Zhao Pochu, "Kangzhan chuqide nanmin gongzuo" (Refugee Work During the Early Period of the War of Resistance), *SWZX* (1981), no. 4: 38.

56. It is, of course, possible that the Party had begun this effort sooner and that we simply do not have access to reports that would tell us so. However, the methods used by the Party in the 1920's do not manifest this understanding, whereas they do during the war.

57. Ma Chunji, "Shanghai nügong."

58. Ma Chunji, "Shanghai gongyunde," pp. 64, 75-76.

59. Interview with Gui Jianying.

60. SGYLW, *Guomian shichang*, p. 10.

61. Materials provided by the Institute for Historical Research, Shanghai Academy of Social Sciences.

62. Ibid.

63. Tang Guifen.

64. SGYLW, *Guomian shichang*, p. 10.

65. Interview with Xu Hongmei.

66. Interview with Chen Zhaodi.

67. SGYLW, *Guomian shichang*, pp. 13-15; Tang Guifen.

68. All China Democratic Women's Federation, *From Struggle to Victory* (Beijing, 1949), p. 50. Cited in Croll, p. 181.

69. Interview with Fan Xiaofeng.

70. Materials provided by the Institute for Historical Research, Shanghai Academy of Social Sciences.

71. Ibid.

72. Tang Guifen, p. 4.

73. Materials provided by the Institute for Historical Research, Shanghai Academy of Social Sciences.

74. Interview with Sun Zhaodi, Shanghai, Mar. 11, 1980.

75. There is no exhaustive study of the postwar labor movement, and this is by no means intended to be one. Future research may more systematically examine patterns of women's participation in the postwar labor movement.

76. Materials provided by the Institute for Historical Research, Shanghai Academy of Social Sciences.

77. SSKJY, *Rongjia*, vol. 2, p. 733.

78. Materials provided by the Institute for Historical Research, Shanghai Academy of Social Sciences.

79. There is some indication that with victory near, the CCP discouraged agitation among workers, but there are no records available to clarify this point.

80. Interview with He Ningzhen.

81. Unless otherwise specified, this account of the strike is based on the following sources: SSKJY, *Rongjia*, vol. 2; SGYLW, "Shenxin jiuchang"; *Shenjiu*; "Shenxin jiuchang er er douzheng jiyao" (Record of the Struggle at Shen Xin Number Nine), *SWZX* (1979), no. 3: 13-25; and *Shen Bao*, Jan.-Mar. 1948.

82. Interview with Chen Zhaodi.

83. ILO China correspondent, Monthly Report, Feb. 1948 (ILO Archives, Geneva).

84. Materials provided by the Institute for Historical Research, Shanghai Academy of Social Sciences.

85. SSKJY, *Rongjia*, vol. 2, pp. 761-63; and Zhang Qi, "Huiyi Shanghai gongrende huchang douzheng," *SWZX* (1979), no. 2: 80-94.

Bibliography

A NOTE ON SOURCES

Personal Interviews

Much of the material in this study is based on interviews conducted during two research trips to Shanghai. Under the auspices of the Committee on Scholarly Communication with the People's Republic of China and the Social Science Research Council, I was an exchange scholar at Fudan University in Shanghai from 1979 to 1981. I then returned to conduct follow-up research from September to October 1982. The interviews with women workers were almost all arranged by Fudan University, and they usually took place at the cotton mills. The Shanghai Academy of Social Sciences, the Federation of Labor, and the Women's Federation also helped arrange the interviews.

I interviewed approximately seventy-five women, most of whom had already retired from their jobs in the cotton mills. Often these interviews were set up as round table discussions, in which I questioned four or five women during a single three-hour session. There was only occasionally an opportunity to conduct follow-up interviews with individual women. Most of the women spoke either Shanghainese or Subei dialect, and usually an official who was present translated into Mandarin. I tape-recorded all the interviews and later had someone familiar with the particular local dialects review the tapes to ensure that the translations were complete and accurate.

*Materials Provided by the Institute for Historical Research,
Shanghai Academy of Social Sciences*

The materials provided by the Institute for Historical Research are an assortment of documents collected as part of an effort to chronicle the history of the pre-Liberation labor movement in Shanghai. The documents are not catalogued. Further information about these materials can be obtained by contacting the author.

Retirement Cards

The retirement cards, a part of the personnel records kept at most cotton mills in Shanghai since Liberation, are filled out at the time a worker retires with the worker's date and place of birth, as well as his or her work history. I had access to the cards of workers who retired from 1949 to 1980 (approximately a thousand workers) at one cotton mill in Shanghai, identified as Cotton Mill A.

WORKS CITED

All About Shanghai and Environs: A Standard Guide Book. Shanghai, 1934.
Anderson, Adelaide Mary. *Humanity and Labor in China: An Industrial Visit and Its Sequel (1923-1926)*. London, 1928.
Ba Jin. *Siqude taiyang* (The Setting Sun). Shanghai, 1949.
Bagwell, May. "An Account of the Industrial Work of the Shanghai YWCA, 1904-1929." (World YWCA Archives, Geneva.)
Bai Baojun. "Shachangli nütonggongde shenghuo" (The Life of Girl Child Workers in the Cotton Mills), *Nü qingnian yuekan*, 13 (1934), no. 5: 65-70.
———. "Shanghai shachang nügong zhi yibande shenghuo" (The General Livelihood of Women Cotton Mill Workers in Shanghai), *Nü qingnian yuekan*, 12 (1933), no. 5: 51-60.
Baoshengongde chouhen (The Hatred of Contract Workers). Shanghai, 1974.
Baoshengongde xueleichou (The Blood, Tears, and Grief of Contract Workers). Shanghai, 1965.
Barnett, Robert. *Economic Shanghai: Hostage to Politics, 1937-1941*. New York, 1941.
Bourne, F. S. A. *Report of the Mission to China of the Blackburn Chamber of Commerce, 1896-1897*. Blackburn, Eng., 1898.
British Economic Mission to the Far East, 1930-31. *Report of the Cotton Mission*. London, 1931.
Bulle, M. O. *Chinese Toiling Women*. Moscow, 1933.
Bush, Richard. "Industry and Politics in Kuomintang China: The Nationalist Regime and Lower Yangtze Chinese Cotton Mill Owners, 1927-1937." Ph.D. dissertation, Columbia University, 1978.
Chan, Ming. "Labor and Empire: The Chinese Labor Movement in the Canton Delta, 1895-1927." Ph.D. dissertation, Stanford University, 1975.
Chang Kuo-t'ao. *The Rise of the Chinese Communist Party, 1921-27*. 2 vols. Lawrence, Kans., 1971.
Chao, Kang. *The Development of Cotton Textile Production in China*. Cambridge, Mass., 1974.
Chapman, S. J. *The Cotton Industry and Trade*. London, 1905.
Chen Da. *Zhongguo laogong wenti* (Labor Problems in China). Shanghai, 1929.
Chen Hansheng. "Zhuinian Chai Jiemin" (Recalling Chai Jiemin), *Renmin ribao* (People's Daily), Mar. 13, 1979.
Chesneaux, Jean. *The Chinese Labor Movement, 1919-1927*. Stanford, Calif., 1968.

———. *Secret Societies in China in the Nineteenth and Twentieth Centuries.* Ann Arbor, Mich., 1971.

Chiao, C. M., Warren Thompson, and D. T. Chen. *An Experiment in the Registration of Vital Statistics in China.* Oxford, Ohio, 1938.

China Forum, 1932-34 (Shanghai).

Chinese Economic Journal, 1927-33 (Shanghai).

"Chinese Labor and the Contract System," *People's Tribune,* 5 (1933), no. 8: 407-10.

Chung Shou Ching and May Bagwell. *Women in Industry in the Chapei, Hongkew and Pootung Districts of Shanghai.* Shanghai, 1931. (YWCA National Board Archives, New York.)

Coble, Parks. *The Shanghai Capitalists and the Nationalist Government, 1927-1937.* Cambridge, Mass., 1980.

Cole, James. "Shaoxing: Studies in Late Ch'ing Social History." Ph.D. dissertation, Stanford University, 1975.

Cressey, George Babcock. *China's Geographic Foundations.* New York, 1934.

Croll, Elizabeth. *Feminism and Socialism in China.* New York, 1980,

Davidson-Houston, J. V. *Yellow Creek: The Story of Shanghai.* London, 1962.

Davin, Delia. *Woman-Work: Women and the Party in Revolutionary China.* London, 1976.

Deng, Cora. "The Economic Status of Women in Industry in China. With Special Reference to a Group in Shanghai." M.A. thesis, New York University, 1941.

———. "A Visit to a Contract Labour Dormitory," *China Christian Yearbook,* 19 (1934-35): 1-4.

Deng Fa. "Zhanhou dihou gongye yu gongrende biandong" (Changes in Industry and Workers Behind the War and Enemy Lines), *Zhongguo gongren yundong shiliao,* 2 (Feb. 1960): 1-51.

Deng Yuzhi. "A Visit to a Silk Filature in Shanghai," *Green Year Supplement,* Industrial Number, 17 (Nov. 1928): 9-12. (YWCA National Board Archives, New York.)

Deng Zhongxia. *Zhongguo zhigong yundong jianshi, 1919-1926* (A Short History of the Chinese Workers' Movement). Beijing, 1953.

Drucker, Alison. "The Role of the YWCA in the Development of the Chinese Women's Movement, 1890-1927," *Social Service Review* (Sept. 1979): 421-40.

Dublin, Thomas. *Women at Work: The Transformation of Work and Community in Lowell, Massachusetts, 1826-1860.* New York, 1979.

Espey, John. *The Other City.* New York, 1950.

Fairbank, John King. *Chinabound: A Fifty-Year Memoir.* New York, 1982.

———. *Trade and Diplomacy on the China Coast.* Cambridge, Mass., 1953.

Fang Fu-an (Fang Fuan). *Chinese Labour.* Shanghai, 1931.

———. "Shanghai Labor," *Chinese Economic Journal,* 7 (1930), no. 2: 853-85.

Fang jian (Textile Reconstruction), 1948-49 (Shanghai).

Fangzhi zhoukan (The Textile Weekly), 1932-48 (Shanghai).
Fangzhiran gongcheng (Textile and Dyeing Technique), 1948-49 (Shanghai).
Fei Hsiao-tung. *Peasant Life in China: A Field Study of Country Life in the Yangtze Valley.* London, 1962.
Feuerwerker, Albert. *The Chinese Economy, ca. 1870-1911.* Ann Arbor, Mich., 1969.
Fong, H. D. (Fang Xianting). *Cotton Industry and Trade in China.* 2 vols. Tianjin, 1932.
———. *Industrial Organization in China.* Tianjin, 1937.
Fortune, Robert. *Three Years' Wanderings in the Northern Provinces of China.* London, 1847; reprint ed., Taipei, 1972.
Funü (Women), 1945-49 (Shanghai).
Gamewell, Mary Ninde. *Gateway to China: Pictures of Shanghai.* New York, 1916.
Geelen, P. J. M., and D. C. Twitchett, eds. *The Times Atlas of China.* London, 1974.
Gipoulon, Catherine. "Integrating the Feminist and Worker's Movement: The Case of Xiang Jingyu," *Republican China*, 10 (1984), no. 1a: 29-41.
Great Britain. Foreign Office. "Memorandum on Labor Conditions in China." London, 1927. (Cmd. 2846.)
Green Year Supplement, 1916-33 (Shanghai; YWCA of China).
Gronewold, Sue. *Beautiful Merchandise: Prostitution in China, 1860-1936.* New York, 1982.
Guo Jianqing and Zhong Zuling. "Shenxin diyichang canguanji" (A Record of a Visit to the Shen Xin Number One Mill), *Qianye yuekan* (The Banking Monthly), 5 (1925), no. 2: 30-42.
Guoji laogong tongxun (International Labor Bulletin), 1931-41 (Shanghai).
Guomian erchang changshi bianxiezu (History of the Shanghai Number Two Textile Mill Editorial Group). *Shanghai guomian erchang shi* (History of the Shanghai Number Two Textile Mill). Shanghai, 1969. Mimeo.
Hammond, Edward. "Organized Labor in Shanghai, 1927-1937." Ph.D. dissertation, University of California, Berkeley, 1978.
Hareven, Tamara. *Family Time and Industrial Time.* Cambridge, Eng., 1982.
Harrison, Agatha. "The Coming of the Factory System to China, 1923." (World YWCA Archives, Geneva.)
Hauser, Ernest. *Shanghai: City for Sale.* New York, 1940.
Hinder, Eleanor. *Social and Industrial Problems of Shanghai.* Shanghai, 1942.
Huang Miding. "Yangshupu gongchang shenghuo diaocha" (An Investigation of Factory Life in Yangshupu). M.A. thesis, Hujiang University (Shanghai), 1947.
Huang Wei. *Shanghai kaibu chuqi duiwai liuyi yanjiu, 1843-1863.* (Research on Early Treaty Port Shanghai's Foreign Trade). Shanghai, 1979.
Huang Yifeng. "Jiu Zhongguo Rongjia zibende fazhan" (The Development of the Rong Family's Capital in Old China), in Huang Yiping, ed., *Zhongguo jindai jingjishi lunwen xuanji*, vol. 4. Shanghai, 1979.
Huang Yifeng and Zhou Shangwen. *Shanghai gongren sanci wuzhang qiyi*

(The Three Armed Uprisings of the Workers of Shanghai). Shanghai, 1979.

Huang Yiping, ed. *Zhongguo jindai jingjishi lunwen xuanji* (Selected Essays on Modern Chinese Economic History). 5 vols. Shanghai, 1979.

Huashang shachang lianhehui jikan (Chinese Cotton Mill Owners' Association Quarterly), 1921-26 (Shanghai).

Institute of Pacific Relations. *Agrarian China*. Shanghai, 1938.

International Labor Organization, China correspondent. Monthly Reports, 1927-49. (ILO Archives, Geneva).

International Labor Organization Archives. Geneva.

Isaacs, Harold. *The Tragedy of the Chinese Revolution*. Stanford, Calif., 1951.

————, ed. *Five Years of KMT Reaction: Gang Rule in Shanghai*. Shanghai, 1932.

Jiu Zhongguode zibenzhuyi shengchan guanxi bianxiezu (The Editorial Group on Capitalist Relations of Production in Old China). *Jiu Zhongguode zibenzhuyi shengchan guanxi* (Capitalist Relations of Production in Old China). Beijing, 1976.

Jones, Susan Mann. "The Ningpo Pang and Financial Power at Shanghai," in Mark Elvin and G. W. Skinner, eds., *The Chinese City Between Two Worlds*. Stanford, Calif., 1974.

Ju Ren (pseud.). "Shanghai zhiye funü shenghuo" (The Life of Female Employees in Shanghai), *Nüsheng*, 3 (1935), no. 12: 6-8; 3 (1935), no. 13: 11-13.

Jue Wusheng (pseud.). *Jinude shenghuo* (The Life of Prostitutes). Shanghai, 1941.

Kelley, David. "Temples and Tribute Fleets: The Luo Sect and Boatmen's Associations in the Eighteenth Century," *Modern China*, 8 (1982), no. 3: 361-91.

Kung, Lydia. *Factory Women in Taiwan*. Ann Arbor, Mich., 1983.

Kyong Bae-tsung. "China's Industrial Women," *Green Year Supplement* (1928), no. 17: 3-4. (YWCA National Board Archives, New York.)

————. "Education of Industrial Women and Girls," *Green Year Supplement* (1928), no. 17: 15-16. (YWCA National Board Archives, New York.)

Lamson, H. D. "The Effect of Industrialization Upon Village Livelihood," *Chinese Economic Journal*, 9 (1931), no 4: 1025-81.

————. "The Problem of Housing for Workers in China," *Chinese Economic Journal*, 11 (1932), no. 2: 139-62.

————. "The Standard of Living of Factory Workers: A Study of Incomes and Expenditures of 21 Working Families in Shanghai," *Chinese Economic Journal*, 7 (1930), no. 5: 1240-56.

Laodong jie (Worker's World), 1920-21 (Shanghai).

Laogong yuekan (Labor Monthly), 1932-36 (Nanjing).

Leung Yuen Sang. "Regional Rivalry in Mid-Nineteenth-Century Shanghai: Cantonese vs. Ningpo Men," *Ch'ing shih wen-t'i*, 4 (1982), no. 8: 29-50.

Li Guowei. "Rongjia jingling fangzhi he zhifen qiye liushi nian" (Sixty Years of the Rong Family Management of Textile and Flour Enterprises), *Gong-shang shiliao* (Historical Materials on Industry and Commerce), 1 (Nov. 1980): 1-15.

Li, Lillian. *China's Silk Trade: Traditional Industry in the Modern World, 1842-1937*. Cambridge, Mass., 1981.

Liu Ta-chun (D. K. Lieu). *The Growth and Industrialization of Shanghai*. Shanghai, 1936.

———. *The Silk Reeling Industry in Shanghai*. Shanghai, 1941.

Luo Chuanhua. *Jinri Zhongguo laogong wenti* (Facing Labor Issues in China). Shanghai, 1933.

Ma Chunji. "Shanghai gongyunde xiankuang baogao" (Report on the Present Condition of the Workers' Movement in Shanghai). Yanan, 1941. Reprinted by Zhonghua quanguo zonggonghui ziliaoshi (Materials Department of the All-China Federation of Labor), Beijing, 1954.

———. "Shanghai nügong gongzuo baogao" (Report on Women's Work in Shanghai). Yanan, 1941. Reprinted by Zhonghua quanguo zonggonghui ziliaoshi (Materials Department of the All-China Federation of Labor), Beijing, 1954.

Ma Zhaojun. *Zhongguo laogong wenti* (China's Labor Problems). Shanghai, 1928.

Manual of Job Descriptions in the Cotton Textile Industry. Australian Industrial Welfare Division, Department of Labour and National Service, July 1946.

Mao Tun. *Midnight*. Beijing, 1979.

Minami manshū tetsudō kabushiki kaisha, Shanghai jimusho chōsashitsu (South Manchurian Railway Company, Shanghai Office, Investigation Department). *Kaisen zengo no Shanghai rōdō kenkei taikei shiryō* (Statistical Materials Concerning Shanghai Labor Before and After the War). Shanghai, 1942.

Morris, Morris David. *The Emergence of an Industrial Labor Force in India: A Case Study of the Bombay Cotton Mills, 1854-1947*. Berkeley, Calif., 1965.

Moser, Charles. *The Cotton Textile Industry of Far Eastern Countries*. Boston, 1930.

Muramatsu, Yuji. "A Documentary Study of Chinese Landlordism in the Late Ch'ing and Early Republican Kiangnan," *Bulletin of the School of Oriental and African Studies*, 29 (1966), no. 3:566-99.

Murphey, Rhoads. *Shanghai: Key to Modern China*. Cambridge, Mass., 1953.

Nelson, Daniel. *Managers and Workers: Origins of the New Factory System in the United States, 1880-1920*. Madison, Wisc., 1975.

Nishikawa Kiichi. *Chūshi rōdōsha no genjō* (Present Condition of Chinese Laborers). Tokyo, 1925.

North-China Herald, 1920-37 (Shanghai).

Nü qingnian yuekan (The YWCA Monthly), 1934-37 (Shanghai).

Nüsheng (Women's Voice), 1932-48 (Shanghai).

Odell, Ralph. *Cotton Goods in China*. Washington, D.C., 1916.

Pai Hsien-yung. *Wandering in the Garden, Waking from a Dream: Tales of Taipei Characters*. Translated by George Kao. Bloomington, Ind., 1982.

Pan Ling. *In Search of Old Shanghai.* Hong Kong, 1982.
Peake, R. J. *Cotton: From the Raw Material to the Finished Product.* London, n.d.
Pengyou (The Friend), 1937-39 (Shanghai).
Pepper, Suzanne. *Civil War in China: The Political Struggle, 1945-1949.* Berkeley, Calif., 1978.
Perry, Elizabeth. *Rebels and Revolutionaries in North China, 1845-1945.* Stanford, Calif., 1980.
Porter, Robin. "The Christian Conscience and Industrial Welfare in China, 1919-1941." Ph.D. dissertation, University of Montreal, 1977.
Pott, F. L. Hawks. *A Short History of Shanghai.* Shanghai, 1928.
Powell, John B. *My Twenty-five Years in China.* New York, 1945.
Prazniak, Roxane. "Weavers and Sorceresses of Chuansha: The Influence of Cash Incomes and Female-Oriented Ideology on Women's Self-Reliance in Traditional Rural China." Paper prepared for Berkeley Regional Seminar in Chinese Studies, Feb. 1983.
Qinghongbang kaoyi (An Investigation and Explanation of the Green and Red Gangs). Taibei, 1973.
"Report of the Shanghai Child Labor Commission," H. G. H. Woodhead, ed. *China Year Book, 1925.* Tianjin, 1925.
Salaff, Janet. *Working Daughters of Hong Kong: Filial Piety or Power in the Family?* Cambridge, Eng., 1981.
Sankar, Andrea. "Spinster Sisterhoods: Jing Yih Sifu: Spinster-Domestic-Nun," in Janet Salaff and Mary Sheridan, eds., *Lives: Chinese Working Women.* Bloomington, Ind., 1984.
Sato Akiko. "Gosa undō ni okeru chugoku fujin" (Chinese Women in the May Thirtieth Movement), *Shikai* (Sea of History). 27 (June 1980): 19-36.
Selden, Mark. "The Proletariat, Revolutionary Change, and the State in China and Japan, 1850-1950," in Immanuel Wallerstein, ed., *Labor in the World Social Structure.* Beverly Hills, Calif., 1983.
Shaffer, Lynda. *Mao and the Workers: The Hunan Labor Movement, 1920-1923.* Armonk, N.Y., 1982.
———. "Modern Chinese Labor History, 1895-1949," *International Labor and Working Class History* (1981), no. 20: 31-70.
Shan Xiren. "Diduban tuibianwei Shaoxingjude laiyou" (The Origins of Shaoxing Peasant Opera Troupes), *Zhejiang yuekan* (The Zhejiang Monthly), 1 (1968), no. 2: 22-23.
Shanghai Bureau of Social Affairs. *The Index Numbers of Earnings of Factory Laborers in Greater Shanghai, July-December 1928.* Shanghai, 1928.
———. *The Standard of Living of Shanghai Laborers.* Shanghai, 1934.
———. *Wage Rates in Shanghai.* Shanghai, 1935.
———. *Wages and Hours of Labor in Greater Shanghai, 1929.* Shanghai, 1929.
Shanghai fangzhi jianshe gongsi (The Shanghai Textile Reconstruction Corporation). *Shanghai dishisi fangzhichang 1946 niandu gongzuo baogao* (Report on Work at the Shanghai Number Fourteen Mill in 1946). Shanghai, 1946.

286 Bibliography

Shanghai fangzhiju, qiershiyi gongren daxue waiyuxi (Shanghai Textile Bureau, July 21 Workers' College, Department of Foreign Languages). *Preliminary Texts on Spinning and Weaving*. Shanghai, 1975.

Shanghai gongren yundong lishi weiyuanhui (Shanghai Labor History Committee). *Guomian shichang gongren douzheng lishi ziliao* (Historical Materials on the History of Workers' Struggles at the Number Ten Textile Mill). Shanghai, 1956. Mimeo.

———. *Kangzhan shenglihou Hengfeng shachang gongrende yixie douzheng qingkuang* (Some of the Conditions of the Workers' Struggles at the Heng Feng Cotton Mill After the Victory Against Japan). Shanghai, 1956. Mimeo.

———. *Shanghai gongren yundong lishi dashiji, 1919-1949* (A Chronicle of the Workers' Movement in Shanghai). 4 vols. Shanghai, 1957. Mimeo.

———. *Shenxin jiuchang gongren er er douzheng lishi ziliao* (Materials on the History of the February 2 Struggle of Workers at the Shen Xin Nine Mill). Shanghai, 1956. Mimeo.

Shanghai heimo yiqian zhong (A Thousand Kinds of Shady Plots in Shanghai). Shanghai, 1939.

Shanghai Municipal Council. *Annual Report, 1938*. Shanghai, 1938.

———. *Annual Report, 1939*. Shanghai, 1939.

Shanghai shehui kexueyuan, jingji yanjiusuo (Shanghai Academy of Social Sciences, Institute for Economic Research). *Hengfeng shachangde fasheng fazhan yu gaizao* (The Birth, Development, and Transformation of the Heng Feng Cotton Mill). Shanghai, 1959.

———. *Nanyang xiongdi yancao gongsi shiliao* (Historical Materials of the Nanyang Brothers Tobacco Company). Shanghai, 1958.

———. *Rongjia qiye shiliao*, vol. 1: *1896-1937* (Historical Materials of the Rong Family Enterprises). Shanghai, 1980.

———. *Rongjia qiye shiliao*, vol. 2: *1937-1949*. Shanghai, 1980.

———. *Shanghai penghuqude biangian* (Changes in the Squatter Areas of Shanghai). Shanghai, 1965.

———. *Shanghai Yongan gongside chansheng, fazhan he gaizao* (The Birth, Development, and Transformation of the Shanghai Yong An Company). Shanghai, 1981.

———. *Yongan fangzhi yinran gongsi* (The Yong An Textile, Printing, and Dyeing Company). Beijing, 1964.

Shanghai shehui kexueyuan, lishi yanjiusuo (Shanghai Academy of Social Sciences, Institute for Historical Research). *Wusa yundong shiliao* (Historical Materials on the May Thirtieth Movement). Shanghai, 1982.

———. *Wusi yundong zai Shanghai shiliao xuanji* (Selected Materials on the History of the May Fourth Movement in Shanghai). Shanghai, 1980.

Shanghai shehuiju (Shanghai Bureau of Social Affairs). *Shanghai gongchang laogong tongji* (Shanghai Factory Labor Statistics). Shanghai, 1946.

———. *Shanghaizhi nongye* (Agriculture in Shanghai). Shanghai, 1933.

Shanghai wenshi ziliao xuanji (Selected Materials on the History and Culture of Shanghai), 1977-81 (Shanghai).

Shanghai zonggonghui nügonbu (The Women's Bureau of the Shanghai

Federation of Labor). *Gonghui nügong gongzuo* (Union Work for Women Workers). Shanghai, 1951.

Shanghaishi gongshang xingzheng guanlihui and Shanghaishi maoma fang- zhi gongye gongsi (The Shanghai Management Bureau for the Admin- istration of Industry and Commerce and the Shanghai Wool-Spinning Company). *Shanghai minzu maofangzhi gongye* (The National Wool-Spin- ning and -Weaving Industry in Shanghai). Shanghai, 1962.

Shanghaishi mianfangzhi gongye tongye gonghui (Bureau of Statistics on the Shanghai Textile Industry). *Zhongguo mianfang tongji shiliao* (Statistics on the History of the Cotton Industry in China). Shanghai, 1950.

Shen Bao (The Huangpu Daily), 1920-49 (Shanghai).

Shenghuo zhishi (Knowledge About Life), 1945-46 (Shanghai).

Shenjiu gongrende guangrong douzheng (The Glorious Struggle of Workers at Shen Nine). Shanghai, 1963.

Shih Min-hsiung. *The Silk Industry in Ch'ing China*. Translated by E-tu Zen Sun. Ann Arbor, Mich., 1976.

Shindo, Takejiro. *Labor in the Japanese Cotton Industry*. Tokyo, 1961.

Shunzo, Yoshisake. "Labor Recruiting in Japan and Its Control," *Interna- tional Labor Review*, 12 (1925), no. 4: 482-99.

Siu, Bobby. *Women of China: Imperialism and Women's Resistance, 1900-1949*. London, 1981.

Stross, Randall. "A Hard Row to Hoe: The Political Economy of Chinese Agriculture in Western Jiangsu, 1911-1937." Ph.D. dissertation, Stanford University, 1982.

Sun Baoshan. "Shanghai fangzhichangde baoshenzhi gongren" (Contract Workers in the Shanghai Textile Mills), *Huanian zhoukan* (The Prosper- ous Year Weekly), 1 (1932), no. 22: 430-32, 467-72.

Sun Yutang, ed. *Zhongguo jindai gongyeshi ziliao, 1840-1895* (Source Mate- rials on the History of Modern Industry in China). 2 vols. Beijing, 1957.

Tang Guifen. "Huxi shachang gongren douzhengde gaikuang" (General Conditions of the Cotton Workers' Struggle in Western Shanghai), *Shang- hai gongren yundong lishi ziliao* (Materials on the History of the Workers' Movement in Shanghai), (1956), no. 9: 1-17.

Tang Hai. *Zhongguo laodong wenti* (China's Labor Problems). Shanghai, 1926.

Tao Juyin. *Gudu jianwen: kangzhan shiqide Shanghai* (Sights and Sounds of a Lonely Island: Shanghai During the Anti-Japanese War). Shanghai, 1979.

Thompson, Edward P. *The Making of the English Working Class*. New York, 1966.

Topley, Marjorie. "Marriage Resistance in Rural Kwangtung," in Margery Wolf and Roxane Witke, eds., *Women in Chinese Society*. Stanford, Calif., 1975.

Torgasheff, Boris. *Mining Labor in China*. Nanjing, 1930.

Tu Shipin, ed. *Shanghaishi daguan* (The Great Spectacle of Shanghai). Shanghai, 1948.

Udaka Yasushi. *Shina rōdō mondai* (Labor Problems in China). Shanghai, 1925.

Wada Ei. *Tomioka nikki* (Tomioka Diary). Tokyo, 1978.

Wagner, Augusta. *Labor Legislation in China*. Beijing, 1938.

Wales, Nym. *The Chinese Labor Movement.* New York, 1945.

Wang Nanbi. "Jiangbei nongcun shikuang" (The True Conditions of Jiang- bei Villages), in Qian Jiaju, ed., *Zhongguo nongcun jingji lunwenji* (Col- lected Essays on the Chinese Village Economy). Shanghai, 1936.

Wang Qingbin et al. *Diyici Zhongguo laodong nianjian* (The First Chinese Labor Yearbook). Beijing, 1928.

Wang, Simine. *Le Travail des femmes et des enfants en Chine* (Female and Child Labor in China). Paris, 1933.

Wang, Y. C. "Tu Yueh-sheng, 1881-1951: A Tentative Biography," *Journal of Asian Studies,* 26 (May 1967): 433-55.

Wolf, Arthur, and Chieh-shan Huang. *Marriage and Adoption in China, 1845- 1945.* Stanford, Calif., 1980.

Wolf, Margery. *Women and the Family in Rural Taiwan.* Stanford, Calif., 1972.

Wolf, Margery, and Roxane Witke, eds. *Women in Chinese Society.* Stanford, Calif., 1975.

"Women zai gongchang" (We Are in the Factory), *Funü,* 3 (1947), no. 10: 17-19.

Woodhead, H. G. H., ed. *China Year Book,* 1924, 1925, 1926. Tianjin, 1924- 26.

World Young Women's Christian Association. Archives. Geneva.

Wright, Tim. "A Method of Evading Management: Contract Labor in Chinese Coal Mines Before 1937," *Comparative Studies of Society and His- tory,* 23 (1981), no. 4: 656-78.

Wu Xiaogu. "Liushi zishu" (A Memoir of Sixty Years), *Zhejiang yuekan* (The Zhejiang Monthly), 5 (1973), no. 8: 33-35.

Wusa yundong bianxiezu (The Editorial Group on the May Thirtieth Move- ment). *Wusa yundong* (The May Thirtieth Movement). Shanghai, 1976.

Xia Yan. *Baoshengong* (Contract Labor). Beijing, 1964.

Xiang Jingyu. *Xiang Jingyu wenji* (Collected Essays of Xiang Jingyu). Changsha, 1980.

Xin qingnian (New Youth), 1919-20 (Beijing).

Xu Huifang and Liu Qingyu. "Shanghai nüxing fande shehui fenxi" (A So- cial Analysis of Women Criminals in Shanghai), *Dalu zazhi* (Continental Magazine), 1 (1932), no. 4: 71-93.

Xu Yinghu and Wang Yangqing. "Shanghai qinghongbang gaishu" (A Gen- eral Description of the Green and Red Gangs in Shanghai), *Shehui kexue* (Social Science) (1982), no. 5: 63-65.

Xue Gengxin. Jindai Shanghaide liumang" (Gangsters in Modern Shang- hai), *Shanghai wenshi ziliao xuanji* (1980), no. 3: 160-78.

Yan Zhongping. *Zhongguo mianfangzhi shigao, 1289-1937* (A Draft History of Chinese Cotton Spinning and Weaving). Beijing, 1955.

Yang Meizhen. "Yangshupu nügong qingkuang" (The Conditions of Wom- en Workers in Yangshupu). M.A. thesis, Hujiang University (Shang- hai), 1930.

———. "Yangshupu nügongde hunyin" (The Marriage of Women Workers in Yangshupu), *Nüsheng,* 1 (1933), no. 9: 6-9.

———. "Yangshupu nügongde yishizhu" (The Clothing, Food, and Housing Conditions of Women Workers in Yangshupu), *Nusheng*, 1 (1933), no. 10: 7-9.

Yang Ximeng. *Shanghai gongren shenghuo chengdude yige yanjiu* (A Study of the Standard of Living of Workers in Shanghai). Beijing, 1930.

Young, Marilyn, ed. *Women in China: Studies in Social Change and Feminism.* Ann Arbor, Mich., 1973.

Young Women's Christian Association. China collection. National Board Archives, New York.

Zhanshi funü (Wartime Women), 1937-39 (Shanghai).

Zhanshi helian xunkan (Wartime Joint Bimonthly), 1937-39 (Shanghai).

Zhe Fei. *Kangzhanzhongde Shanghai nügong* (Shanghai Women Workers During the War Against Japan). N.p., n.d.

Zhong Shaoqin (Helen Zhong). "Wosuo kanjiande nügong shenghuo" (What I Have Seen of the Life of Women Workers), *Nü qingnian yuekan*, 12 (1933), no. 5: 42-50.

Zhongguo fangzhi jianshe gongsi (The China Textile Reconstruction Corporation), *Shanghai diersan fangzhichang gaikuang* (The General Conditions at the Shanghai Number Two and Three Textile Mills). Shanghai, 1947.

———. *Shanghai diliu fangzhichang gaikuang* (The General Conditions at the Shanghai Number Six Textile Mill). Shanghai, 1947.

———. *Shanghai diliu fangzhichang lukan* (A Survey of the Shanghai Number Six Textile Mill). Shanghai, 1948.

———. *Shanghai dishisi fangzhichang 1946 niandu gongzuo baogao* (Report on Work at the Shanghai Number 14 Mill in 1946). Shanghai, 1946.

———. *Shanghai diyi fangzhichang gaikuang* (The General Conditions at the Shanghai Number One Textile Mill). Shanghai, 1947.

Zhongguo gongren yundong shiliao (Materials on the History of the Chinese Workers' Movement), 1960-62, 1979-81 (Beijing).

Zhongguo jingji quanshu (The Complete Book of the Chinese Economy), translated from the Japanese, *Chūgoku keizai zensho*, N.p., 1908.

Zhongguo kexueyuan, jingji yanjiusuo (Chinese Academy of Sciences, Institute for Economic Research). *Zhongguo jindai nongye shi ziliao* (Materials on the History of Chinese Agriculture). 5 vols. Beijing, 1957.

Zhou Erfu. *Morning in Shanghai.* Translated by A. C. Barnes. Beijing, 1962.

Zhu Bangxing, Hu Linge, and Xu Sheng. *Shanghai chanye yu Shanghai zhigong* (Enterprises and Workers in Shanghai). Hong Kong, 1939.

Zhu Zuotong and Mei Yi, eds. *Shanghai yiri* (A Day in Shanghai). Shanghai, 1939.

Zui ede jiu shehui (The Evil Old Society). Shanghai, 1978.

Index

Library of Congress Cataloging-in-Publication Data

Honig, Emily.
Sisters and strangers.

Bibliography: p.
Includes index.
1. Women textile workers—China—Shanghai—History—
20th century. 2. China—Economic conditions—1912-1949.
3. Trade-unions—China—Shanghai—Political activity—
History—20th century. 4. Shanghai (China)—Economic
conditions. I. Title.
HD6073.T42C64 1986   331.4'87721'0951132   84-51711
ISBN 0-8047-1274-3 (cloth)
ISBN 0-8047-2012-6 (pbk.)